SETTING THE RISING SUN

SETTING THE
RISING
SUN

HALSEY'S AVIATORS STRIKE JAPAN, SUMMER 1945

KEVIN A. MAHONEY

STACKPOLE
BOOKS
Guilford, Connecticut

STACKPOLE BOOKS

Published by Stackpole Books
An imprint of The Rowman & Littlefield Publishing Group, Inc.
4501 Forbes Blvd., Ste. 200
Lanham, MD 20706
www.rowman.com

Distributed by NATIONAL BOOK NETWORK
800-462-6420

British Library Cataloguing in Publication Information available
Library of Congress Cataloging-in-Publication Data available

Names: Mahoney, Kevin A., author.
Title: Setting the rising sun : Halsey's aviators strike Japan, summer 1945 / Kevin A. Mahoney.
Other titles: Halsey's aviators strike Japan, summer 1945
Description: Guilford, Connecticut : Stackpole Books, [2019] | Includes bibliographical references and index.
Identifiers: LCCN 2018050357 (print) | LCCN 2018050724 (ebook) | ISBN   9780811768429 | ISBN 9780811738422 (hardcover)
Subjects: LCSH: World War, 1939-1945—Campaigns—Japan. | World War, 1939-1945—Aerial operations, American. | Halsey, William F. (William Frederick), 1882-1959. | Aircraft carriers—United States—History—20th century. | World War, 1939-1945—Naval operations, American.
Classification: LCC D767.2 (ebook) | LCC D767.2 .M2354 2019 (print) | DDC 940.54/252—dc23
LC record available at https://lccn.loc.gov/2018050357

Printed in the United States of America

CONTENTS

Preface

Research for this book began ten years ago at the National Archives, College Park, MD, and the Archive of the Naval Historical Center in Washington, DC. The prospect of reviewing thousands of pages in hard copy in the poorly managed Main Research Room, or on microfilm in the antiquated Microfilm Research Room, at Archives II led me to write two other books first. Fortunately, the website Fold3.com digitized the microfilm of the War Diaries and placed them online, making research for this book feasible and efficient. In addition, archivists Michael Rhodes and Timothy Duskin at the Naval History and Heritage Command provided invaluable assistance for the completion of this book.

Obviously not all the combat missions flown by carrier-borne aircraft over the Japanese Home Islands during the last month of World War II are described in this book. An effort has been made, however, to include all those missions during which an aircraft was lost. The Aircraft Action Reports in the War Diaries, the main source for this book, often refer to the men involved in these actions by their initials and last name, or last name only. To completely identify these airmen, a variety of sources have been consulted to determine their first names, with success with all but a handful.

May 2018

Task Force July 1945

Task Force August 1945

Chapter One

Soon after 6:00 AM on December 7, 1941, eighteen Dauntless dive-bombers from Scouting Squadron 6 took off from the aircraft carrier *USS Enterprise*, located 200 miles west of the island of Oahu, to patrol the waters west of Hawaii before landing at Ford Island, in the middle of Pearl Harbor, later that morning. At about the same time, Japanese fighters, bombers, and torpedo planes were taking off from six Japanese carriers 200 miles north of Oahu to attack the American fleet anchored in Pearl Harbor.

The American aircraft flew in pairs to patrol different sectors of the patrol area. The commander of the aircraft on the *Enterprise*, Lieutenant Commander Howard Young, flew with Ensign Perry Teaff. Both Dauntlesses completed their patrol and flew over Oahu on the way to Ford Island. As they flew past Ewa Field, about twenty-five minutes after the Japanese began the attack on Pearl Harbor, they saw a number of aircraft over the field and assumed they were Army Air Force planes. Shortly thereafter, however, a fighter attacked Teaff's Dauntless. "The [enemy] plane pulled up directly astern of me.... At about seventy-five feet he opened fire." The Japanese pilot hit neither Teaff nor his radioman, but the Dauntless collected a number of machine-gun holes. As the Zero turned to make another attack, Teaff turned and his radioman fired a burst at the enemy, dissuading the Zero from making a second run on their plane. The enemy flew past them and attacked Lieutenant Commander Young's plane.[1]

Young had just noticed antiaircraft fire over Pearl Harbor when the Zero's cannon and machine-gun fire began to hit his plane, from the rear. He recognized the large red circle insignia on the Zero's fuselage and dove for the ground, jinking back and forth to throw off the enemy pilot's aim. The evasive action succeeded and he hugged the ground as he continued to Ford Island, under constant American antiaircraft fire as the defenders were firing at anything in the air. Young could not contact the tower at Ford Island, then under attack by Japanese dive-bombers and strafing fighters, so he landed without permission, as did Ensign Teaff.[2] Machine-gun fire had holed both Dauntlesses. Thirteen of the eighteen SBDs dispatched from the *Enterprise* eventually reached Ford Island that day, some after considerable adventures.

Ensign Eugene Roberts flew with Ensign Edward Deacon. As Roberts passed over Barbers Point, he saw a flight of green planes with red insignia and one waggled its wings as it went past. He continued on toward Ford Island, but while passing over Fort Weaver, antiaircraft guns began to fire, hitting Deacon's Dauntless. Fuel began to stream from a wing and the engine began to smoke as Roberts immediately sought safety on the ground. He landed at nearby Hickam Field, shortly before the second wave of the Japanese attack began and his rear-seat man, AMM1c D. H. Jones, remained in the rear seat of the Dauntless after landing and fired his .30 caliber machine gun at the attackers until his ammunition ran out.[3]

As Deacon passed over Barbers Point, he heard another Dauntless pilot, Ensign Manuel Gonzalez, shout over their radio frequency: "Don't shoot—Navy plane!" He immediately charged his guns and headed for Ford Island. Spotting Japanese planes as they came off the attack on Pearl Harbor, he flew near the ground and headed for Hickam Field. As he passed over Weaver Field, antiaircraft fire hit his Dauntless and the engine began to sputter. He was barely able to ditch, in a few feet of water, just off Hickam Field. American troops on the beach began to shoot at him, wounding his radio operator, RM3c Audrey Coslett, in the wrist and neck, and also grazing Deacon. He later reported: "After landing I was under rifle fire and machine gun fire from the beach some two hundred yards away." The troops soon realized their error and stopped firing. Deacon used a radio cord as tourniquet on Coslett's arm, broke out the life raft, and helped the wounded man into it. He then began to paddle toward the shore, but a crash boat, stationed nearby, intercepted him. The boat landed them on a dock and both went to the Hickam hospital.[4]

Lieutenant Commander Hallsted Hopping, commander of Scouting Squadron 6, also heard Gonzalez, flying with his wingman, Ensign Frederick Weber. As Hopping neared Barbers Point, he heard Gonzalez exclaim over the radio: "Do not attack me. This is Six Baker Three [his aircraft number and radio call sign] an American plane." Hopping recalled, "The same voice then told his gunner to break out the boat [life raft] as he was landing in the water." Hopping then saw Japanese planes attacking Ewa Field and reported the attack over the radio. He scooted for Ford Island, flying close to the ground, and landed.[5] Gonzalez's wingman, Ensign Weber, had lost sight of the former when the action started and circled around to locate him. When a Japanese fighter then flew at him, he recognized the red circle painted on it and dove for ground. He flew toward Barbers Point, where he joined up with another Dauntless, flown by Ensign Wilmer Gallaher. Weber and Gallaher joined with other pilots on the mission and the small flight made their way to Ewa Field and landed. The Marines on the field told them it was too dangerous to remain on the field, so they immediately took off again for Ford Island, but intense antiaircraft fire forced them back to Ewa, where they landed again.[6]

Other Dauntlesses had even more trouble that morning. Lieutenant Frank Patriarca, flying with Ensign Walter Willis, saw many aircraft in the air as they neared Ewa Field, as did other *Enterprise* pilots. As his radioman pointed out antiaircraft smoke over Pearl Harbor, tracers shot by Patriarca's aircraft, followed by a Zero. He dove for the deck, then started back to the *Enterprise*, until he realized his wingman was not with him. After a fruitless search, he headed for Ford Island, but low fuel forced him to land at Burns Field. He later learned a Japanese fighter had shot down Willis's aircraft, killing him and his radioman, Coxswain Fred J. Duclon.[7] Japanese Zeros also shot down the Dauntless flown by Ensign John Vogt, killing him and his radio operator, RM3c Sidney Pierce.

The Dauntlesses of Lieutenant Clarence E. Dickinson and Ensign John R. McCarthy were also shot down; only the two pilots survived. McCarthy's plane went down after Japanese planes attacked them near Barbers Point, but he managed to parachute to safety, although he broke a leg while landing. Dickinson and his radio operator, RM1c William Miller, were also shot down, but claimed the first Japanese plane shot down by Navy airmen during World War II. As he approached Pearl Harbor, Dickinson noticed antiaircraft bursts over Pearl Harbor and smoke rising from *USS Arizona*, bombed and sunk only minutes earlier. He then saw McCarthy's Dauntless on fire, circling after two Zeros attacked it. McCarthy's parachute had just opened when the fire of up to five other Zeros distracted Dickinson as they came straight at him. Miller, in the rear seat, returned their fire and reported that he had hit one of the Zeros and that he, himself, was wounded. Dickinson saw the Zero on fire and losing altitude. The Zeros continued to pound the Dauntless, hitting Miller a second time. One of them flew in front of Dickinson and he managed to fire two bursts from the two wing guns. By now, the dive-bomber was on fire, so he ordered Miller to bail out, later casually reporting: "My left tank being on fire and my controls being shot away, I told the gunner to jump." The badly damaged aircraft went into a spin, but Dickinson managed to bail out, landing safely near Ewa Field. Miller, unfortunately, went down with the aircraft.[8]

Five of the Dauntlesses that took off from the *Enterprise* were shot down, either by Japanese fighters or American antiaircraft fire, with eight men killed and three wounded. Most of the Dauntless crews that landed safely took part in abortive searches for the Japanese fleet later in the day, all in a day's work for these intrepid aviators. The Zero shot down by Miller was the first recorded aerial victory by a naval aviator during World War II. More than four and half years later, the last aerial melee of the war took place, just after the cease fire on August 15 that led to the Japanese surrender.

After a month of air strikes against the Home Islands of the Japanese Empire, one of the last missions flown that day, by Hellcats of VF-88, took off from the carrier *USS Yorktown* at 4:15 AM and rendezvoused with Corsairs from two other carriers for a mission to airfields around Tokyo, the Japanese capital. The planes encountered heavy overcast and the Hellcats circled the clouds for a short while until they spotted a small break that allowed them to continue in formation. While penetrating the clouds, the two VBF-88 flights became separated. The section led by

Lieutenant Marvin Odom headed for the briefed target, the airfield at Takahagi, after frustrating attempts to understand garbled transmissions from the strike leader, Lieutenant Howard Harrison. Odom's section reached Sagami Wan, a way point, but found no other American aircraft there. While in the area, another pilot in the section radioed Odom that he heard a message indicating that clouds covered the briefed target and aircraft should strike targets of opportunity instead. Odom took his flight along the coast until they spotted a factory near the town of Shimoku. The Hellcats attacked the factory with rockets, then strafed a lighthouse. Just after the attack, the section got word by radio to return to the *Yorktown*. Admiral Chester Nimitz, Commander in Chief of the Pacific Fleet, had just ordered that all offensive action against Japanese forces cease, after he received word that the Japanese government had accepted the Allied terms of surrender.[9]

The other section of Hellcats, led by Lieutenant Harrison, continued on to the Tokyo area until they also got word to return to the *Yorktown*. About twenty-five minutes after these planes had turned for home, they were jumped by about eighteen Japanese fighters, apparently part of a dedicated Japanese aerial patrol intent on fighting American planes up to the last minute, perhaps sparked by a revolt against the surrender that had taken place at Atsugi Airfield that morning. Most of the enemy fighters were Japanese Army Ki-84s, or "Franks," believed to have been part of the Japanese Army Air Force's 70th Air Regiment, with a few Navy Jack fighters.[10]

The American fighters were cruising at 8,000 feet, near the Japanese airfield at Atsugi about twenty-five miles southwest of the center of Tokyo, when the Japanese fighters dove from the rear to attack them. The Hellcats immediately turned to engage the attackers and a free-for-all aerial engagement ensued, led by Lieutenant Harrison.

Two members of the American flight flying as wingmen, Lieutenants (jg) Theodore Hansen and Maurice Proctor, waded into the enemy with the rest of the flight, Harrison, Lieutenant (jg) Joseph Sahloff, and Ensigns Wright Hobbs and Eugene Mandeberg. Proctor immediately shot the wing off a Frank, while Hansen dispatched two more. Immediately afterward, as Proctor later reported, he "saw a Jack that was on Lt.

(jg) Sahloff's tail. I opened up at about 700 feet and the [enemy] plane immediately exploded."[11] Sahloff, his Hellcat badly damaged and smoking, headed for the coast.

While Proctor engaged the Jack, a Frank managed to get on his tail, but his wingman, Hansen, blew it out of the sky. Proctor then turned and ran into six more Franks head on. The six pulled up to avoid a collision as Proctor took on the seventh he spotted flying away from him. He fired at the Frank, which caught fire, but he didn't see it crash as the six enemy fighters turned and came at him again. "I found myself virtually alone with several (I think six) Franks, so I high tailed it for the clouds below with all the [enemy] planes chasing and firing at me."[12] The enemy fire damaged his Hellcat as Hansen, his fighter also damaged, joined Sahloff's damaged aircraft as an escort, as the latter made for the coast. When Sahloff reached Tokyo Bay, he bailed out as his aircraft rolled a few times before crashing into the water.

The other three pilots, Harrison, Hobbs, and Mandeberg, also failed to return to the *Yorktown* with Proctor and Hansen. All three had gone down during the dogfight. Japanese on the ground later reported to American occupation authorities that a Japanese fighter (referred to as a "suicide plane" in a report) collided with Mandeberg's Hellcat. Although Sahloff had successfully bailed out, a rescue mission failed to locate him.

Besides the five Japanese fighters shot down by Proctor and Hansen, four more went down in the melee, including the plane that collided with Mandeberg. It was impossible, however, to determine who of the four missing men shot them down, so the Navy appropriately credited each man with shooting down one enemy aircraft.[13]

Chapter Two

By the summer of 1945, Allied forces, overwhelmingly American, were poised to invade the Japanese homeland. The initial six months of Japanese successes gave them control of the Philippines, East Indies, Southeast Asia, Micronesia, and large portions of Melanesia. By early 1943, the Americans blunted their advance on the island of Guadalcanal and, with Australian forces, on the north coast of the island of New Guinea. During the next two and half years, the Allies fought a two-pronged assault from the southwest Pacific and central Pacific, aimed at the heart of the Japanese Empire, the Home Islands of Japan. By June of 1945, American soldiers, Marines, airmen, and sailors had either captured or bypassed Japanese-held islands in Micronesia, Melanesia, and the Volcano Islands (including Iwo Jima) and liberated all but a portion of northern Luzon and a few smaller islands in the Philippines. The island Okinawa, part of the Japanese Home Islands and only 300 miles from them and also in American hands, was to become the springboard for the invasion of Kyushu, planned for the fall of 1945. The British, who had recaptured most of Burma, were poised to invade Singapore, on the Malay peninsula.

At the Second Quebec Conference of the Big Three in September 1944, American president Franklin Roosevelt, British prime minister Winston Churchill, and Soviet premier Joseph Stalin agreed on the strategy to force the unconditional surrender of Japan, following an invasion of the Home Islands. The strategic aim was to destroy the Japanese military and any hope they might have of continuing to resist the Allies, thus forcing unconditional surrender. The precursor to the invasion was the establishment of an air and sea blockade of the Home Islands, along with the strategic bombing of Japanese industry and the destruction of the Japanese army and navy air forces and the Navy.[14] The Joint Chiefs of

Staff formulated the American component of the strategy. It included the use of B-29 bombers from the new 20th Air Force and carrier aviation raids to eliminate Japanese industries, blockade the Home Islands, and cut sea communications with Korea and China.[15]

The blockade and aerial bombardment of the Home Islands, carried out by the U.S. Navy, was the only strategy on which all senior commanders agreed, seen as the precursor to the actual invasion.[16] In 1944, the Navy thought a blockade and strategic bombing would force the Japanese to surrender while Army planners believed an invasion of the Japanese Home Islands was necessary. After the Second Quebec Conference, the Joint Chiefs of Staff agreed to continue a blockade with strategic bombing, followed by an invasion of the island Kyushu in late 1945. The Navy, however, still viewed an invasion as only a possibility, used to gain more airfields to increase the level of bombing of Japanese cities and industries. By 1945, the Army, under Generals George Marshall and Douglas MacArthur, believed a strategy limited to blockade and aerial bombing would take too long to induce the Japanese to surrender. Admiral Nimitz, commander of the Pacific Fleet, joined them in supporting an invasion of Kyushu, but only after the blockade and bombing had created the most favorable condition. Although Allied policy had been the unconditional surrender of Japan, an assessment by the Joint Intelligence Staff in the spring of 1945 concluded that Japan could surrender before the end of the year, but not unconditionally. In addition, it also determined that pursuing a policy of rigid unconditional surrender using only a blockade and aerial bombardment would make the war last several more years. Roosevelt died in mid-April and Vice President Harry S. Truman became president. The same month, the Joint Chiefs of Staff ordered planning for the invasion of Kyushu to commence. Wrangling about whether the Army or Navy would command the invasion ensued, but by June both services agreed that the Army would have the major command responsibility for a contingency they hoped would never be carried out.[17]

The bombardment plan depended on strategic bombing by AAF, as well as attacks by Army Air Force and Navy aircraft on tactical targets, primarily airfields, but also the remnants of the Imperial Fleet, shipping, and railways.[18] Admiral William Halsey expected attacks by carrier planes on shipping and ports, as well as the shore bombardments carried out by battleships and cruisers, to close Japanese coastal shipping routes, further restricting the movement of supplies and reinforcement of the island of Kyushu. He believed the destruction of the remaining capital warships in the ports of Kure and Yokosuka was necessary to prevent these ships from slipping out and harassing supply convoys scheduled to ply the north Pacific that fall, although the Army dismissed this threat as minor.[19]

The Japanese Imperial Staff began to plan for the invasion of Japan in January 1945, a few days after American forces landed on Luzon, in the Philippines. Potential landing places began to be fortified and plans to raise another forty divisions finalized. The defense of the Home Island of Kyushu, a plan called Ketsu Go, aimed to defeat an invasion on the beaches. The plan called for the reinforcement of troops and the stock-piling and dispersal of aircraft for *kamikaze* missions and the creation of new, hidden airfields. This soon became evident to the Allies through intercepts of Japanese communications and aerial reconnaissance. The Japanese government mobilized the civilian population along the coast of the Home Islands in March 1945 to build fortifications and a civilian defense corps created to help with the defense once an invasion occurred.[20]

The Americans became aware of these defensive plans through Allied intelligence intercepts of Japanese communications, code-named "Ultra" for military messages and "Magic" for diplomatic intercepts. The intercepts revealed the extent to which the Japanese military refused to acknowledge the war was lost and their intention to fight to the death in the Home Islands, or at least inflict so many casualties on the American invaders that a negotiated peace would become a practical eventuality.[21] Information about the rapid increase in the number of Japanese troops in Kyushu to oppose the invasion also became evident through intercepts. The prospect of increasing numbers of American casualties from the increase in Japanese troop strength became an important factor in the decision to drop the atomic bomb on a Japanese city. During the Potsdam Conference in July 1945, General Marshall told President Truman that the invasion of Kyushu, and the landing on the Kanto plain near Tokyo, planned for early 1946, would cost a minimum of 250,000 American casualties and potentially up to a million.[22]

THE AMERICAN FORCES

The air component of the strategy to prepare for the invasion of Japan involved full-scale strategic bombing by the 20th Air Force, begun in November 1944 from the Mariana Islands, 1,500 miles from the Japanese Home Islands. Following mixed success with traditional high-altitude bombing, low-level attacks with incendiary bombs began in March 1945. By mid-June 1945, the big bombers had flatted the major cities of Tokyo, Nagoya, Osaka, Yokohama, and Kobe with incendiary raids, so the Super-fortresses turned to secondary cities with populations between 100,000 and 200,000 people. Attacks on these medium-size cities during the first ten days of July destroyed almost fifty percent of their area. By war's end, B-29s had attacked sixty-six cities and destroyed forty-three percent of their areas,[23] as well as strictly military targets during this period: oil refineries, aircraft and other industrial plants, and arsenals.

The B-29s also began to drop mines outside ports and in the Inland Sea and Shimonoseki Straits in March 1945. This effort soon began to severely affect Japanese shipping. Part of the blockade of Japan preventing the shipping of vital war supplies from Southeast Asia, China, and Korea, about two-thirds of the Japanese merchant ships sunk or damaged between March and August 1945 were victims of mines dropped by B-29s.[24] Navy patrol planes based on Iwo Jima and Okinawa also took part in this sea blockade, attacking Japanese shipping in the East China Sea, Yellow Sea, Sea of Japan, and Inland Sea between Kyushu and Honshu. The operation of so many Army Air Force and Navy planes over the same seas, and the Home Islands, led to the creation of operational boundaries in June to prevent Navy planes from flying into areas raided by B-29s and Army Air Force fighters and bombers of the Far East Air Force. The latter's B-24 bombers, along with long-range P-47 and P-51 fighters, were, by then, attacking airfields in Kyushu and southern Honshu from new bases on Okinawa, only 325 miles from Kyushu.[25]

The Japanese had expended many planes, most as *kamikazes*, during the Okinawa campaign. Beginning in June, the number of missions the Japanese flew declined, as they began to hoard their aircraft strength for the impending invasion of the Japanese Home Islands. The absence of Japanese aircraft in the air made it necessary for the Allies to seek out and destroy the Japanese air force over the Home Islands themselves to prepare for the invasion. Besides the Army Air Force bombers and fighters attacking enemy airfields on Kyushu and southern Honshu that summer, Navy carrier-based planes of Task Force 38, called the Fast Carrier Task Force of the American Pacific Fleet, attacked airfields on the island of Kyushu for three days at the beginning of June. The next attacks by carrier aircraft of the Task Force took place in early July, as we shall see.

Three Task Groups composed Task Force 38, with each containing three or four aircraft Essex-class carriers and two Independence-class light carriers.

The Essex-class *USS Bennington* with Air Group 1, *USS Hancock* with Air Group 6, and *USS Lexington* with Air Group 94 sailed in Task Group 38.1. The two light carriers were *USS Belleau Wood* with Air Group 31 and *USS San Jacinto* with Air Group 49. Task Group 38.3 also had three Essex-class carriers: *USS Randolph* with Air Group 16, *USS Essex* with Air Group 83, and *USS Ticonderoga* with Air Group 87. This Task Group's light carriers were *USS Monterey*, Air Group 34, and *USS Bataan*, Air Group 47. The last Task Group, 38.4, included the Essex-class carriers *USS Shangri-La* with Air Group 85; *USS Wasp* with Air Group 86; *USS Yorktown* with Air Group 88; and *USS Bon Homme Richard* with Air Group (N) 91, the air group trained for night operations. Task Group 38.4's two light carriers were the *USS Independence*, Air Group 27, and *USS Cowpens*, Air Group 50.

Each Essex-class carrier air group had four squadrons: a fighter (VF), fighter-bomber (VBF), dive-bomber (VB), and torpedo (VT) squadron. Fighter and torpedo squadrons made up the flight lines of the light carrier air groups. With some exceptions among the VF and VBF squadrons, F6F-5 Hellcats equipped the VF squadrons and F4U Corsairs the VBF squadrons. The usual complement of aircraft on an Essex-class carrier in mid-1945 was thirty-six fighters, thirty-six fighter-bombers, fifteen dive-bombers, and fifteen torpedo bombers.

The Hellcat was the mainstay of Navy fighter squadrons during 1943 and 1944. Bearing six .50 caliber machine guns, it had a high diving speed because of a heavier airframe, had good rate of climb, and could absorb considerable damage and still reach home. Not as fast as the Corsair, it still performed well at high altitude. The Navy was initially leery of the Corsair, believing it to be a poor carrier aircraft as the pilot sat toward the rear of the cockpit and closer to the deck. The Corsair was more likely to stall at the slower speeds required when landing on an aircraft carrier. The Marines initially got the aircraft, but once they had proven its worth in combat, the Navy reconsidered the Corsair and began to equip carrier air groups with the plane by late 1944. The aircraft composition of two air groups in Task Force 38, Air Groups 85 and 87, however, differed from this norm. VF-85 flew Corsairs, while Air Groups 16 and 87 still had Hellcats equipping their fighter-bomber squadron, VBF-16 and VBF-87.

All dive-bomber, or VB, squadrons flew the SB2C Helldiver, or "Beast," with a two-man crew: the pilot and a radioman-gunner behind, facing the tail of the plane. The Helldiver had teething problems, like the Corsair, but joined the fleet in late 1943. Armed with two 20mm cannons in the wings, it also had two flexible .30 caliber guns in the rear.

Crews of torpedo squadrons flew the TBM Avenger, also nicknamed the "Turkey" because of its stout appearance. The TBM had a gunner in an electrically operated turret armed with a .30 caliber machine gun, and a radioman in a compartment in the bowels of the aircraft. It was a sturdy aircraft with an internal bomb bay and wings that folded electrically.[26] The usual bomb load for all four aircraft during the summer operations was either two 500-pound bombs or one 1,000-pound bomb. They also carried rockets that were used to great effect against aircraft on the ground and small ships.

The pilots of these aircraft generally received better training than other services during the war, particularly those qualified for carrier landings that required more skill than landing in a stationary air strip, a source of pride for the pilots of carrier air groups.[27] The experience of the crews assigned to air groups in Task Force 38 in the summer of 1945, however, varied. Most air groups had flown in combat earlier in the war. After each combat tour, the air group would return to the United States, where they reformed before returning to combat. After working up to combat requirements, the reformed air group was assigned to a new aircraft carrier. Several of the air groups in Task Force 38 that summer had begun their last combat tour of World War II before the final raids on Japan.

Air Groups 6, 47, 83, and 86 entered combat during Fifth Fleet raids on Japan in March. In May, Air Groups 34, 49, 85, and 87 began their combat tours, while Air Group 50 began combat operations in early June. The combat initiation for the reformed configurations of Air Groups 1, 16, 27, and 31 came during the July 10 missions to Japan. Air Groups 88 and 94, both formed for the first time in 1944, also flew their first combat missions in July.

The air groups and their carriers were the main part of the Task Group. Five carriers with one to three battleships, light cruisers, and destroyers as escorts were the usual components of a Task Group. The three Task Groups—38.1, 38.3, and 38.4—plying the waters off the coast of Japan that summer usually sailed about ten miles apart, to remain with the line-of-sight range of TBS (talk between ships) communications. Ships would sail in one direction to launch planes, then turn around to land them, repeating this cycle throughout a day and remaining in the same general area so pilots would know where to return to their carriers.[28]

Combat air patrols (CAPs) were flown from carriers throughout the day, from dawn until dusk, to patrol for submarines and enemy aircraft, as were CAPs over surfaced lifeguard submarine stations off the coast of Japan to rescue downed flyers. Planes flying the latter, called "SubCAP" missions, usually attacked targets of opportunity on the Japanese coast in the vicinity of the submarine they had protected once their patrols were complete. Weather flights flew daily, and replacements for those aircraft lost in combat, or written off in flight deck crashes, often landed while the Task Force steamed off the coast, in between combat strikes. When not engaged in combat operations, air groups flew daily and training flights and accidents were not uncommon. The flight deck of a carrier was a place of constant activity, and danger, to flight deck personnel and air crews alike. Aircraft accidents usually involved ditching at takeoff or landing crashes, with planes either piling up on the flight deck of a carrier or going over the side of the ship. Men were injured or killed, an unfortunate part of the day-to-day routine of aircraft carriers at sea during wartime.

On a day of combat operations, a first wave of fighter and fighter-bomber sweeps would take off around dawn, followed by the first strikes of the day, flown by more fighters and fighter-bombers, as well as dive-bombers, and torpedo planes. After the first sweeps and strikes returned, guided to a safe landing by the Landing Signals Officer on each carrier, more sweeps took off later in the morning. A second wave of strikes usually took to the air in the very early afternoon. Combat and operational losses on the morning missions often reduced the number of planes flying the afternoon mission. Sometimes, more sweeps would follow the afternoon strikes, before darkness brought a halt to air operations on most carriers. The exception was Air Group (N) 91 on *USS Bon Homme Richard*, specially trained for night flying. Most strikes and many sweeps included several Hellcats employed as photo aircraft, to record the target before and after an attack so damage could be accurately assessed. These aircraft also took reconnaissance photos of potential targets for use in planning future attacks.

Of course, American aircraft were not the only planes in the air off the coast of Japan that summer. Japanese planes often tried to attack the Task Force, as they had during the *kamikaze* suicide attacks made on the American fleet during the battle for Okinawa that spring. The first line of defense against Japanese air attack was the radar picket destroyer line, stationed between twenty to fifty miles from the carrier Task Groups. Their radar often detected enemy planes approaching from the Empire with enough time to alert the combat air patrols orbiting overhead. When Japanese planes penetrated this first line of defense, the combat air patrols over the Task Force took a hand and usually shot down the intruders, sometimes braving American antiaircraft fire to do so. Although these American, and British, flyers stopped most *kamikaze* attacks, sailors manning the antiaircraft guns on ships of the Task Force defended themselves against the few that did get through, using several basic antiaircraft weapons. Japanese pilots first encountered heavy antiaircraft fire from five-inch antiaircraft guns with a range of 18,000 yards that could fire up to twenty rounds per minute with an experienced crew. As they drew closer to the fleet, the 40mm Bofors gun, with a range of three miles, joined in followed by the 20mm Oerlikons that could fire 600 rounds per minute. No Japanese planes, nor bombs, hit any of the ships in the carrier task groups of the Task Force while steaming off the coast of the Home Islands of Japan during July or August 1945.[29]

Attempts to hit the fleet began with "snooper" flights by Japanese reconnaissance planes attempting to locate the fleet so *kamikaze* flights could follow. A Japanese bomber would then follow up, leading planes with poorly trained but dedicated pilots who would aim at an American ship. The ideal method was shooting down the snoopers, often very successful that summer, to prevent suicide attacks from taking place.[30]

Besides the *kamikaze* attacks on the Task Force, the Japanese also maintained an antiaircraft defense of the Home Islands, although in 1945 it was still, in some respects, rudimentary and fragmentary. A number of the strikes described here surprised the Japanese defenders of airfields and ports, as the effectiveness of Japanese radar was limited, ineffective in locating fighters and the smaller aircraft flown by Task Force 38.[31] They used two types of radar, vertical scanning and horizontal scanning, but neither could detect planes approaching at either very high or very low altitude. Radar coverage was not continuous in Japan, except near important potential targets like Tokyo. The gaps often allowed American planes to approach the Empire undetected. Many Japanese picket boats stationed several hundred miles offshore to provide the first word of an attack had been sunk by the summer of 1945. As a result, military and civilian aircraft observers on shore often gave the first word of an approaching attack. Fighter control was inadequate, with poor communication between operations rooms that tracked American aircraft and the fighter units intended to intercept them. So the Japanese had great difficulty in concentrating fighters to oppose American strikes, a necessity for an efficient defense.[32, 33]

Among the fighters encountered by American Navy pilots over Japan that summer was the venerable Mitsubishi A6M Reisen or Zero, code-named "Zeke," in service since 1940. Maneuverable at lower altitudes, it was less nimble above 15,000 feet but had a good rate of climb. Without armor plating or self-sealing fuel tanks, it caught fire easily. Although armed with 20mm cannons, they were not all that effective. The Hellcat surpassed the Zero when it appeared in combat in 1943.[34] The Japanese Army also employed the Ki-43 Hayabusa, code-named "Oscar," over the Home Islands that summer. Very light weight and maneuverable, with a good rate of climb, it was slower than Zero and relatively poorly armed with two 13mm (.50 caliber) machine guns, and also did not have armor or self-sealing fuel tanks. Allied pilots feared it early in the war and it was still a formidable adversary in the hands of experienced pilots, although these were in increasingly short supply that summer.

The Japanese Army Kawasaki Ki-61 Hien, code-named "Tony," first appeared in 1943. Based on the German Me 109, the Army's Tony, or Ki-61, had an inline, water-cooled engine that provided good high-altitude performance. The plane dove well and, equipped with self-sealing fuel tanks and four 13mm machine guns, was effective against American bombers in the last year of the war.[35]

The Navy's Mitsubishi J2M Raiden, code-named "Jack" by Americans, also took part in many air battles that summer. Japanese pilots preferred the Jack because of its armament, four 20mm cannons on most models, high performance, and improved protection for the pilot. A Japanese Army fighter, the Ki-84 Hayate ("Gale" or "Frank") also had good pilot protection. With high speed, good maneuverability, and four 20mm cannons, it held its own against American planes that summer. American pilots also encountered the Kawanishi N1K Shiden, or "George," armed with two machine guns and two 20mm cannons. The plane had some success against Hellcats at lower altitude, but lost performance at higher altitude.

Without a rotation policy for combat pilots, few experienced Japanese pilots remained by the summer of 1944. Navy pilots had half the experience of those flying at beginning of the war, as did Army pilots, brought about by the decline in pilot training.[36] The result could often be a one-sided encounter with American pilots during a dogfight, often fought at ranges of 300 yards, or less. American pilots, with more flight training and, often, more combat experience often had a distinct edge in a dogfight, particularly when they had an altitude advantage.[37]

Only a few Navy missions met fighter opposition that summer, however, since the Japanese hoarded most of their remaining aircraft as *kamikazes* to oppose the impending invasion. By early August 1945, Japanese forces in the Home Islands had 800 fighters and 2,000 *kamikaze* aircraft available to oppose an invasion. Most were camouflaged and hidden on, or near, small airfields undiscovered by American reconnaissance or dispersed up to more than four miles from established airfields. Once the invasion fleet appeared off the coast, these aircraft would move closer to the American invasion armada. The pilots of these *kamikaze* units had insufficient training to oppose American naval aircraft, and the communications necessary to get them into the air to do so had broken down by the summer of 1945. With experienced pilots growing scarce, less-experienced pilots took part in normal combat operations, as well as *kamikaze* attacks, and often faced American flyers in air battles that summer.[38]

These aerial melees often occurred over airfields, the prime target of Navy fighters, where antiaircraft gunners generally took over the defense of airfields since the Japanese were conserving aircraft to oppose the impending invasion. These antiaircraft gunners used two types of antiaircraft guns: heavy 75mm and 120mm guns to reach high altitude and medium- to small-caliber 20mm and 40mm guns to fire at lower altitudes. The Japanese discovered, however, that these antiaircraft weapons were generally not that effective against planes below 7,000 feet (3,000 meters), so antiaircraft units with automatic cannon began to be placed on some airfields that summer.[39] Regardless of the type of guns employed, many of the planes of the Task Force lost that summer went down to guns on airfields, around ports, and on ships.[40] Navy pilots found Japanese naval antiaircraft gunners particularly annoying during attacks on shipping and harbors. The intensity, and accuracy, of their fire was often superior to guns onshore, manned by Army gunners. Both the Japanese Army and Navy used radar-guided antiaircraft guns for barrages fired at attacking American planes. Their effectiveness varied as the American planes dropped small strips of aluminum, called window, and very long strips, called rope, to throw off the radar.[41]

Chapter Three

JULY 10 WAS A LONG DAY FOR AVIATORS AND SAILORS OF THE TASK FORCE, the first day of a month-long campaign attacking a wide variety of targets in the Home Islands of Japan.

Carrier aircraft flew 1,303 sorties against airfields from Hamamatsu, south of Tokyo, northward to the city of Koriyama, more than 200 miles from the Japanese capital. Japanese fighters did not rise to oppose the attacks, but American flyers managed to destroy more than one hundred aircraft on the enemy's airfields.[42] VF-50 accomplished the only confirmed shootdown of an enemy plane on the 10th, as the Japanese hoarded their aircraft for the expected invasion of the Home Islands.

Lieutenant Charles Brock shot down a two-engine Dinah during a combat air patrol near the Task Force. At about 1:00 PM, a flight of Hellcats spotted the Dinah flying at an altitude of about 28,000 feet, seventy miles from the Task Force, apparently on a mission to locate the American fleet. The Hellcats went after the enemy bomber, catching up with it after a two-minute chase. The first section of the flight attacked, scoring hits from more than 1,000 feet away. Almost immediately, the second section, led by Lieutenant Brock, overtook the first section, closing to about 600 feet when Brock opened fire. His rounds hit the wing roots near the Dinah's fuselage and the plane immediately caught fire, went into a spin, and headed down toward the sea. Brock followed it down and saw one crewman bail out, before returning to his flight.[43] The enemy crashed into the sea, becoming the first aerial victory for the Task Force in this final offensive against the Home Islands of Japan.

The usual defensive combat air patrols flown around the Task Force began at sunrise and the first aircraft lost that day had just begun such a mission. A Hellcat of VF-6 ditched soon after takeoff from *USS Hancock*.

The submarine *USS Caperon* rescued the pilot, Lieutenant (jg) James Long, within a few minutes. Another fighter, a Corsair from *USS Hancock*'s VF-6, also ditched later in the morning. Lieutenant Harvey Odenbrett came down in the drink inside the Task Force. The destroyer, *USS John Rodgers*, immediately rescued him.

The air strikes and sweeps began very early as fighters and bombers took off from carriers in predawn darkness at 4:00 AM, almost half an hour before sunrise.[44] Seventeen different strike and sweep missions to enemy airfields took to the air during the next hour: 134 Hellcats and 103 Corsairs. Planes from Air Group 83 took off first, from *USS Essex*. Sixteen Corsairs from VBF-83 attacked the Japanese airfield at Atsugi, near Tokyo. Despite heavy antiaircraft fire from medium antiaircraft guns that fortunately missed the mark, the F4Us dropped fragmentation bombs over about sixty aircraft caught in the open on two parts of the field. Although pilots saw a number of bombs explode directly over planes, they couldn't easily see the damage they inflicted since fragmentation bombs required planes pull out at higher altitudes than other bombs, usually about 4,000 feet, to avoid damage to the attacking aircraft. *Essex* Hellcats, taking off twenty minutes later, got word of the large number of planes at Atsugi, in flight, and arrived at the field as the Corsairs finished up. They immediately spotted a large, four-engine plane on the field, heavily damaged by the Corsairs' bombs. Japanese antiaircraft gunners greeted them with intense fire as they also dropped fragmentation bombs on clusters of enemy aircraft, again without seeing specific results. On the way home, a few Hellcats strafed the airfield at Nii Shima.[45]

Seven Hellcats and four Corsairs from Air Group 6 mounted a sweep mission to airfields in the Tokyo area early that morning and pilots were in the air for four hours. Fog encountered on the Japanese coast dissipated as they flew inland. The first airfield they attacked, at Kiryu, put up strong but inaccurate antiaircraft fire as the American fighters dove on about twenty enemy fighters sitting in a dispersal area. Dropping 250-pound fragmentation bombs from an altitude of 5,000 feet, the Hellcats destroyed three planes and damaged at least two more. The flight then moved on to Kodama Airfield. Having dropped all their bombs on their first target, as was the case with most sweeps and strikes, the American fighters strafed a group of fifteen to twenty enemy planes with rockets and machine guns, destroying one plane and damaging several others As the flight turned toward home, the Corsairs made a pass at a third airfield, at Shimodate, firing the remainder of the rockets. The mission resulted in claims of five enemy aircraft destroyed, two by the Corsairs and three by the Hellcats, as well as four more damaged.[46] Flights often encountered moderate to heavy enemy antiaircraft fire while crossing the coast but varying opposition at the airfields they attacked.

Besides these early sweeps, aircraft from different air groups joined forces on several strike missions early that morning. Fighting Sixteen (VF-16) took off from *USS Randolph* just before 4:00 AM, then rendezvoused with Hellcats from VF-34 from *USS Monterey* for a strike against airfields on the Chiba Peninsula, near Tokyo. The flight leader from VF-16 acted as the strike leader. Hitting Miyakawa Airfield first, where no enemy planes were in the open, the Hellcats dropped fragmentation bombs and fired rockets at well-camouflaged enemy aircraft revetments, as well as hangars and other buildings. After reforming over the ocean, the flight set out for the second target, the airfield at Naruto, where they rocketed and machine-gunned hangars and repair shops. Before heading back to their carrier, they turned to a third target, a small fighter strip at Choja. Again finding no enemy planes in the open, the Hellcats "viciously strafed" and fired rockets at what appeared to be the operations building on the field, setting it on fire. Antiaircraft gunners did little firing at the attacking planes, their efforts described by pilots as "meager."[47]

More fighters from the *Randolph*, Hellcats from VBF-16, teamed up with Hellcats from VF-47 for a sweep of Mobara and Kisarazu Airfields on the Chiba Peninsula, including photographing other enemy airfields in the area. The Americans bombed and rocketed Japanese transport planes in the field at Kisarazu first, damaging two of them, then turned to Mobara, where they attacked aircraft revetments with rockets and machine-gun fire, also not observing any readily apparent results in the cleverly camouflaged revetments. Antiaircraft fire gunners at Kisarazu were fairly accurate, but didn't hit any American planes, while pilots reported little resistance at Mobara. All planes returned safely to their carriers.[48]

Many pilots on these early morning missions complained of the difficulty of communicating with each other as the Japanese jammed the frequencies they used, as well as filling the air with numerous bogus "tallyhos," but without using any of the call signs of Navy air groups or squadrons.[49] During the attacks, the American planes dropped window, aluminum strips employed to distort the wavelengths of the Japanese radar that often guided their antiaircraft guns, but pilots later reported it was as not very effective.[50]

<hr />

Following the early fighter sweeps, the first wave of strikes that added dive and torpedo bombers to the fighters took off between 6:45 and 7:15 AM. One hundred forty-two Avengers and ninety-three Helldivers from all carrier air groups in the Task Force took off from their carriers for thirteen airfield strikes, escorted by forty-eight F4Us and sixty-nine F6Fs not already committed to the earlier strikes. All these missions encountered enemy antiaircraft fire, but flak claimed only two American planes.

All four squadrons of Air Group 94, flying from *USS Lexington*, took part in a strike on Utsunomiya Airfield, the third attack on the airfield by the group since the dawn. All "pushed over" to attack the field from an altitude of 12,000–13,000 feet, encountering intense Japanese antiaircraft fire from heavy guns in their dives. Helldivers dive-bombed the field while the Avengers, never designed for dive-bombing, executed glide-bombing attacks at about 40 degrees. Bombs hit an antiaircraft emplacement and damaged, if not destroyed, several aircraft. Enemy antiaircraft gunners shot down Lieutenant Edward Clancy, flying a Corsair from VBF-94. Hit while diving on the airfield, other pilots saw a wing fly off his Corsair, which then dove into the ground, killing him instantly.[51]

Nine Avengers of VT-34, flying from *USS Monterey*, joined Air Group 83 planes—fourteen TBMs, fifteen SB2Cs with seven Hellcats and eight Corsairs as escort—in an attack on Atsugi Airfield. Japanese antiaircraft fire harassed the American planes from the time they made landfall, becoming extremely heavy at Atsugi. Its intensity made it difficult to observe the results of the attack, but pilots saw two "burners," their term for enemy aircraft that caught fire when hit, among the enemy aircraft bombed. Some of the VF-83 Hellcats stayed at high altitude to provide cover if enemy fighters tried to break up the attack while other Hellcats, and the Corsairs from VBF-83, attacked antiaircraft positions to suppress enemy antiaircraft fire as the Helldivers and Avengers dropped their bombs. Although only two enemy planes were on fire after the attack, it is likely the fragmentation bombs used inflicted damage to other planes that did not catch fire.[52]

Japanese antiaircraft fire at Atsugi claimed four Avengers from VT-34. One, flown by Ensign Joel Wasson with crewmen ARM3c Robert Miller and AMM3c Walter Selberg, went down near the target but the three fortunately survived to become prisoners of war. Three more TBMs, badly damaged by enemy fire, tried to return to the *Monterey*, escorted by some VBF-83 Corsairs, but eventually ditched off the coast of Japan. Two of the "Turkeys," flown by Ensigns Hugh Lang and John Jahnke, flew together, escorted by two more VT-34 TBMs. When they reached the location of a submarine on "lifeguard" duty at Suno Saki, off the coast of Honshu, both planes ditched together. The sub, *USS Galiban*, rescued both crews. The last Avenger, piloted by Ensign Homer Winter, had too much damage to reach the *Galiban* and ditched eighteen miles off the coast, in the Sagami Wan. Fighters from Air Group 83 circled the flyers in their raft and radioed the position to the sub. A short time later, the *Galiban* effected their rescue, too. The VT-34 report of the mission stated that the squadron pilots' and crewmen's "faith in the calm courage and seamanship of the officers and men of the lifeguard [submariners knew] ...no bounds."[53]

Air Group 1 made a fairly standard, single air group attack on the enemy at Hyakurigahara Airfield, nicknamed "Hari Kari" by the group's pilots "to avoid tongue-twisting radio reports." Approaching the enemy field along the coast, air group planes turned westward over the coastal town of Mito to attack the field a few miles inland.[54]

Eleven Helldivers attacked in three divisions. One targeted antiaircraft positions that put up little opposition, the second bombed aircraft revetments on the southern side of the airfield, while the third dropped their bombs on revetments on the eastern side. Bombs destroyed up to nine Japanese planes. A Helldiver pilot who had trouble during his dive flew over these revetments at low altitude and observed the damage. He reported that the camouflage of enemy planes in the field was extremely good, making targets difficult to locate.[55] The six Hellcats on the mission dropped fragmentation bombs on dispersal areas while the eight Corsairs bombed aircraft parked near hangars as well as revetments.[56] The Avengers, using their usual glide-bombing technique, bombed the northeast and west sides of the field, hitting several enemy aircraft.[57]

As an alternative to the combined force of a single air group, larger attacks could also combine squadrons from several air groups, a large force intended to overwhelm enemy defenses. One hundred six planes took part in the early morning attack on Kasumigaura Airfield northeast of Tokyo: sixteen Hellcats from Air Groups 27, 50, and 88; seventeen Corsairs and twenty-seven Helldivers from Air Groups 85 and 88; and forty-six Avengers from all the air groups involved. The strike leader, Lieutenant Commander Wallace Sherrill of Air Group 85, led the Corsairs of VBF-85 to reconnoiter the assigned airfields, then rendezvoused with the main force just before the attack began. The American crews spotted Kasumigaura while they were still twenty miles away and the attack began as planes from Air Groups 50 and 85 dove on the field, followed closely by Air Groups 27 and 88 to overwhelm the defenders. Squadrons bombed different parts of the field packed with enemy planes, each starting their dives from different altitudes, varying from 12,000 to 8,000 feet to throw off Japanese antiaircraft gunners. Crewmen on the bombers threw out window to further confuse the radar that controlled the heavier AA guns.

The Americans pulled out of their dives between 5,000 and 3,500 feet, higher than in the past because of the variable time, or VT, fused bombs they carried. This was an advantage to the Navy flyers since medium and light antiaircraft fire was less accurate at this higher altitude. Squadrons reported variable, less-accurate antiaircraft fire that only damaged a few planes. One pilot from VT-88 remarked that it was as if the Japanese gunners "closed their eyes and fired." With no enemy fighters to oppose them, the Hellcats strafed antiaircraft positions, no doubt reducing the accuracy, if the not the volume, of fire that they could level at the American bombers. The Helldivers of VB-85, who dove together to their war cry "Let's go, Dragons!" further disrupted the aim of antiaircraft gunners. VT-27 pilots reported that a smoke screen over the portion of the field they attacked, near the aircraft factory located next to the airfield, made it very difficult for crews to see how many planes were in the aircraft revetments they bombed. Close examination of strike photos taken during the attack later revealed ten twin-engine planes hidden in these revetments. The TBMs' fragmentation bombs exploded directly over the revetments, undoubtedly damaging some planes. But among all the squadrons involved in this attack, crews could only claim seven enemy planes as definitely destroyed.

The Corsairs had ammunition to spare on the return flight, so they strafed the enemy seaplane bases at Kashima and Shimazu, claiming three enemy aircraft destroyed. Because of the difficulty in determining the damage done to enemy aircraft by fragmentation bombs, from both photos and aerial observation during the attack, it was difficult to assess the damage inflicted on planes on an enemy airfield, particularly if they were not fueled and would not catch fire.[58]

One of the Avengers from VT-85 had an officer with a voice recorder on the mission. He described the attack as it unfolded, also recording conversations between the crew of his Avenger as well as the chatter between planes. The recording was later broadcast in the United States.[59]

Between 8:30 and 10:45 AM another 126 Hellcats and eighty-five Corsairs took off from their carriers to continue sweeps and attacks against Tokyo-area airfields. Two Hellcats failed to return from these missions. Four Hellcats and eight Corsairs of Air Group 1 took off at 9:00 AM to hit several airfields. Dropping bombs on a group of ten planes identified from reconnaissance photos at Ishioka Airfield, they damaged them, but couldn't claim any as destroyed as none caught fire. Moving on to Ishioka West Airfield, they rocketed and strafed planes in revetments, hitting one. The Americans took part in an oft-repeated coda to missions that summer, attacking targets of opportunity on the coast during the flight home. Two Corsair pilots strafed and sank a sampan, another damaged a barge, and a third "liquidated a lone hapless Jap fisherman and sank his twenty-foot boat." Pilots reported antiaircraft fire as "moderate" during the mission, but none of the twelve fighters was damaged.[60]

VF-88 lost a Hellcat, flown by Lieutenant (jg) Raymond Gonzalez, during another sweep of three Japanese airfields flown in tandem with Hellcats from VF-85. *Yorktown's* Hellcats attacked Kashima Airfield, followed closely by *Shangri-La's* Hellcats. Moderate antiaircraft fire made it inadvisable for the planes to stick around to assess the effect of the fragmentation bombs they dropped on aircraft revetments and dispersals, as well as antiaircraft positions. The few aircraft visible to them were obvious wrecks or dummies. Some *Yorktown* pilots, enthusiastic during their first combat mission, made another strafing pass, a practice not recommended by more experienced pilots when dropping fragmentation bombs.

Following the bombing at Kashima, the flight turned to Imba Airfield, where they did find some operational aircraft to burn. Firing rockets and machine guns, a VF-88 pilot set one plane on fire, but couldn't claim it as destroyed, while VF-85 made no claims. The airfield at Shiroi was the next stop. At this airfield, VF-85 destroyed a Betty bomber and one pilot strafed antiaircraft positions, silencing one. *Yorktown* pilots also dropped more fragmentation bombs on gun positions and revetments, fired more rockets on the latter, and set two planes on fire by strafing. Here flak damaged Gonzalez's plane, leaving his belly gas tank dangling underneath his Hellcat. Ordered to return to the *Yorktown* with another Hellcat experiencing engine trouble, Gonzalez got as far as the destroyer radar pickets when he ran out of fuel. He ditched his fighter between two destroyers. One of them, *USS Wadleigh*, immediately picked him up safely.

The level of resistance reported on this sweep varied between the two squadrons. *Yorktown* pilots on their first mission reported it as intense, while the more experienced VF-85 pilots, flying combat operations since May, described it as generally moderate. The fact that flak shot down a VF-88 Hellcat may also have influenced the squadron's characterization of flak on the mission.[61]

The other Hellcat lost was from VF-31, on a 10:00 AM strike to hit Kumagaya Airfield, northeast of Tokyo. Hit by "meager" flak while strafing the field, the pilot, Ensign E. H. Caywood, bailed out only 400 feet above the ground. His comrades saw his chute open just before he landed in a dry riverbed, but unfortunately he was killed. The squadron bombed camouflaged aircraft revetments during their first pass on the airfield, then returned for two more strafing passes. They set one enemy plane, hidden under trees and camouflage netting off the main airfield, on fire. One Hellcat strafed a train chugging along near the airfield during the attack, but inflicted little obvious damage.[62]

Two minor but interesting incidents occurred during one of the second wave of strikes that took off between 8:30 and 10:45 AM that morning. The first involved an encounter with an American plane captured by the Japanese. Thirteen Hellcats of VF-49 flew a sweep to Koga and Tsukuba Airfields, also northeast of Tokyo. At the first field, Koga, half the Hellcats attacked Japanese aircraft parked on field, hitting a two-engine Betty bomber parked in the open that exploded when a bomb landed directly on it. The remaining Hellcats stayed at altitude to provide top cover during the bombing that also destroyed two more enemy planes parked in front of hangars. Roles then reversed as the top cover planes made their own attack on Tsukuba West Airfield, bombing revetments and aircraft dispersals, but with no obvious results. After leaving Tsukuba, on the flight home, the squadron observed aircraft parked on Miyakawa Airfield, so several Hellcats strafed the field. Close observation revealed the aircraft were not operational, but one looked to most pilots to be an American B-24 four-engine bomber, in characteristic Japanese brown and green camouflage. The circumstances of the bomber's capture are unknown, but similar instances occurred in the Pacific and Europe during the war.[63]

The other incident involved a Corsair pilot from *USS Shangri-La*. VBF-85 and VBF-88 bombed and strafed two enemy fields near Tokyo during their 10:45 AM strike. Facing moderate flak, the F4Us dropped bombs and strafed the field at Tokorozawa, with VBF-85 claiming five planes destroyed while *Yorktown* pilots hit hangars. Following the rendezvous after their first pass on Tokorozawa, the planes moved on to Irumagawa Airfield. Although none of the aircraft attacked burned, pilots thought they had destroyed five with their thorough strafing. The flight then returned to Tokorozawa for a third pass, strafing the field and hitting a Helen bomber.

Immediately after the attack at Tokorozawa, the engine of Lieutenant (jg) John Loeffler's Corsair quit. He guided his planed to the Tone River, which he thought would lead him to the sea. It soon became apparent that he was heading into the intense antiaircraft defenses of Tokyo itself. He spotted an open field along the river and prepared to crash land when he fortunately discovered that his "disabled" engine had quit because he had inadvertently placed it in "idle/cut off" during the strafing run. He restored the proper setting and returned safely to the *Shangri-La*.[64]

A lull in attacks, lasting several hours, permitted the landing of aircraft from the morning strikes and preparation for the second strike, early in the afternoon. The latter took off beginning at about 1:00 PM: 166 Hellcats, ninety-two Corsairs, 143 Avengers, and eighty-six Helldivers, all continuing attacks on airfields. The Americans lost five aircraft on these missions. A sixth, an Air Group 94 Helldiver, crashed on takeoff and ditched near the carrier. Fortunately, *USS Ringgold* rescued both crewmen, Ensign William Nicholson and ARM2c Julius Wofford.[65]

One of the aircraft lost was from VBF-88, part of another combined strike on Konoike Airfield, near Osaka, by three of the four air groups dispatched to Kasumigaura that morning: Air Groups 27, 50, 85, and 88. Twenty-two Corsairs, twenty-eight Helldivers, and forty-four Avengers took part. On the flight to the target, the target changed to Konoike, where earlier missions spotted forty planes that morning. Arriving over the field, it was quickly evident that most of the aircraft reported were wrecks or dummies, so the target coordinator, Commander Seth Searcy of Air Group 88, ordered bombing of aircraft revetments containing camouflaged twin-engine planes. The *Yorktown*'s Corsairs bombed and strafed antiaircraft positions to suppress their fire, then the Helldivers went in shortly before VB-85. When only half of *Yorktown* Helldivers were in their dive, the commander of the *Shangri-La* Helldivers told them to attack so they would not lose their attack position. The result was saturation of the defenses with two squadrons attacking at once. Both squadrons dropped fragmentation bombs on aircraft revetments. The Avengers from all four air groups followed up, hitting bombed hangars, aircraft dispersals, and aircraft revetments. Because of smoke, and the higher altitude at which planes dropped fragmentation bombs, crews generally could not see the effect of the attack. VT-50 did set two planes on fire in revetments, while VBF-85 bombed several more containing up to twenty enemy aircraft that no doubt suffered varying degrees of damage. Air Group 88 claimed two planes known destroyed and TBMs from the carrier *Independence* left a hangar burning.

The air groups reported Japanese antiaircraft fire to be moderate and it cost Ensign Charles Emhoff of VBF-88 his life. Antiaircraft rounds hit his Corsair as he dove to attack a gun position on the field, although it is possible fragments from a prematurely detonating fragmentation bomb, dropped by another plane, struck his aircraft. In any event, his plane crashed on the field.[66]

One of the other planes lost that afternoon was an Avenger of VT-1 that went down attacking Hyakurigahara Airfield, northeast of Tokyo, when all four squadrons hit the enemy airfield. Corsairs hit different parts of the field first. Bombing revetments and hangars, they started fires in the hangar area that were still raging several hours later. Helldivers and Avengers concentrated on aircraft revetments but could not assess any damage they might have caused. Japanese flak gunners fired a "meager" barrage, but still managed to shoot off part of the tail of Ensign Robert Haughton's TBM as the plane dove to drop its bombs. The plane crashed about a mile and a half from the enemy field. Although one crewman parachuted from the stricken aircraft just before it crashed, none of the three crewmen—Haughton, AMM3c Joseph Ciccarelli, and ARM3c George Clegg—survived. Flak also damaged four other Avengers that did return safely to their carrier, the *Bennington*.[67]

Air Group 16, flying with a dozen Hellcats, fourteen Avengers, and fourteen Helldivers from *USS Randolph*, lost two planes during their 2:00 PM strike on enemy airfields at Mobara, Naruto, and Miyakawa, carried out with eight Avengers from VT-47. The strike split into three sections to hit all three airfields at the same time. Although bombs and rockets hit aircraft revetments, runways, and some buildings, crews could not note specific damage. Part of the intense antiaircraft fire reported during the mission, flak at Miyakawa hit the Hellcat of Ensign William Lange, of

VF-16, as he flew a strafing run on the airfield. The fighter rolled on its back at a very low altitude and crashed in a corner of the enemy field, killing the pilot instantly.[68] Another *Randolph* plane on this mission, an Avenger, suffered an oil leak as it pulled out of glide-bomb attack on Naruto Airfield. This mechanical problem forced the pilot, Lieutenant William Holmes, to ditch about sixty miles off the coast of Japan. Holmes and the other two crewmen, AMM2c Robert Zern and ARM2c Neil Hanley, got out of the aircraft safely and into a life raft. Three other VT-16 Avengers circled the men for several hours until darkness fell, but search and rescue aircraft didn't locate the downed men with their aerial escort later that day. The aerial search continued for two more days without success and the three crewmen were lost.[69] The F6F of Lieutenant Robert Talbot developed engine trouble at the start of the return flight and decided to ditch near a lifeguard submarine known to be on duty in the vicinity. After that successful ditching, *USS Galiban* picked him up, the fourth rescue by this submarine on July 10.[70]

Air Group 6 flew a strike that afternoon with all four of its squadrons: eight Hellcats, four Corsairs, ten Helldivers, and ten Avengers. Briefed for another airfield in the Tokyo area, at Maebishi, they arrived to find the enemy field covered by clouds. Upon discovering a hole in the clouds, the group dove through to attack an enemy field they could see that turned out to be Takasaki Airfield, located close to Maebishi. Two of the TBMs on the mission had to jettison their bombs due to faulty release mechanisms, over Maebishi town, but the remaining planes bombed the field. The Hellcats dropped fragmentation bombs and fired rockets on aircraft revetments and hangars. The Corsairs split into two sections, one leading and the other following the Helldivers and Avengers, also dropping fragmentation bombs and firing rockets, but increasing cloud cover prevented the pilots from viewing the results. The Helldivers preceded the Avengers in the attack, pushing over into their dives from 10,000 feet altitude, firing rockets and dropping fragmentation bombs on aircraft revetments. Like most groups on the day's strikes, crews had great difficulty in seeing any concrete results from their efforts, namely, enemy aircraft destroyed by fire or explosions.

One Helldiver had a very close call as the aircraft went into a spin during the dive. The pilot only recovered control a frightening 200 feet from the ground. Unable to release their bombs, the pilot and gunner both "strafed like mad" as they flew away from the enemy field, eventually jettisoning their bombs at sea. The remaining Helldivers dropped their bombs and fired rockets, hitting hangars and aircraft revetments. The only enemy opposition encountered was a few antiaircraft bursts on the way to the target.[71]

The score for the day was good, with American planes claiming 109 Japanese aircraft destroyed on the ground, along with the destruction of hangars and repair shops on the airfields.[72] The ability of the Japanese to successfully hide their planes frustrated American airmen, who hoped for better results for their efforts. Not only were dummy aircraft, made from wood or even straw, employed, but the Japanese hid operational aircraft some distance from the runways of fields, using the topography of the surrounding area to conceal them. This frustration is evident in a comment in the mission report from the *Yorktown*'s Corsair squadron following one of the morning attacks on Kashima Airfield mentioned above, where it was impossible for pilots to see if their bombs and rockets had hit any enemy aircraft. "The known results of the sweep [to Kashima Airfield] make it nothing less than a discouraging effort. We had lain awake at nights thinking of the spectacular air battles over Japan. We actually saw two enemy planes airborne [apparently in the distance, as they are not specifically mentioned elsewhere in the report] and were confronted by a non-spectacular opposition in the form of little to moderate AA and intense light and medium AA. Although over one hundred individual attacks were made on the various targets, not one pilot can say with any certainty that he destroyed a single operational aircraft or killed a single Jap."[73]

Following these missions, one squadron commander recommended low-level strafing, as the only effective way to locate these Japanese planes was to use "tree top" bombing and strafing to destroy them, a distinctly more dangerous endeavor than dive- and glide-bombing attacks that leveled out above the accurate range of medium and light antiaircraft fire. The practice became more common as the campaign continued.[74]

As mentioned earlier, air crews found it difficult to observe the damage caused by fragmentation bombs, primarily because of the altitude from which they dropped these bombs. Although hundreds of fragments could damage enemy aircraft, if they had no fuel, they wouldn't burn. From the usual pull-out altitude of 4,000–5,000 feet, it was almost impossible to determine the effect of the bombs on enemy aircraft that were not on fire.[75]

After a satisfactory day's work, the Task Force steamed northward that night to prepare for the next series of strikes, scheduled for July 13 against targets in northern Honshu and Hokkaido. Extremely bad flying weather, however, forced postponement of the strikes until the following day.

Chapter Four

WITH THE WEATHER IMPROVED BUT STILL FAR FROM IDEAL, EARLY ON the morning of the 14th carrier aircraft again attacked airfields, this time on northern Honshu and Hokkaido, previously immune from American aircraft attacks as they were beyond the range of even the B-29s flying from the Marianas. Almost 700 strike sorties flown down that day added shipping, ports, and railroads to the airfields already on their target list. The ferries that transported coal from the island of Hokkaido to Honshu, vital to the Japanese war effort, were the one of the main targets of strikes on the 14th. American planes attacked the ports of Hakodate, Aomori, Kushiro, and Muroran, along with shipping in the Tsugaru Strait between the two islands, as well as airfields and some industrial targets. These attacks destroyed twenty-seven Japanese aircraft on the ground, as well as four warships, a destroyer and three frigates, and twenty-five merchant ships.[76]

The Task Force used an approaching typhoon to mask its approach. Forecasts and observations indicated the storm would curve toward the Home Islands, so the Task Force remained in the area and launched attacks behind the storm, achieving surprise as the Japanese expected the fleet to retreat from the storm as they had in the past. The Task Force also used the fog line, the point where water temperature changed rapidly, producing fog to the north of it, to mask its location by remaining to the south.[77]

❧

By 4:05 that morning, seventeen sweep and strike missions had already taken off to cover a large area, as intelligence on Japanese airfields and military installations on Hokkaido was incomplete. VBF-1's Corsairs from *USS Bennington* ranged along the east coast of Hokkaido, beginning at the town of Shiranuka, which they strafed before moving on to the town of Kushiro, in search of an airfield believed to be in the vicinity. Failing to locate it, the flight strafed Kushiro town and boats in the harbor. Their next stop was then the seaplane base at Akkeshi, farther north along the coast. Although no enemy planes were at the base, strafing set an oil dump on fire. Two five-inch guns near the town fired at the flight as it left the town, anxious to strike back at the enemy. After the seaplane base, the Corsairs returned to Kushiro, this time concentrating on the harbor, where the pilots strafed docks, ships, and boats. One small freighter blew up during the attack, believed to be the *No. 2 Tamazono Maru*. The Corsairs rounded out the mission with an attack on a trawler as pilots fired a few rockets and then strafed the craft mercilessly, damaging it to the extent that it grounded near the shore.

Fog complicated the return flight to the *Bennington*. One of the Corsairs, damaged by antiaircraft fire at Akkeshi, had to ditch. The plane's engine stopped while in the landing circle. The pilot, Lieutenant (jg) Frank Kingston, made a successful "dead stick," ditching about a mile and a half from the carrier, and immediately got out of the plane before it sank. The cold temperature of the water made it difficult to inflate the raft, but he did so, got in it, and awaited the rescue that was not long in coming. Within fifteen minutes the destroyer *USS Brush* picked him up.[78]

Two fighters went down on the dawn sweeps, one from VF-85, the other VF-88, when both squadrons flew a sweep over Hokkaido. Unable to rendezvous because of the poor weather, each squadron proceeded independently. VF-85 split into two, six-plane sections and attacked ships near the port of Otaru.

One flight had good luck and sank two small cargo ships and a tugboat. The Hellcats bombed and strafed the first ship they found and quickly sank it. Looking for more prey, they next spotted a tugboat towing a barge. Strafing blew up the tug's boiler and the craft sank. A near miss by a 500-pound bomb and several rocket strikes sent another small cargo ship to the bottom. The section's last victim was a mid-size troop transport. Another near miss with a bomb and follow-up rocket attacks left it on fire and beached, with a large hole in its side.

The other six Hellcats also found a small cargo ship to strike from Japanese merchant shipping rolls. One pilot scored a direct hit with a 500-pound bomb on the vessel, followed by ten rocket hits scored by other planes. The Japanese vessel caught fire and sank.

Resistance to these attacks was very minimal and the only loss was Lieutenant Duncan McPhee's plane. He ran out of fuel and had to ditch near the Task Force. After an hour in his life raft, *USS Metz* picked him up.[79]

Yorktown's VF-88 also lost a fighter on the mission, but had even better luck with targets than VF-85. Reaching Hokkaido, the flight came down through the overcast and spotted land, but no readily available targets. Flying along the coast, they found a marshalling yard in the clear. Carrying only rockets, the eleven Hellcats on the mission fired at a number of locomotives in the yard and more pulling trains, destroying at least eight locomotives. One exploded directly in front of the attacking plane and threw mud and dust on the cockpit. Another train had two engines, one at either end. Two pilots, one of them Lieutenant Raymond Gonzalez, who was back in the game after his ditching and dunking on the 10th, fired rockets that blew up both engines.

While some pilots entertained themselves with the locomotives, Lieutenant Howard Harrison, whom we met in chapter one, saw a harbor in the distance. The squadron flew over it, after completing the destruction of the rail targets, to find it was Hakodate Harbor, packed with ships. Overcast at about 3,000 feet over the harbor made an attack feasible as antiaircraft gunners would have little time to lay their sights on diving planes. The flight dove through the overcast and several pilots rocketed a small cargo ship, scoring six hits. At the beginning of the strafing run, another plane dropped a bomb on the vessel's bow and two more pilots scored near misses. The vessel sank before the *Yorktown* pilots could make another pass. At the same time, other VF-88 pilots attacked shore installations, rocketing a large building near the docks, one of the train ferries at dock, and another merchant ship that caught fire.

Following these attacks, the aviators saw a destroyer, subsequently identified as the *Tachibana*, sailing out of the harbor. Several pilots made a strafing run that reduced the volume of antiaircraft fire coming from the warship considerably. Two more attacks followed and, during the third, the vessel suddenly exploded, broke in two, and sank.

The squadron then turned for home, satisfied with the morning's accomplishments. Flak from the destroyer had damaged the Hellcat flown by Ensign Ralph Koontz, creating a large hole in the wing. He reached the Task Force but had to abandon the fighter, as a damaged hydraulic system would not let the flaps down. Waved off from a landing three times, he chose to bail out. He parachuted safely and a plane-guard destroyer soon picked him up.[80]

A Helldiver from VB-94 also ditched during the early morning strikes. Poor weather prevented the squadron from reaching their target and they turned back to the carrier. Ensign Edward Williams and ARM3c Elmer Minwell went into the drink during the mission, but the destroyer *USS Ringgold* fortunately rescued them.[81]

Five more sweeps took off early that morning, including a mission by eight Hellcats from VF-34 tasked to photograph and attack several airfields on the west coast of northern Honshu. Led by Lieutenant (jg) John Ryan, the fighters took off at 5:45 and flew across Hokkaido to the three airfields. Total overcast covered all three, so after taking a few photos of two, from a distance and under the overcast at an altitude of 300 feet, they returned to the east coast to strike the enemy field at Misawa.

Forming up for the attack offshore, the flight penetrated the overcast at 3,000 feet and spotted Misawa only five miles away. To start the attack, seven of the F6Fs bombed the hangar area while Ryan strafed a runway, destroying five Bettys and damaging five, without any opposition from antiaircraft but certainly disconcerting Japanese mechanics seen working on a plane in the middle of the airfield.

Reforming over the ocean, Ryan divided his flight into two divisions and assigned different parts of the airfield to each for the next attack. For the next fifty-five minutes the Hellcats worked the field over, still without any antiaircraft fire, as the pilots "had a field day" with attacks made "on the deck," claiming twenty planes destroyed and more damaged. When the American planes turned for home, there were only a few enemy planes that appeared to be undamaged on the airfield. It seemed that most of the Japanese planes had fuel, as they burned very easily.

Toward the end of the attack, two pilots noticed a ten-car passenger train south of the airfield and attacked it, too. They fired rockets at the engine, scoring hits that brought it to a halt, then spotted a second six-car freight train in a marshalling yard about a mile farther on and attacked it as well. One rocket hit the locomotive just before Lieutenant (jg) Lowell Wessels scored a direct hit with a 500-pound bomb, from only 500 feet. The engine blew up as Wessels flew through the debris blown into the air, but fortunately there was no damage to his Hellcat.

The assessment of the results, from photos taken during the raid, was at least thirteen, and up to twenty, enemy planes destroyed. The photos also revealed what photo interpreters believed to be two Japanese Baka suicide bombs, normally carried by Betty bombers, on the field. As most of the planes on this airfield burned readily, indicating they had fuel, VF-34 may well have forestalled an imminent suicide attack on the Task Force.[82]

Strike missions followed the usual early morning sweeps, several targeting ports. Air Group 6, flying from *USS Hancock*, got off to a difficult start when they lost a Helldiver that crashed taking off. Ensign Robert Wikstrund spun in and crashed near the carrier. Unfortunately, Wikstrund was killed in the crash but *USS Brush* rescued his radioman, ARM3c John Backstrom.

Like it did to other groups that morning, the bad weather separated five Helldivers from the main formation on the flight to Hokkaido. These planes found the town of Obihiro in the clear and bombed a large factory in the town, knocking down a chimney and a bridge. Bombs struck alongside the latter, destroying the supports, and it collapsed.

The remaining planes, eight Corsairs, three Hellcats, three Helldivers, and six Avengers, reached their briefed target: airfields at Kennebetsu. Minimal antiaircraft fire failed to hit any planes as they dove on the field. Although the aircraft on the field were cleverly hidden, the attackers bombed, rocketed, and machine-gunned them anyway. Since none caught fire, crews did not make any specific claims, but they did set three hangars on fire and also damaged the control tower. Near the field, two Hellcat pilots fired rockets at a locomotive partially hidden in a railway tunnel and left it steaming.

During the return flight, a Japanese fighter made a pass at one Helldiver. The flight leader, Lieutenant Commander Gordon Chase, turned toward the enemy plane only to find his machine guns jammed, but pressed on and chased the enemy plane away; it disappeared into the clouds.[83]

Air Group 16 Hellcats, equipping both VF-16 and VBF-16 as mentioned in chapter two, flew an early morning strike with VT-47 to the port of Hakodate, intent on attacking the town and the ferries that used the harbor. Eight Avengers from VT-47 joined eleven Hellcats, fifteen Avengers, and thirteen Helldivers from Air Group 16 and reached the town around 6:30 AM. Poor visibility from a low cloud ceiling prevented the Helldivers from dive-bombing, so they turned to glide-bombing with the Avengers.

The Hellcats strafed a cargo ship and a destroyer, or destroyer escort, as they drew near the target and left both burning and dead in the water. In Hakodate Bay, they bombed another warship as they flew on to the town. The Corsairs also attacked a destroyer escort off the coast, leaving it burning and dead in the water as well, before continuing on to hit several ferries in Hakodate Harbor. Despite intense and accurate antiaircraft fire that harassed all planes on the mission, the only loss was on the flight back to *Randolph*. The Corsair piloted by Ensign Glen Haynes disappeared when the flight entered heavy clouds, or "pea soup," about forty miles from the carrier. The cause of his loss remained unexplained, although antiaircraft fire that damaged some other aircraft on the raid may have been responsible. Unfortunately, Air Sea Rescue efforts to locate him were unsuccessful.

Randolph's Helldivers had a rocky start to the mission when the SB2C flown by Ensign Lewis Whitaker and radioman ARM3c Edward Dubois spun in on takeoff. Regrettably, attempts to find and rescue the flyers by *USS Bullard* were unsuccessful. Two more planes missed the rendezvous and didn't take part in the strike, leaving ten Helldivers to continue on to

Hakodate. Four of these planes, separated from the others, arrived at the harbor by themselves. Three attacked a ferry underway (the third didn't drop, as his position was poor), leaving the ferry slips, but missed it. The fourth Helldiver went after another ferry, but antiaircraft found the mark and damaged the auxiliary fuel tank, causing the engine to quit. The pilot switched to the secondary tank and made a second attack, but did not see a hit. The Helldiver trio attacked their ferry again, but only Lieutenant Robert Birch dropped his bomb; no one saw where it hit, as flak struck his plane and smashed the instrument panel and set a wing fire that burned a four-foot hole in the surface. The fire went out shortly, so Birch stayed with the aircraft and began the return flight to the carrier, escorted by another two Helldivers from his squadron. The damage to the aircraft was too great to reach the *Randolph*, so Birch ditched along the crest of some large swells near a radar picket destroyer, *USS McKee*, that rescued him and his radio operator, ARM1c William Hisler.

Antiaircraft rounds hit another of these four Helldivers, flown by Ensign Keith Moore with radioman ARM3c Charles Lux, and it flew back to the carrier alone. He also failed to reach *Randolph* and ditched close to the Task Force, where *USS Melvin* rescued both men.

The last of the four, flown by Lieutenant Lewis Williams, still had two bombs aboard, so he dropped one on one of the ferries underway, believed to be the *Hiran Maru*, scoring hits with both between the stacks, at almost the same time that a VT-47 Avenger, flown by Ensign Robert Graham, hit it from masthead height with two more bombs that had a five-second delay to allow him to clear the ship before they exploded. Williams then made a second pass firing rockets that hit the stern, and the vessel then turned over and sank. After this success, Williams then attacked another ferry, hitting it amidships, leaving it burning.

The remaining VB-16 Helldivers arrived after the first four. One escorted Birch home, as mentioned earlier, as the other five attacked warships in the harbor. Three bombed a destroyer, scoring two direct hits and two near misses that left the vessel on fire and dead in the water. The other two bombed a ferry underway just outside the harbor. Antiaircraft fire hit one of the two, flown by Lieutenant Warren Langley with radioman ARM3c Charles Milnor, and the bombs he dropped missed the ferry. The plane immediately caught fire and went into a turn and one man, who turned out to be Langley, succeed in bailing out. He was taken prisoner of war but Milnor was, unfortunately, killed. No one saw the result from the bombs dropped by the second SB2C. After using the remainder of their ordnance on a radio station at Oma Saki, the planes then returned to their carrier.

The poor weather led VT-16's Avengers to split into three sections. One group of four planes also glide-bombed a ferry at the entrance to the harbor. Although none of the crews observed their results, a VB-16 pilot reported that the bombs dropped by one of the four hit the ferry, believed to be the *Matsumae Maru*, and sank it.

A second flight of four Avengers damaged ferry slips and docks in Hakodate, as did the last group of five TBMs. The last five also attacked a small cargo ship on the return flight, last seen dead in the water.[84]

VT-47's Avengers followed VT-16 and also struck the docks and ferry slips at Hakodate. The squadron report commented on the opposition, particularly from warships in the harbor that "aggravated the situation by sending up a great volume of fire." Their bombs damaged the ferry terminal and docks, and two of the TBMs bombed a small cargo ship in the harbor, setting it on fire. As recounted earlier, Ensign Graham took part in the sinking of the ferry near the harbor, believed to be the *Hiran Maru*.

Flak damaged the wing and tail of the plane piloted by Lieutenant Benjamin Douglas, but he was able to return to the Task Force. The damage, however, forced him to ditch near a destroyer. Douglas and his radioman, ARM2c William Brewer, exited the plane readily, inflated their life raft, and jumped aboard. They paddled to *USS McNair* and the crew of the destroyer took them aboard five minutes after they went into the drink.[85]

Air Group 83 and VT-34, flying from *USS Monterey*, flew another combined mission to the Honshu end of the ferry line across the Tsugaru Strait. The *Essex* air group contributed seven Hellcats, eight Corsairs, thirteen Helldivers, and a dozen Avengers. With VT-34's eight TBMs, they arrived over open water north of Honshu and made a coordinated attack on several ships they sighted. The *Essex* Hellcats and Corsairs attacked one (either the ferry *Seikan Maru No. 10* or cargo ship *Seikan Maru No. 3*) with rockets and bombs, followed by the Avengers and Helldivers. Hellcats made three hits with rockets and the Corsairs scored twice with 500-pound bombs. The Helldivers made a total of eight bomb strikes on the vessel and VT-83 five more, three on the stern and two amidships. Bombs dropped by the last two Avengers caused the vessel to blow apart and the unlucky craft rolled over and sank. VT-34 found another ferry and scored several direct hits, and more near misses close aboard, with 500-pound bombs, that damaged the hull. The ship soon sank.

After these successes, with the coast of northern Honshu socked in by clouds, the strike planes turned north to search the Tsugaru Strait for more targets. They found, and attacked, a destroyer escort off Fukushima, scoring near misses. Several *Essex* fighters, whose bombs had hung up during attacks on the ferries, also went after this warship. Although their bombs were also near misses, their rockets and strafing seriously damaged the enemy warship. Two more destroyer escorts got the attention of *Essex* Helldivers and Avengers and also suffered serious damage.

The Hellcats strafed and sank several small wooden cargo ships in the strait, while the Avengers and Helldivers also attacked the destroyer escort off Fukushima. The Corsairs, not to be denied additional prey, sank two more sea trucks and strafed a lighthouse.[86]

Four air groups flew a combined strike to another port on Hokkaido, at Muroran. Air Groups 27, 50, 85, and 88 took part, with the commander of Air Group 85 in the role of strike leader. The poor flying weather and low overcast prevented some squadrons from reaching the town. The strike leader ordered those that did reach the town to act independently, as there was no possibility of a coordinated strike.

Four Helldivers of VB-85 turned back before reaching Muroran, as did an Avenger from VT-85. The remaining Avengers continued on to the vicinity of Muroran by flying between fifty and one hundred feet above the waves, the report of the mission declaring, "This hop produced navigators, not heroes." In the event, the Avengers could not find Muroran itself and attacked three luggers that crews later reported "had lost some skin off their collective face." The Corsairs of VBF-85 bombed and rocketed several trains as Muroran remained elusive to them. Nine Hell-divers from VB-85 did locate the town and five went in to attack small craft near the harbor, hitting some. The other four attacked targets on the shore, strafing trains in the vicinity of Tomakomai on the coast, about forty miles north of Muroran. One of the Helldivers, flown by Lieuten-ant (jg) Howard Eagleston, Jr., with radioman ARM1c Oliver Rasmus-sen, disappeared into the low clouds that hampered the mission from the start. During a pass on a train, the SB2C crashed on a mountain, killing Eagleston. Rasmussen, however, was uninjured and proceeded to accom-plish a unique feat for air crews flying over Japan: evading capture. He was on the run for over two months. Thwarted in a valiant attempt to sail to Okinawa, over a thousand miles away, he settled into the hills around the town, taking food, when he could, from five farms in the area, as well as milk from a cow he called Daisy. Some days after Rasmussen had an encounter with a farmer early in September, the presence of American planes overhead without Japanese antiaircraft fire instilled the notion that the war might over. On September 15, he spelled out the word "help" on the sand of a beach on the coast, waiting nearby for rescue. Four days later, another encounter with a farmer confirmed that the war was indeed over, and the next day, U.S. Army troops stationed in the town of Chitose found him.[87]

The planes from Air Group 50, three Hellcats and nine Aveng-ers, reached the Muroran area. The Hellcats did so by dead reckoning. While looking for a break in the overcast, two of them spotted a Japa-nese destroyer underway near Urakawa and attacked it with bombs and machine guns. It put up a spirited defense with intense antiaircraft fire, the only enemy opposition seen by any of the four groups on the mission. This fire ceased, however, during the second attack pass and both planes dropped their bombs close to the destroyer, which rolled toward one side but then righted and continued underway with smoke pouring from the stern.[88]

Air Group 50's Avengers lost the fighters as they reached the Muro-ran area, but managed to join with some Hellcats from Air Group 85, although two of the F6Fs had to return to base shortly thereafter. Two

VT-50 Avengers went with the fighters as escort but both managed to drop their bombs on a small factory in the area before setting out for home. The remaining bombers eventually located some "Sugar Dogs," small cargo ships, but scored no hits, a disappointing result after the flyers had stuck with the mission despite the bad weather.[89]

The two Hellcats and nine Avengers dispatched by Air Group 27 from USS Independence also had trouble finding Muroran, but upon finding a break in the overcast at Arakawa, the planes attacked small cargo craft and wharves in the harbor without any opposition. Unfortunately, they couldn't see what damage they may have done. Then, finding another small cargo ship underway near the harbor, the planes strafed and bombed it. As they flew away, they saw it beached on the shore.[90]

All four squadrons of Air Group 88 took part in the combined strike, but only the Corsairs of VBF-88 succeeded in eventually attacking the port. After the strike leader told the squadrons to hit targets of opportunity, VBF-88 joined with VBF-85 in attacking rail targets, hitting the marshalling yard in the town of Oshambi. Splitting off from Shangri-La's Corsairs, the Yorktown Corsairs strafed some small cargo ships off the town of Nishi, then went on to the Muroran area, where they rocketed yet another small vessel at a pier.[91]

The Yorktown's Hellcats experienced a tragedy before they even reached the assigned rendezvous for the mission. As the squadron was climbing through the overcast, the planes of the squadron commander, Lieutenant Commander Richard G. Crommelin, and Ensign Joseph Sahloff, whom we met in chapter one, collided. Crommelin's Hellcat crashed into the sea, killing him, but Sahloff managed to keep his damaged plane under control and continued with the mission. The squadron history emphasized: "The weather was extremely hazardous . . . visibility was so poor that Sahloff did not actually see Crommelin's plane hit the water." Not finding Muroran through the overcast, they settled for bombing and strafing factories and locomotives at Tomakomai, the town also attacked by VB-85.[92]

The Helldivers of VB-88 had had a difficult time from the start. Among the ten that didn't complete the mission, two couldn't locate the others during form-up after leaving the Yorktown and joined some

Avengers from Air Group 31. The latter jettisoned their bombs over the sea because of the poor weather and, according the VB-88's mission report, almost blew the two *Yorktown* Helldivers "out of the sky," hastening their return to the carrier. Other mishaps included another Helldiver returning because of a faulty compass and another returning after it had a close call with a Hellcat while still over the Task Force. Four Helldivers persevered and continued the mission, eventually joining up with the Avengers of VT-85, taking part in the attack on the small cargo ships mentioned earlier.[93]

The *Yorktown*'s Avengers also had bad luck that morning. All fifteen reached Hokkaido, but couldn't find Muroran through the overcast. With their fuel running low, they attacked a bridge spotted through a break in the cloud cover: "Skirting just below the overcast at 1,100 feet, the nine Torpeckers peeled off in their dives, pulling out at 1,000 feet." Unfortunately, the bombs dropped missed the bridge, but did hit its approaches. One TBM, flown by Lieutenant William Thurston, set out on its own for Muroran, but as the weather began to improve, he decided a lone attack on the town with its bristling antiaircraft guns would be unwise. He chose, instead, to bomb rail targets in the town of Arakawa, also attacked by VB-85. He bombed the marshalling yard, tearing up tracks that rained down on the station, then strafed a locomotive, causing steam to erupt from its boiler before he turned for home.[94]

Ships of the Task Force also got into action for the first shore bombardment of the Japanese Home Islands, late that morning. Task Group 34, composed of battleships, cruisers, and destroyers, carried out the first shore bombardment of the Japanese Home Islands, shelling the vital steel works in the coastal city of Kaimaishi, in northern Honshu.

Before 11:00 AM, air groups providing observation for the bombardment and their fighter cover took off. Air Group 1 provided eleven Helldivers to carry observers, from the observation squadron assigned to the battleships and cruisers, during the bombardment. Air Groups 6 and 94 provided fighters to protect the SB2Cs from interference from enemy fighters that fortunately failed to appear. The only Japanese opposition was from antiaircraft guns located in the city and on ships in the harbor. Their fire, initially described as intense to moderate, dwindled as the bombardment continued.

The Helldivers circled Kaimaishi for several hours during the bombardment, directing salvos onto the iron works, oil facilities, and docks of the city. The battleships sailed in a column, with the first salvos from the battleships creating so much smoke over the iron works that it became difficult for the spotters in the air to observe the results and adjust fire. The cruisers hit the oil facilities, starting fires, as did one salvo that hit inside the city. Observers on the battleship *Missouri* could follow the shells fired from the warship with binoculars. During the bombardment, they saw some men running down to the piers in the port, waving at the ships offshore. A surmise that they were American prisoners, signaling for rescue, later proved to be correct after the war ended.[95]

When the shore bombardment ended, the fighters on patrol were let loose to strafe in the area. Four Corsairs from VBF-1 attacked a destroyer escort in the harbor that was shooting at the Helldivers carrying the observers. The attack was intense, leaving the ship on fire and beached in a cover in the harbor. Japanese sailors, however, managed to take some revenge, shooting down one of the Corsairs, piloted by Ensign Stephen Komar. His plane crashed into the bay, killing him instantly.[96]

Another group of light cruisers and destroyers sailed along the coast of Honshu, from the coastal town of Rikusentakata and past Kaimaishi during the bombardment, sweeping for enemy shipping, northwards to the vicinity of the small town of Noda. Neither operation encountered shore opposition, although Destroyer Squadron 96 found a tug and barge that they quickly dispatched to the bottom. Air Group 91 covered these warships with combat air patrols by its night fighter.

——❦——

The second wave of strikes, twelve in all, took off from the carriers around 1:00 PM. Air Group 16 returned to Hakodate for the early afternoon attack, flying twenty-five Hellcats from both VBF-16 and VF-16, thirteen Avengers, and nine Helldivers. VT-47 was on this mission again, with two Hellcats and seven Avengers.

The weather at Hakodate was still poor in the afternoon, so VF-16 attacked a coastal freighter in the Tsugaru Strait, damaging but not sinking it. Three Avengers from VT-16 appeared soon after and sank it. The Helldivers spotted a ferry, the *Tsugaru Maru*, underway in the strait. The bombers went in, in flights of three at masthead height, with two SB2Cs strafing while the third dropped its bombs, then alternating position until all three had dropped their bombs. After a number of hits, the *Tsugaru Maru* turned over and sank quickly. After this major accomplishment, the SB2Cs sank a small cargo ship and a lugger as an encore.

The Avengers of VT-16 went on to Hakodate Harbor, where they found a hole in the overcast through which they could attack ships in the harbor. They blasted several small ships, but Japanese antiaircraft gunners had "bore sighted" their guns on the small bit of clear sky through which the Avengers dove, and some of the intense light antiaircraft fire met throughout the mission damaged the TBM flown by Ensign Burton Noah. He was able to clear the harbor but soon had to ditch in Tsugaru Strait. He and his crewmen, ARM3c Harry Leake and AOM3c Charles Hester, were able to get in their raft but could not be rescued before nightfall. The next morning, just before noon, the lifeguard submarine *USS Cero* rescued them only two miles off the coast, almost forty miles from their ditching location.

The mission report of VB-16 closed with this: "Two ships and one small craft sunk and one coastal freighter damaged was only partial revenge for the four planes and two crews lost on the morning attack." Fortunately, only one crew was lost that morning, as we have seen.[97]

The final score for the day at Hakodate, as tallied by Third Fleet, was an old destroyer, a *Seikan Maru* class ferry, two coastal freighters, and fourteen Sugar Dogs. They were sunk at a cost of three Helldivers and one crew, lost to the formidable antiaircraft defense put up by batteries on the shore and particularly ships in the harbor.[98]

━━━━━

The harbor of Muroran on Hokkaido got limited attention during the morning sweeps and strikes because of the poor weather. The afternoon attack, carried out in greatly improved weather, produced much better results. The same four air groups assigned to the town that morning returned in the early afternoon, with the Air Group 85 commander acting again as strike leader. All aircraft bombed in the face of intense antiaircraft fire, coming from ships and the hills surrounding the harbor. Japanese gunners again aimed at breaks in the overcast hanging over the harbor, through which American planes made their attacks.

The thirty-five planes, including four Hellcats acting as photo planes, from *USS Yorktown* went into attack before Air Group 85. Told to hold their bombs, the Corsairs strafed antiaircraft positions to some effect as the intense antiaircraft damaged a few planes but failed to shoot any down. Afterward, the F4Us were let loose and bombed and rocketed two luggers that had the misfortune to be underway outside the harbor, sinking both. With their remaining ammunition, the F4Us then destroyed a fishing boat and two more luggers at the village of Sawara.

Several Helldivers from VB-88 bombed an iron works near Muroran, before all ten aircraft that attacked continued on the harbor. The SB2Cs executed a line-abreast glide-bombing attack, as some overcast still persisted, against warships and cargo ships. Five pilots got hits on armed merchant ships, setting all on fire, and also hit a destroyer escort. The Avengers' attack set an armed merchant ship on fire, as well as a cargo ship. After this, the TBMs struck eight Sugar Dogs tied up near the shore. After they dropped their bombs, only a few were left as "the others just weren't there anymore."[99]

Air Group 85 contributed a dozen Corsairs, a dozen Avengers, and another dozen Helldivers that attacked after Air Group 88. The Corsairs fired rockets and dropped bombs on small warships and cargo ships, claiming a merchant ship sunk and another small patrol craft and a number of small cargo ships damaged. Crews of the Helldivers described their successful efforts to evade antiaircraft fire as "standard evasive tactics of 'zig and zag and go like mad.'" They also claimed damage to a coastal defense vessel, as well as two more merchant ships. *Shangri-La's* Avengers attacked ships at low level, sinking two frigates and damaging two freighters.[100]

Air Group 27 contributed nine Avengers and four Hellcats. On reaching the harbor, these aircraft bombed some of the more than thirty warships and merchant vessels seen in the harbor during the raid. Their bombs hit and damaged two destroyer escorts, causing a large explosion on one as well as an explosion on a coastal cargo ship.[101] The Avengers from VT-50 also bombed two warships at masthead height that crews identified as a destroyer and a destroyer escort, but they did not see any hits. Post-strike intelligence indicated both ships were actually coastal defense vessels.[102]

The total for the day at Muroran was one frigate, one armed merchant ship, and seven small cargo ships sunk.[103]

Planes from *USS Essex* and the *Monterey* achieved excellent results during the afternoon strikes. Three Air Group 34 Hellcats and six Avengers joined twelve Hellcats, eight Corsairs, thirteen Avengers, and fourteen Helldivers from Air Group 83 to sink several ferries that usually plied the waters between Hokkaido and Honshu. Prior to scoring this bonanza, VT-34 Avengers found a small cargo ship off Oma Saki. Their strike leader, Lieutenant (jg) Lester Lampman, dove on the ship and dropped one bomb that was a direct hit. The hull of the Japanese vessel "blew out" and it immediately sank.

Shortly later, the entire flight sighted four ferries sailing in a circle in Aomori Bay, Honshu, to avoid being bombed. When they saw the approaching American planes, each began to take violent evasive action, in the same manner as Japanese warships, but to no avail. Air Group 83's planes attacked all four ferries, with the *Monterey* aircraft assisting in the demise of one. *Shangri-La* fighters attacked the ferries first, dropping bombs, firing rockets and their machine guns. The ferries offered very little antiaircraft fire in return. The Helldivers and Avengers, splitting into groups to attack all ships simultaneously, directed the same ordnance at the four ships. Some Avengers dropped their bombs from only 300 feet. One 500-pound bomb exploded in the water, underneath a ferry, and broke it in half. An Avenger pilot from Air Group 34 described the bombing by the American planes as resembling nothing more than a "traffic pattern." Along with the ferry that broke in half, the flyers claimed another two as sunk, the *Seikan Maru No. 1* and *Seikan Maru No. 2*, with a third beached, down by the stern and burning fiercely. American crews could not see any survivors in the water. Six Japanese ferries went down to American bombs and rockets on the 14th: *Hiran Maru*, *Seikan Marus No. 1*, *No. 2*, and *No. 10*; *Tsugaru Maru*; and *Matsumae Maru*.[104]

———

Besides the enemy shipping destroyed, strikes and sweeps to enemy airfield destroyed or damaged aircraft on the enemy fields. Corsairs from VF-85 also destroyed one enemy plane in the air during a combat air patrol over the radar picket destroyers guarding the periphery of the Task Force. The encounter took place after noon when two "bogies," or unidentified aircraft, were reported approaching the Task Force. Four Corsairs on patrol intercepted the pair, which turned out to be two Japanese twin-engine Betty bombers. Two of the Corsair pilots, Lieutenant Elvin Hatfield and Ensign Leon Devereux, immediately attacked one bomber, flaming its right engine. The other two pilots followed up, hitting it as well, although the bomber managed to escape.

In the meantime, Hatfield and Devereux went after the second Betty, whose waist and tail gunners fired furiously at the oncoming Americans, without success. On their second pass, Hatfield scored hits on the bomber's port engine, which caught fire. Devereux followed up and hit the right engine. The Betty then went out of control and crashed into the ocean, with no sign of survivors.[105]

Air Group 47 lost a Hellcat and an Avenger, with four air crew, to unknown causes during the day: Lieutenant John Wright, Jr., piloting the Hellcat, and the crew of the Avenger—Lieutenant (jg) Clifford Fluitt, CAERM William Browning, and AOM2c Robert Thomas.

Both planes took off for a routine weather reconnaissance mission after dawn, flying southeast of the carrier for several hundred miles. Fluitt made several contacts with the pilot of a fighter flying a combat air patrol over the Task Force before noon. The last contact occurred shortly before 1:00 PM, when Fluitt reported he had only eighty gallons of fuel left on board the Avenger. After that, there was only silence and nothing more was heard from any of the crew. Search planes combed the area during the afternoon and next morning, but no sign of either aircraft, or any crewmen, was ever found. Presumably, both aircraft ran out of fuel and either ditched or crashed into the sea.[106]

Chapter Five

SHORTLY AFTER MIDNIGHT ON JULY 15, FOUR NIGHT-FIGHTER HELL-cats from Air Group 91 took off from *USS Randolph* to provide air cover for cruisers and battleships off the port of Muroran, on Hokkaido. Air Group 1 Hellcats and Corsairs from *USS Bennington* took over the job before 4:00 AM and flew several air cover missions during the morning. Fighters from VF-6, VBF-6, and VF-49 covered the retirement of the ships as the Task Force moved away from the coast.

USS Iowa, Wisconsin, and *Missouri,* with the light cruisers *USS Atlanta* and *USS Dayton,* and nine destroyers as escort began to bombard the steel and iron factories and a coal liquefaction plant at 9:37 AM. For almost an hour the Task Force steamed leisurely along shelling the town, unhindered by any Japanese counterfire.[107]

Air Group 1 Helldivers flew "spotting" missions, carrying observers from the battleship's float reconnaissance planes who directed the fire from the ships offshore. Low overcast at only 300 feet forced the SB2Cs to fly below the clouds, underneath the trajectory of the sixteen-inch shells that were pummeling factories in the city. Although Japanese coastal guns did not fire on the ships, antiaircraft crews did fire on the American planes over the city, but did not score any hits.[108] The bombardment destroyed eight buildings in the Wanishi Iron Works and caused an explosion in the Nihon Factory that damaged shops.[109]

As the bombardment ended, *Bennington*'s fighters went in search of targets of opportunity in the area. After rocketing a railroad tunnel, they attacked some small cargo ships in harbor about fifteen miles northwest of Muroran. One of the pilots, Lieutenant Roy Morgan, spotted two armed merchant ships and attacked them solo after radio trouble prevented him from contacting the other planes. He made two runs on the enemy ships, hitting both of them with two rockets on the second pass. As he pulled away, two 40mm shells struck his Corsair. One round damaged a wing while the second hit underneath the cockpit, breaking Morgan's leg, opening an artery and blowing off the canopy and the top of the control stick. The plane then began to burn. As he lowered the flaps in preparation for ditching, hydraulic fluid from broken lines in the damaged cockpit began to squirt in his face. Unfazed by the bath and his serious injuries, Morgan discovered his plane could stay in the air, so he placed a tourniquet on his leg to stem to stream of blood and set out for the ships from the Task Force, then about thirty miles away. Reaching them within minutes, he prepared to ditch near one of the escorting destroyers, but realized that shock and loss of blood, which was blurring his vision, had weakened him to the point that he would have trouble getting out his parachute and pulling out his life raft. He unstrapped his parachute, then landed the Corsair in the ocean while holding his head to one side as the hydraulic fluid continued to stream into the cockpit. Unfortunately, Morgan had not tightened his cockpit straps when he unstrapped the parachute, and the crash impact threw him forward. He struck the gun sight, fracturing his skull. Undeterred by his multiple serious injuries, the intrepid airman climbed out the cockpit before the Corsair sank, inflated his Mae West, and awaited rescue that was only minutes away. *USS Frank Knox* appeared and a sailor jumped into the sea to help Morgan aboard the destroyer, which returned him to *USS Bennington* the next day.[110]

Throughout the day, American crews flew almost 750 combat sorties, despite the low overcast that covered most enemy airfields. Attacking aircraft sank a minesweeper and a frigate as well as twenty merchant ships, including six large cargo vessels, and also destroyed six aircraft on the ground.[111]

The usual morning sweeps, and a few strikes, took off beginning at 3:30 AM with sixteen missions airborne by 4:45 AM. The lousy flying weather forced one air group strike to turn back; another dropped their bombs through the overcast by radar. Many, however, did manage to attack some targets on either Honshu or Hokkaido.

Briefed to sweep airfields at Sapporo and Otaru on the west coast of Hokkaido, with a dozen Corsairs from VBF-88, twelve F4Us from

VBF-85 first flew to Sapporo but found it heavily covered by overcast. A few aircraft did manage to attack the field, but only one dummy plane was visible. Using rockets and 500-pound bombs, they hit a hangar and some aircraft revetments. The flight then flew on to Otaru, about ten miles northwest of Sapporo, only to find it also covered by overcast. By flying out to sea, however, they managed to find a hole in the "mattress," Navy flyers' nickname for heavy overcast clouds, that allowed them to get under the clouds and attack the seaplane base near the town. With no aircraft on the enemy base, the Corsairs turned to ships and luggers in the harbor, strafing them with rockets and machine-gun fire. The result was a troopship set on fire and several small vessels damaged. Antiaircraft defenses were formidable and intense, light and medium caliber that always proved a danger to low-flying aircraft. Enemy rounds hit several Corsairs. Lieutenant (jg) John Weeks's plane suffered severe damage and he immediately ditched in the bay, abandoning the Corsair just before it sank. Two of this comrades stayed overhead, but one developed engine trouble and soon had to leave. Lieutenant (jg) Cecil Moore remained, dropping his seat pack life raft and some dye markers to Weeks as Japanese antiaircraft gunners continually tried to bring down his plane. Two Corsairs from VBF-88, from a 7:00 AM mission, joined Moore as he was about to leave, as his fuel was low. Then word came that a destroyer was on the way to rescue Weeks. The airman then spotted a Japanese destroyer escort coming out from Otaru Harbor to capture Weeks. Moore and one of the VBF-88 pilots, Lieutenant (jg) Clifford Roberts, Jr., both attacked the enemy vessel. Moore dropped a bomb and both strafed the enemy vessel. Although the bomb missed, the strafing set the vessel on fire and forced it back to port. In a short time the American destroyer arrived on scene and rescued Weeks.[112]

Moore succeeded in reaching the destroyer pickets of the Task Force when he ran out of fuel and ditched. As he had dropped his raft and dye markers to Weeks, he had only his Mae West to keep him afloat. Despite the difficulty in locating a man in the water, fighters flying cover for the destroyers located him and radioed his position. Soon one of the picket destroyers rescued him.[113]

The same luck did not attend VF-88 during the same mission. They began by strafing a few locomotives, a powerhouse, and a pulp factory near the town of Tomakomai, on the way to Sapporo Airfield. Here they strafed aircraft revetments and hangars, as no aircraft were visible on the field. The flight then turned to the harbor at Otaru. On arriving over the port shortly after VBF-85, the flyers saw it still covered by overcast, but the planes also succeeded in flying underneath the clouds to make an attack on ships in the harbor.

Japanese antiaircraft gunners greeted them with an intense antiaircraft barrage. Pilots described flak from ships in the harbor as particularly severe as small and medium cargo ships, as well as a few small frigates and patrol vessels, packed the harbor. The strike leader, Lieutenant Hoke Sisk, went after an armed merchant ship, scoring hits with four rockets at the waterline, then strafed a patrol boat as his wingman hit an armed merchant ship. Other pilots reported hits on a small tanker and small cargo ships. Antiaircraft fire hit the Hellcat of Lieutenant Herman Chase, who was leading another section of the flight, but despite the damage he pressed on, firing four rockets that hit a coastal tanker. Just after the attack, his Hellcat caught fire and he bailed out, or was pulled out of the cockpit by his parachute, only 200 feet above the water over the outer harbor. Although possibly injured, he inflated his Mae West as two squadron mates circled above him. Two hours later, however, when their fuel gauges told them it was time to return to the carrier, Chase was no longer moving in the water. Unfortunately, he did not survive, listed as killed in action. When the two Corsairs reached the *Randolph*, both planes had less than five gallons of gasoline in their tanks.[114]

Lieutenant Roberts, of VBF-88, remained over Weeks for about two hours, until Corsairs from VBF-88 that had taken off on a later mission appeared over Otaru Harbor when Japanese antiaircraft shot down a VBF-88 Corsair, in an action that will be described shortly. As he turned for home, Roberts found time to knock out two locomotives near the town of Oiwake, from such low altitude that he brought "home a high tension cable on his bomb rack."[115]

Weeks and Moore were not the only *Shangri-La* pilots to ditch near the Task Force that morning. Another *Shangri-La* Corsair, from VBF-85, ditched when it also ran out of fuel earlier in the morning, on the way home from an anti-shipping sweep flown by planes from several air groups: Corsairs, Avengers, and Helldivers from Air Group 88, Hellcats and Avengers from Air Groups 27 and 50, and Avengers and Helldivers from Air Group 88.[116]

Assigned to hit the ports of Hakodate and Muroran on Hokkaido again, the attackers were stymied by bad flying weather but managed to strike targets of opportunity. Japanese resistance was minimal or absent from the targets they found. A VB-88 Helldiver found a railroad tunnel to bomb. The pilot, Lieutenant Louis Miller, planted three 500-pound bombs inside the tunnel's mouth, starting an avalanche that sealed the tunnel entrance. Another *Yorktown* pilot flew his Avenger, alone, to Hakodate and bombed a large building in the port. Two VBF-88 Corsair pilots, not detailed to cover the downed pilot floating near Otaru, found a Japanese frigate to strafe, damaging it severely, and destroyed two bridges.

Shangri-La's Corsair pilots sank a medium tonnage cargo ship, a small coastal freighter, and four picket boats (SSDs) near Uchiura Wan. One of them, Lieutenant Jerome Feeley, had to ditch after his engine developed an oil leak. He landed in the water near the Task Group bombarding Muroran and one of the escorting destroyers promptly rescued him. Three VB-85 Helldivers found an armed merchant ship. All three scored hits on the vessel, which was soon enveloped in flames. A *Shangri-La* Avenger, flying below the solid overcast that covered the entire area from 200 to 2,000 feet, found a small freighter. Lieutenant Richard Paland attacked only seventy-five feet above the water and hit it amidships. The Japanese ship broke in two and sank. Air Group 50 pilots also attacked shipping near Uchiura Wan and Shikabe, north of Hakodate, from low level under the overcast. Four small ships went down to their bombs, including a small cargo ship and a small tanker.

The highlight of the mission, however, was the sinking of a Japanese destroyer escort near Hakodate. Avengers came upon the unlucky vessel, still smoking from an earlier strafing attack. It fired only "meager" antiaircraft fire as a defense. TBMs from *USS Independence* and VT-88 attacked the enemy vessel from a bow angle, only one hundred feet off the water. VT-27 claimed five direct hits and VT-88 two. The vessel exploded from this pounding, broke up, and quickly sank by the stern.[117]

Shortly before the Corsairs, Helldivers, and Avengers took off from *USS Yorktown* for the strike that netted the destroyer, eight VF-88 Hellcats took off on a photo mission, at 6:45 AM. After searching in vain for airfields in the clear to photograph along the west coast of Honshu, they flew north to look along the north coast. While flying over the Tsugaru Strait, near Shiriya Point, one of the pilots spotted a life raft in the strait. While circling the raft, they attempted to contact a lifeguard submarine, without success, but soon another plane in the air heard them and relayed their message. Two planes remained over the raft while the rest continued the photo mission. Lieutenant Fred C. Sueyres and his wingman remained, but soon Sueyres flew toward the submarine's position, as radio contact with it was poor. As he neared the sub's position, he saw the Japanese destroyer escort in the vicinity just as the Avengers from VT-27 and VT-88 sank it. He returned to the raft, strafing a few targets along the way. The pair then continued to circle the raft, but occasionally one would fly over to Shiriya Point and strafe the radar station there, or some small boats near it. Around 10:30, the other planes returned from their photo mission. The photo section flew back to the *Yorktown* as four planes from the flight, still including Sueyres and his wingman, remained over the raft. The submarine soon appeared and rescued the three men, who were, in fact, Ensign Burton Noah and his crew of VT-16, whom we met in chapter four when the Avenger ditched late in the afternoon on July 14 from flak damage during the afternoon strike on Hakodate Harbor. The raft had drifted almost forty miles across the Tsugaru Strait, ending only a few miles from the northern coast of Honshu.

Before the four Hellcats returned to the *Yorktown*, two pilots, Sueyres and Ensign Hollis Eldridge, took time to strafe a gun position that had annoyed Sueyres during his strafing at Shiriya Point. Another pilot, Lieutenant (jg) Edward Chamberlin, strafed the radar station and an oil storage tank.[118]

The Hellcat from VF-83, flown by Ensign William Kingston, Jr., also went into the drink, when it ran out of fuel after antiaircraft fire damaged the aircraft during an attack on the enemy airfield at Matsushima that destroyed two Japanese planes and damaged several hangars. Japanese antiaircraft gunners put up intense fire that damaged the fuel line on

Kingston's Hellcat, but he managed to fly about thirty miles east toward the Task Force before he ditched. He got into his life raft as one plane of the flight circled above him while two more flew toward the Task Force, radioing his exact position to the submarine *USS Trepang* on lifeguard duty. The sub rescued Kingston soon after.[119]

Of course, there were no aircraft losses on many missions, such as the early morning sweep and attack briefed for the ports of Hakodate and Aomori, already struck the day before. A dozen Hellcats of VBF-16 took off from *USS Randolph* at 3:30 AM. Once over Japan, the flight discovered zero ceiling except over the port of Hachinhoe, where the overcast hung at 800 feet. The Hellcats flew under the mattress and attacked ships in the harbor, as well as the airfield near the town. Both targets offered only meager antiaircraft fire in response. All planes took part in a vicious attack on a small cargo ship. Three direct hits left the ship burning fiercely and headed to the shore to beach itself before sinking. Pilots also strafed small vessels tied to piers in the port, and then, with ammunition to spare and hungry for more targets, they turned to a railroad yard nearby. Their bombs blew up a rail junction and damaged a roundhouse.

After these accomplishments, the flight turned to the airfield near the town, but didn't observe any operational aircraft or flak. The F6Fs bombed and strafed camouflage-covered aircraft revetments that photo analysts later believed to contain dummy aircraft, as well as hangars. Turning to the harbor to round out the mission, the Hellcats bombed and strafed a lighthouse at Same Saki before all returned safely to their carrier.[120]

⌐◆⌐

Later in the morning, with a 9:00 AM takeoff, Corsairs from *USS Yorktown* with *Shangri-La* Corsairs flew a sweep of the Sapporo area. The poor weather forced the two squadrons to separate and each proceeded to locate targets independently. VF-85 found few targets, but also no antiaircraft fire, eventually striking a previously damaged small tanker, as well as some small boats and docks, in the coastal town of Mori.

VBF-88, however, had more action and lost two aircraft during the mission. After locating a hole in the thick overcast that affected all the day's missions, the *Yorktown* flight found a hole in the clouds and attacked the harbor in the town of Suttsu, on the western coast of Hokkaido. All twelve planes on the mission went after a small tanker in the harbor and scored four hits with rockets that immediately set the vessel on fire. An armed merchant ship also got their attention. The Corsairs swooped down, again firing rockets that struck the ship's stern, setting it on fire.

With no more targets at Suttsu, VBF-88 flew northeast along the coast to the port of Otaru, taking time to strafe a tugboat, a fishing boat, and some luggers on the way. The flight spread out as they flew into Otaru Harbor, encountering heavy antiaircraft fire from ships and positions on the shore. The attackers scored four hits on an armed merchant ship, but antiaircraft fire hit two planes. Ensign Robert Shepherd went down in flames, crashing into the harbor. Flak damaged the engine of the F4U flown by Ensign Maurice Springer, but he managed to stay in the air for a few minutes before ditching about seven miles offshore, outside the harbor. Enemy fire also damaged another Corsair that headed for home, escorted by another plane. The remaining Corsairs flew over Springer for a time, waiting for two OS2Us already dispatched for another rescue. Unfortunately, the latter never appeared as they couldn't find Otaru because of the poor flying weather, and the Corsairs eventually had to head for home. The current appeared to be taking Springer out into the Sea of Japan where he was, unfortunately, lost.[121]

<hr />

Midmorning strikes by seven air groups included an attack by Hellcats, Avengers, and Helldivers of Air Group 16, accompanied by three Avengers from VT-47 briefed to hit the port of Hakodate. The Corsairs became separated from the Avengers and Helldivers near the northern coast of Honshu. Finding the area to the north and west covered by overcast, the F4Us headed south to the eastern coast of Honshu and struck the port and airfield at Hachinhoe. The Corsair flight leader, Lieutenant Commander Elmer Kraft, leading one section of the squadron, bombed a small cargo vessel, leaving it dead in the water. Turning to the airfield, the flight strafed one aircraft spotted on the field, then turned to industrial targets in the town. Ensign William Rogers strafed and destroyed three locomotives in a rail yard near the town, as two others joined him in strafing the yard. Still looking for targets, Kraft directed them to targets in the town, where they destroyed a large oil tank. As they left for home, the flight strafed small ships in Hachinhoe Harbor.

The Helldivers and Avengers found Hachinhoe, too, after realizing that they also would never locate Hakodate under the overcast. The Helldivers made low-level attacks on ships in the harbor since the low overcast prevented conventional dive-bombing. Executing daring attacks at less than one hundred feet from the water, one section of three SB2Cs sank a coastal freighter with a direct hit, while a second section sank another. As a follow-up, some planes bombed small ships at dock, sinking about half a dozen, while other Helldivers turned to oil tanks, docks, and warehouses. The *Randolph*'s Avengers hit a factory in the town, starting a fire that grew in intensity as the raid, which lasted a leisurely thirty minutes, continued. They also sank a small coastal freighter and nine small vessels in the harbor.[122]

Although they had only three Avengers on the mission, VT-47 claimed the largest cargo ship in the harbor as sunk, following a direct hit forward of amidships. Two TBMs went after the ship, the first getting two near misses just before the second, flown by Ensign Kenneth Loring, hit and sank it. Two of the Avengers also bombed a factory in the town, setting it on fire, while the third bombed a small oil refinery before also strafing a rail yard a few miles outside the town. The last plane then strafed the refinery again, starting a fire. The squadron report of the mission described the attack as a "happy half hour, in spite of moderate AA from light weapons" that fortunately did not shoot down any American aircraft. Air Group 16 crews reported very little flak.[123]

The remainder of the Corsair flight didn't have to fly as far to find targets. Their first victim was a small cargo vessel that rose out of the water when a bomb hit its bow. When it settled again, it had a pronounced list. One of the F4Us found a railroad terminal a few miles from Hachinhoe where it destroyed three locomotives before some other planes on the flight joined in, strafing more trains. Moving on to a gas works in Hachinhoe, the Corsairs bombed and rocketed the facility, eventually causing a storage tank to disappear in an explosion as flames rose several hundred feet into the air.

Two divisions of the flight added some Japanese aircraft to their squadron's tally for the day. As they flew over the small port of Kominato Wan, on the north coast of Honshu, they spotted four Japanese "Jake" single-engine seaplanes moored in the port. Four planes promptly attacked and destroyed all four Jakes, along with a dredge in the immediate vicinity. After this, the quartet then rocketed a train, destroying the locomotive and setting the cars on fire. Another Corsair bombed gas storage tanks that instantly blew up. Over the harbor, one pilot attacked a small cargo ship in the harbor itself, hitting it amidships with a 500-pound bomb that broke the vessel in half. At the same time, a squadron mate took on a similar cargo ship, leaving it listing and apparently sinking.

All aircraft returned to the carrier except the Hellcat flown by Lieutenant (jg) George McKenzie. He had sustained flak damage during the mission and had to ditch before reaching the Task Force. Fortunately, an OS2U Kingfisher from *USS Pasadena* rescued him.[124]

Ten of the usual early afternoon strikes and sweeps took off from their carriers between 12:40 and 1:30 PM, targeting towns and harbors rather than airfields. Only one incurred a loss, a strike by three squadrons of Air Group 1 composed of eight Corsairs, fifteen Avengers, and four Helldivers. The flight flew to the small town of Rumoi, Hokkaido, on the Sea of Japan, to hit a reported synthetic oil refinery. Upon reaching Rumoi, they found there was no refinery near the town. Eleven Avengers bombed Rumoi anyway, well underneath the overcast blanketing the town at an altitude of 1,000 feet, while four others bombed the nearby village of Opirashike. At Rumoi, the extremely low bombing altitude led to damage to two TBMs from fragments from their own bombs, since the fuses were not set for such a low-altitude attack. Ensign Clifford Mehelich and his two crewmen, ARM3c Joseph Dortsch and AOM3c Ernest Davis, Jr., turned out to sea and ditched successfully in the Sea of Japan. All three crewmen got into their life raft and two Avengers dropped two more rafts and survival equipment to the men, but the men were not rescued. Mehelich and Dortsch became prisoners of war, but Davis was later reported as killed in action, although the circumstances are unknown. The second damaged Avenger managed to return to the *Bennington* and crash land on the flight deck. This was the only damage to planes on the mission, as crews encountered little, if any, Japanese antiaircraft fire.

Meanwhile, the Corsairs and Helldivers headed for several small towns to the south. The Helldivers bombed the small village of Ishikari, hitting a small powerhouse. The Corsairs struck two other towns, Hachiman and Ebetsu. Rockets fired into the former set some buildings on fire. At Ebetsu, rockets hit a paper mill and its powerhouse, setting the latter on fire.[125]

Besides strikes, sweeps, and photo missions, Task Force aircraft also flew combat air patrols over so-called "lifeguard" submarines, plying the surface off the coast of Japan while awaiting the call to rescue ditched flyers. The planes assigned to such patrols could look for targets of opportunity if not given other tasks such as searching for downed flyers, as did two Hellcats from VF-50 on the morning of July 15. After the relief planes arrived over the sub, the two F6Fs followed orders to search for a life raft off Shiriya Point, a reference to Ensign Kingston, whom we have already met. Upon their arrival, the pair spotted what they thought was a life raft in the distance with a Japanese destroyer escort bearing down in it. They immediately attacked, strafing the enemy vessel, which put up a valiant defense with intense antiaircraft fire. Several strafing runs left the vessel dead in the water with the crew abandoning ship. Turning to the suspected life raft, the F6Fs realized upon close inspection that this identification was mistaken. Asking the Task Force for a better position for the raft they were seeking, they were directed to Shiriya Point, where they spotted Kingston in his raft. They directed the submarine *USS Trepang* to the raft. When they saw the sub drawing close to Kingston, they headed for home. More fighters arrived to take over covering the rescue, which was, as we've seen, successful.[126]

The final aerial loss of the day occurred shortly before 4:00 PM when an Avenger from VT-31 crashed while landing on *USS Belleau Wood*, going over the side. Fortunately, the *USS McKee* was on hand to rescue the crew.

The raids of July 14 and 15 on Hokkaido and northern Honshu dramatically reduced coal shipments from Hokkaido to industries on Honshu, by more than eighty percent. This was an accomplishment of great strategic value in preparation for the invasion and the effort to degrade Japan's ability to wage war.[127]

Chapter Six

ON THE 16TH, THE DAY THE FIRST ATOMIC BOMB EXPLODED DURING A test in the desert of New Mexico, the Task Force withdrew from the Japanese coast, steaming south while refueling as the British Pacific Fleet, with a battleship, four carriers, light cruisers, and destroyers, joined them. The highlight of fleet action during the day was the sinking of a large Japanese submarine about 650 miles east of Tokyo. Hellcats and Avengers on patrol spotted the sub on the surface and forced it to submerge by attacking with rockets and depth charges. The destroyer escort, *USS Lawrence C. Taylor*, joined in the attack and sank the sub with several depth charge attacks.

Early that morning, TBMs from VC-13 on the escort carrier *USS Anzio* were flying a routing antisubmarine patrol to protect the Task Force. About seventy miles from the *Anzio*, one Avenger spotted a large Japanese submarine, later identified as the I-13, on the surface. The plane, piloted by Lieutenant (jg) William McLane, radioed his find to the *Anzio*, then immediately attacked, dropping depth charges and a Mark 24 mine during three passes on the sub, which immediately submerged. McLane fired his wing guns, striking the sub's conning tower, as well as four rockets. One rocket scored a direct hit on the conning tower. As the Avenger turned away, the turret gunner fired at the conning tower.

The I-13 began to dive but remained on a fairly even keel as it did so, so it had not gone under much when McLane made his second pass, dropping two depth charges that exploded a short distance from the sub. The I-13 was now almost out of sight, diving for the safety of the depths, so McLane dropped a sonobuoy to track it, then went in for a third pass, but failed to drop the Mark 24 mine on board, as the weapons switch was not properly set. After a quick correction, he successfully dropped the mine only a minute after the sub's conning tower had completely disappeared under the waves.

These attacks certainly damaged the sub, as it began to leave a trail behind it and floating yellow objects, resembling uninflated life rafts, bobbed to the surface. Another *Anzio* Avenger on patrol joined McLane and they both dropped several more sonobuoys to continue tracking the enemy vessel. A third Avenger, piloted by Lieutenant Rex Nelson, reached the scene at about 10:00 AM. When the noise of the sub's propellers became loud through the sonobuoys, he also dropped a Mark 24 mine. The propeller noises continued for about a minute and a half, then air crews overheard a loud explosion, described by one crewman as "the dull roar of a depth charge explosion." The sound from the sub's propeller stopped, bubbles came to the surface of the sea, and the oil trail reaching the surface stopped and began to spread over the water. Two more Avengers arrived to relieve McLane and the other Avenger flying over the sub with him, but Nelson, with more fuel remaining, remained and marked the position of the I-13 with a smoke light for the two destroyer escorts, *USS Lawrence C. Taylor* and *USS Robert F. Keller*, now arriving at the scene.

At about 11:40, the *Taylor* made a hedgehog depth charge attack, firing twenty-four depth charges on the submerged submarine. Sonar operators heard the sub's screws speed up, then the crews of both ships heard, and felt, two small explosions quickly followed by two more. The *Taylor* went to flank speed to clear the spot and only seconds later, two explosions occurred, of such violence that they temporarily knocked out the sonar gear and the electric panels in the *Taylor*'s engine room. Nelson's Avenger overhead also felt these explosions and he and his gunner noted a ripple in the water below, emanating from the source of the explosion, that resembled those made by a stone dropped in still water. The *Keller* then moved in and fired another salvo of hedgehog depth charges, but without any subsequent underwater explosions. The sonar contacts became indistinct as sonar operators heard several more small explosions during the next ten minutes. Flotsam soon appeared that included deck planks, candles, Japanese magazines, bundles of newspapers and letters, and a photo of a Japanese family. Three hours after the last depth-charge attack, the oil slick that marked the watery grave of the I-13 and all its crew covered an area about five miles wide.[128]

———

On July 17, Task Force aircraft, including the first strikes flown by British aircraft, attempted to hit airfields around Tokyo and the Japanese battleship *Nagato*, anchored at Yokosuka Naval Base near Tokyo. Bad weather, however, hampered the attacks and only 146 American and sixty-five British aircraft from the first two strikes launched that morning succeeded in hitting any targets before air operations halted about noon. The *Nagato* was damaged and the old heavy cruiser *Kasuga* sunk, but the bag in aircraft by Navy pilots was low: only five single-engine floatplanes destroyed at Kitaura. British aircraft destroyed nine aircraft on the enemy fields and sank a few small vessels.[129]

Flyers of Task Force 38 flew only ten missions, both sweeps and strikes briefed for airfields north of Tokyo, before the weather closed in by noon. Two strikes returned to their carriers without hitting a target, and those that did attack hit targets of opportunity instead, such as enemy shipping off the coast and small towns.

Nineteen Hellcats from VF-6 took off from *USS Hancock* at 4:20 AM to sweep the airfields at Kiryu and Koizumi, northwest of Tokyo, encountering only a few antiaircraft bursts as the flight crossed the coast during the entire mission. Arriving over the airfields, they discovered both totally covered by overcast. After returning to the eastern coast of Honshu, the planes then flew south from the town of Tomioka looking for targets. Spotting a train, the sweep commander ordered one division to attack. Two pilots fired rockets at the locomotive and missed, but the remaining Hellcats then strafed the train, hitting the boiler, stopping it. Other divisions of the flight continued south, hitting factories, small vessels, and warehouses. One Hellcat strafed a picket boat offshore as another part of the flight bombed the small town of Kuji. After this, they came upon three small cargo ships a few miles offshore. Attacking the unfortunate vessels with rockets, they scored a direct hit with a rocket on one, sinking it.

More F6Fs hit the town of Isohara, where they rocketed and bombed a factory and warehouses. One warehouse blew up after several rockets hit and the factory caught fire. On one attack run, Ensign Marlyn Kinder dropped his fragmentation bombs from very low altitude and pieces struck the wings and fuselage of his Hellcat. He succeeded in flying his heavily damaged F6F to the destroyer picket line offshore and ditched near a destroyer. The *USS John Rodgers* quickly picked him up.[130]

⁓

Kinder's Hellcat was the only aircraft lost on a strike or sweep that morning. A Corsair flying from *USS Hancock* exploded just after being catapulted for a combat air patrol from the carrier shortly before the Hellcats took off, killing the pilot, Ensign Nathan Edmonson. Another fighter was lost during another CAP in the afternoon. Hellcats from VF-34 took off from *USS Monterey* shortly before 3:00 PM. During the patrol the Hellcat flown by Ensign Oscar Northington suddenly dropped from the formation and crashed into the sea, killing him. Although the cause of the crash was unknown, a failure of the oxygen system may have caused the mishap.

After the cancellation of strikes at noon on the 17th, American flyers did not fly any more missions over Japan until that night, when Air Group 91 again went into action, flying the first so-called "Heckler" mission to interdict enemy airfields, as well as a nighttime combat air patrol over another shore bombardment that will be described shortly.

The Heckler mission took off after 6:00 PM that evening: two Avengers with two Hellcats as escort. One Avenger with a Hellcat harried enemy airfields near Tokyo, including Kasumigaura, Hyakurigahara, and Hokoda. After an hour in the air, the flight reached the vicinity of the airfields, but cloud cover made it impossible to identify any of them. Rain had soaked the cables for the radar on the Avengers, rendering them inoperable. After one circuit of the area, one of the Hellcats, piloted by Ensign Henry Sohrweid, became separated from the other three aircraft. He radioed the flight leader for permission to strike out on his own, to use his rockets and ammunition on targets of opportunity. With permission granted, he flew off, not to be seen again.

The Avenger crew then spotted a small town with all lights burning brightly through a momentary break in the overcast during their second round of the area. They dropped two bombs on an industrial area in what they believed was the town of Tamatsukuri. One struck among factories, the other fell into what crews believed was a residential area. The city blacked out just after the bombs struck.

The second Avenger and Hellcat attempted to harass Katori Airfield, but could not find it through the heavy clouds below. Shortly thereafter they tried to locate another airfield, but again failed to see it through the clouds. On their third attempt to locate an enemy airfield, fortune smiled on them, as they succeeded in finding the airfield at Tateyama. The Hellcat made a rocket attack on the field, followed by a few strafing runs, but total darkness prevented the pilot from observing the results. The Avenger got into the act as well, dropping several bombs on the runway. These two planes, as well as the TBM that bombed the town, returned safely to the *Bon Homme Richard*. Apparently unused to small nighttime nuisance raids such as this one, not one Japanese antiaircraft gun fired at the intruders during the entire mission.

Besides the combat loss, Air Group 91 suffered another air crew's fatality that night when a Hellcat, piloted by Lieutenant Charles Canham, Jr., crashed into the sea while circling the carrier, waiting to land from a combat air patrol over the Task Force.[131]

Surface ships had better results with two shore bombardments during night of the 17th. *USS Iowa, Wisconsin,* and *Missouri,* with their cruiser and destroyer escorts and joined by *HMS King George V,* shelled enemy factories at Mito and Hitachi for about half an hour just before midnight. Radar aimed the guns and tracked the flight of the shells that were clearly visible on radar sets.[132] Japanese aircraft were active, dropping window in an attempt to throw off the aim of the American ships, but this was the extent of their opposition to the attack.

A shipping sweep that began before midnight on the 18th encountered no Japanese ship. Task Group 35.4's four American cruisers—*USS Topeka, Oklahoma City, Atlanta,* and *Dayton*—with destroyer escort, however, bombarded Japanese radar stations and coastal artillery positions around Nojima Saki, without any response from Japanese defenses.

American and British aircraft had a little better luck with the weather on the 18th as it improved late in the morning. Flyers from both nations attacked airfields in the Tokyo area, to keep Japanese fighters from coming up to oppose the highlight of the day's action: a strike by aircraft of all three American Task Groups against the Japanese battleship *Nagato*, moored at Yokosuka Naval Base, on Tokyo Bay. American planes flew a total of 557 attack sorties on the 18th, almost 200 to Japanese airfields around Tokyo and 372 to attack Yokosuka. British aircraft also attacked airfields. The strikes at Yokosuka badly damaged the *Nagato* and sank the old heavy cruiser *Kasuga*, a submarine at anchor, and several merchant ships, including two fair-sized cargo ships. British flyers destroyed thirteen aircraft on the ground.[133]

Following hours on standby for a mission on the 17th and the early morning of the 18th, aircrews finally got the chance to go into action by midday, with fifteen strikes taking off by 12:45 PM. Of the aircraft dispatched, ninety-seven Hellcats and eighty-eight Corsairs struck airfields around Tokyo to prevent enemy fighters from intercepting the large attack on Yokosuka.

Tsukuba West Airfield was the target of VF-49 from *USS San Jacinto*. Making high-speed attack runs from about 1,000 feet, they spotted several two-engine planes and more single-engine fighters cleverly camouflaged with foliage. American bombs and rockets pummeled these aircraft, damaging if not destroying them. Moving on to their next target, Shimodate Airfield, the flight strafed hangars and aircraft revetments as no enemy planes were visible on the field. Their last airfield visited, before returning to the *San Jacinto*, was Hokoda Airfield, soon to be attacked by planes from Air Group 1. Pilots quickly recognized the airplanes seen on the field as "duds," or previously destroyed planes, so the Hellcats strafed hangars. After the attack, on the flight back to the carrier, pilots saw several Japanese "Rufe" floatplanes on a beach near Kitaura Seaplane Base. Zooming in to attack, the Hellcats strafed them all, set two on fire, and then headed out to sea and home. Pilots noticed only two bursts of anti-aircraft fire during the missions that damaged one Hellcat slightly.[134]

Hellcats from *USS Randolph* also found operational enemy aircraft at Katori Airfield after finding their briefed targets, airfields on the Chiba Peninsula, covered by overcast. The F6Fs bombed, rocketed, and strafed the field, hitting hangars and two single-engine planes that must have been fueled and ready to take off, as they immediately burst into flames. After this first attack, the squadron reformed over the ocean to make a second attack, to take out two training planes that appeared to be land-ing on Katori. As they made landfall, an intense antiaircraft barrage from guns not previously seen near the field forced them to break off the attack. Not deterred, they turned south to find another airfield, soon rewarded when four Hellcats spotted Mobara Airfield under the cloud overcast. The four promptly attacked aircraft revetments with rockets and machine-gun fire as their squadron mates rocketed and machine-gunned hangars and buildings on the field, but did not see the results.[135]

More Japanese planes went up in smoke before they could inter-fere with the impending strike on Yokosuka when a dozen Hellcats from VF-31 attacked Kumagaya Airfield. The fighters initially bombed hangars on the field, but seeing few tangible results, they scoured the area until they spotted several planes in revetments, three or four miles from the main airfield, where earlier reconnaissance photos had revealed Betty bombers. The *Belleau Wood* pilots worked over this area for about an hour, making between fifteen and twenty strafing runs, firing about 10,000 rounds of ammunition. They claimed fifteen planes as destroyed, including five that caught fire during the attack. Another section of the squadron hit Katori Airfield, as did other squadrons on the 18th, bomb-ing hangars and destroying a Betty bomber parked near one.

During the hour-long attack on Kumagaya, a few pilots saw a train entering the station at the nearby town of Chichibu and decided to attack the marshalling yard, a change from repeated strafing runs on the aircraft. They hit several locomotives and trains with rockets, and two planes also found time to fire rockets at a power station nearby. Although reports do not specify the target, the Japanese welcomed these American visitors with antiaircraft fire that damaged seven planes during the mission.[136]

Although the Hellcats were lucky on these airfield suppression missions, five Corsairs went down while working over Japanese airfields. Nine Hellcats and eight Corsairs from Air Group 1 hit the airfields at Hokoda and Hyakurigahara. Their first stop was Hokoda Airfield, where the Corsairs and four Hellcats dropped 500-pound bombs on hangars at the field, soon after VF-49's visit. The flight then continued on to Hyakurigahara. Pilots initially saw only dummy and previously destroyed aircraft on the field, so they decided to rocket hangars. Japanese antiaircraft gunners met them with light- and medium-caliber antiaircraft fire, potentially deadly to aircraft attacking at a low altitude. During one of these attack runs, two pilots found and strafed two undamaged planes, then spotted a few more a mile from the runways. When they returned to strafe the latter, Japanese antiaircraft fire, described as intense by returning pilots, hit three Corsairs. One managed, despite serious damage, to return to the *Bennington* and land safely, but the badly damaged aircraft was jettisoned over the side of the carrier. Two others were not as fortunate. Squadron mates last saw two pilots, Lieutenant Richard Eason and Ensign William Carney, during the second strafing run. The possibility of a midair collision between the two could not be discounted, as both men never returned; they were later reported as killed in action.[137]

Two more Corsairs from VBF-88 also failed to return from another airfield strike, carried out with Corsairs from *USS Shangri-La*. The briefed field, at Kashiwa, was totally cloud covered, so the sweep attacked the alternate, Katori Airfield.

VBF-85 made two passes on the airfield, firing rockets into aircraft revetments and hangars as Japanese defenders responded with moderate antiaircraft fire that slightly damaged one plane. Their rockets found a number of targets in revetments and parked near the runway, destroying twenty-one and damaging more.

Yorktown's Corsairs also rocketed aircraft revetments and hangars, but none of the aircraft they hit burned. After the first pass, the strike leader gained altitude to radio a weather report to the *Yorktown* while two pilots made a second run on the enemy airfield. Lieutenant Leon Christison found and destroyed one enemy aircraft, confirmed by his wingman, who rejoined the strike leader to return to the *Yorktown*. Christison never made it back to the ship, killed in action. The remaining Corsairs then flew over to their original target, Kashiwa, and found the field now open for attack. Pilots again fired rockets at Japanese planes in revetments near the field, but didn't get the satisfaction of seeing any of them burn. During the attack, Japanese antiaircraft fire hit the Corsair of Lieutenant (jg) Theron Gleason, which exploded in midair, killing him.

Undeterred by this loss, the squadron returned to Katori again, after the strike leader had reported the location of several more enemy planes hidden off the main airfield. The Corsairs went in again to attack as antiaircraft fire damaged three of them, but pilots didn't see obvious results, as none of the enemy aircraft hit began to burn. Two enemy aircraft were destroyed on the ground at Katori, one of them credited to Lieutenant Christison.[138]

The last Corsair lost during the attacks on the airfields was from VBF-83. The squadron hit Atsugi Airfield, finding about forty enemy aircraft in plain sight, Betty and Nell bombers, as well as "a four-engine job." Japanese opposition here was unusual, as pilots reported aerial mines that exploded as flaming red bursts below the attackers, while there was little conventional flak. Pilots bombed the enemy planes but later determined that most of them were derelicts destroyed in earlier raids. On the way back to the *Essex*, the squadron strafed a destroyer escort in Sagami Wan. The destroyer fought back with two bursts of heavy, and less effective, automatic antiaircraft fire. One of the heavy rounds hit Lieutenant David Horton's Corsair during the attack, blowing off an aileron, part of the tail. The plane crashed into the sea only a few hundred feet from the enemy vessel. The pilots could not claim the enemy ship as destroyed, but they certainly damaged it with machine-gun rounds.[139]

Planes from all the air groups of the three Task Groups of the Task Force attacked the *Nagato*. The total number taking part in the three coordinated strikes by all three Task Groups was 103 Hellcats, forty-nine Corsairs, 139 Avengers, and eighty-one Helldivers. Planes dispatched from Task Group 38.3 attacked first, followed by aircraft from Task Group 38.4. Planes from Task Group 38.1 dove last.[140] The commander of the entire strike was Commander Harman Utter of Air Group 83. Strike commander for Task Group 38.3 aircraft was the commander of

VT-83, Lieutenant Commander Henry Stewart.[141] Commander Wallace Sherrill of Air Group 85 commanded Task Group 38.4's strike.[142] Planes from *USS Independence* followed those from *Shangri-La*, *Cowpens*, and *Yorktown* during the attack.[143]

Commander Henry "Hank" Miller of Air Group 6 from *USS Hancock* commanded the last strike force, from Task Group 38.1. Fighters from several air groups remained at altitude to cover the dive-bombers and Avengers during the attack.[144]

During takeoffs from carriers, three Helldivers crashed into the sea. From *USS Bennington*, the Helldiver flown by Lieutenant (jg) Joyce Bardelmeier spun in and crashed near the carrier. Fortunately, destroyer *USS Brush* rescued the pilot and his radioman quickly.[145] Air Group 6 lost two SB2Cs during their takeoff from *USS Hancock*, both flown by newly arrived replacement pilots. Ensign Howard Harrison and his radioman, ARM3c Raymond Predmore, and Ensign Stephen DeCoste with his radioman, ARM3c John Backstrom, who had also ditched July 14, all ended up in the drink just after they took off, but all four were soon rescued by the destroyers *USS Blue* and *USS Samuel L. Moore*. The air group report of the mission ascribed both of these crashes to the lack of training in taking off from a carrier with a full combat bomb load.[146] Besides these ditchings, a flight deck mishap occurred when a propeller chopped off the tail of a Hellcat from VF-88 preparing for takeoff.[147]

The strike forces from the three Task Groups formed up for the flight to Yokosuka over the radar picket destroyers, then proceeded up the Sagami Wan, to fool the Japanese into thinking their target was the airfields at Atsugi and Tachikawa, before turning west as they neared Yokosuka. Fighters escorted the bombers on the way to the target by weaving back and forth, to reduce their speed to remain with the slower bombers. Once over Yokosuka, the battleship's position moored near a dock, with the bow pointing northwest, dictated the direction of the attacks on the *Nagato*, but air groups approached it from all directions of the compass. Many planes, armed with 1,000-pound bombs, intended to drop them in the water just next to *Nagato* as intentional near misses, to create the effect of a mine and hole the vessel below the waterline with the aim of rolling it over.[148,149]

Aircraft from Task Group 38.3 led the aerial armada of almost 400 planes, with the air groups from *USS Essex* and *USS Monterey* in the lead, followed by planes of *USS Randolph* and *USS Bataan*.[150]

A major task for some groups during the attack was to attack antiaircraft positions on shore and the *Nagato*, to suppress flak for following planes that dive-bombed the ship. These planes faced the most vicious flak not only because they were the first to attack, but also since they aimed directly at the antiaircraft guns. Avengers and some Hellcats from Air Group 83 bombed these positions, the first planes to do so during the attack, against intense antiaircraft fire. The Avengers released their bombs from the prudent altitude of 6,000–7,000 feet, but crews still saw puffs of smoke directly over the gun positions as their fragmentation bombs exploded on target.[151]

Monterey TBM pilots were assigned AA positions near the *Nagato*, as well as on nearby Futtsu Island. Crews reported that it was not difficult to pick out their assigned antiaircraft gun position targets, as each gun clearly identified itself by gun flashes. One pilot, Ensign George Tuffanelli, went around twice. Overshooting on his first glide attack, he opted to go around and try again, despite the intense antiaircraft fire and plethora of aircraft in the air around him. He bombed gun positions on Futtsu Island on his second run. Although Japanese defenses were intense, pilots of VT-34 observed that they "did not shoot AA guns as well when the AA gun crews were being shot at [from fragmentation bombs aimed directly at them]."[152] VT-16 and VT-83 also bombed antiaircraft positions on hills on the shore, with crews from the *Essex* reporting they saw their fragmentation bombs explode directly over the positions.

Corsairs, Hellcats, and Avengers from the groups of Task Group 38.3 dive-bombed the battleship itself, with VBF-16 Corsairs releasing their bombs 3,500 to 3,000 feet above *Nagato*. One of the trailing pilots saw three explosions in the water near the hull of the vessel, exactly where they had been aimed. Other Corsairs dropped more fragmentation bombs on flak positions in the immediate vicinity of the ship.[153]

Corsairs from VBF-83 dive-bombed with the carrier's Helldivers. Three bombs hit the ship and two landed in the water near it. The *Essex's* Helldivers dove in formation, spotting a large explosion of what they believed was an aerial mine during their dives. All the planes had good visibility as they were the first to attack, and six bombs dropped by VB-83 landed close to the *Nagato*. As the formation pulled out of their dives, flak burst directly in front of one, piloted by Ensign Ernest Baker. He headed east with his engine smoking.

After the *Essex* and *Monterey* air groups dived on *Nagato*, Helldivers from VB-16 were to bomb the battleship, but planes from another air group got there first, so the SB2Cs broke off their attack and circled the target once. Half the squadron's planes went into their dives while the remainder circled *Nagato* three times before doing the same. Pilots reported that the danger from midair collisions at this point was almost as great as that posed by the intense antiaircraft fire. The VB-16 report of the strike concluded, "There were too many planes in the small area [over *Nagato*] under the conditions" to bomb accurately. "Every pilot on the strike reports having to be constantly on the alert for other planes to avoid mid-air collisions." VT-34 crews also reported that "Diving planes were everywhere, at all altitudes and on a variety of courses."[154] VB-16 crews reported they could not discern the *Nagato* through smoke until they were about 5,000 feet above it. They released their bombs from 3,000 feet, claiming three hits[155] as antiaircraft fire damaged six of their Helldivers.[156] The SB2C flown by Ensign George Dean was hit in wing and wheel well, the latter starting a fire that swept to the rear of the plane and the radioman. The radioman prepared for a ditching and threw out equipment in the process, including the camera he used to photograph the attack. Fortunately, the fire went out as they flew toward Tokyo Bay and the plane landed safely on their carrier.[157]

After their bombs were gone, VB-16 crews flew "on the deck" over the southern part of the Chiba Peninsula to avoid more Japanese flak by flying between Tateyama and Mobara Airfields in what they called "Flak Free Valley." At such low altitude, it seemed natural for them to strafe several small ships as they flew over Tokyo Bay and they left one small cargo vessel on fire.[158]

The four groups of Task Group 38.3 lost only one aircraft during the attack. Ensign Baker's flak-damaged VB-83 SB2C made it to Sagami Wan, when he reported his plane was losing power and he would have to make a water landing. He did so successfully and both he and his radioman, ARM3c Walter Owens, got into their raft. As their squadron mates continued on to their carrier, VF-83 Hellcats arrived and proceeded to circle the life raft until their fuel ran low and they had to return to the *Essex* as well. Although alerted of the position of Baker and Owens by VB-83, the lifeguard submarine in the vicinity was busy with another rescue and couldn't reach the men before the Japanese captured them. They spent the next few weeks as prisoners of war.[159]

The planes of Task Group 38.4 attacked after those from 38.3. Following the established pattern, planes went in to hit antiaircraft positions before the dive-bombing.

Just before takeoff, the *Yorktown* air group received word of a flak barge with medium and light guns spotted in the harbor and radioed the news to the target coordinator of Task Group 38.4, Lieutenant Commander Sherrill of Air Group 85. Sherrill responded, "I'll get the flak barge." As they approached Yokosuka, crews of Air Group 88 saw Sherrill, with his escort, dive on the barge, which "seemed to explode" believed sunk.[160]

The Avengers bombed antiaircraft positions and a TBM pilot in Air Group 85 described his squadron's role in bombing flak guns as "blocking back for its group." As VBF-85 and VT-85 from *USS Shangri-La* hit antiaircraft positions, flak blew off the canopy of the Avenger flown by Lieutenant Donald Macinnes, but despite this event he still bombed his target.[161]

As the bombing of antiaircraft positions was well underway, dive-bombing attacks on the Japanese battleship began. *USS Shangri-La's* VB-85 Helldiver crews couldn't see if they scored hits on the battleship, but flak damaged five of their planes. Flak hit Lieutenant William Gauvey's aircraft during his dive but he continued on and dropped his bomb, then pulled up, delighted to find that he still had control of the

SB2C although flak had knocked out his radio. The flak burst mortally wounded his radioman, ARM3c Alfred Bonoconi, who unfortunately bled to death before they regained the carrier, despite the fact that Gauvey flew straight on to the carrier. An antiaircraft burst damaged another Helldiver, flown by Lieutenant Commander Arthur Maltby, Jr., cutting all the control cables on the left side of the plane. He managed to fly back to the *Shangri-La* and land safely, without a tail hook, by holding both feet on the right side of the rudder pedals.[162]

VT-50 Avengers released their bombs at the *Nagato* from an altitude of 4,500 to 5,200 feet. The bombs took seven to eight seconds to reach the battleship, and during this time the Avengers were taking evasive action to avoid flak, so it was difficult for crews to gauge if they scored any hits. Flak hit the Avenger flown by Ensign Melvin S. Harder during the dive but he continued on and dropped his bomb, then returned safely to the carrier.[163]

VT-88 Avengers, following the *Cowpens* Avengers, hit the *Nagato* as well. The flak suppression was effective, as crews later reported a slackening, and reduced accuracy, of enemy fire after these attacks began, with light flak more troublesome. They dove at a sharper angle than usual, up to 60 degrees, with their "fifteen big-belled, supposedly antiquated Avengers [that] converged on the heart of the once great twenty-nine-year old BB" in four sections, attacking different parts of the battleship. The last section saw five bombs hit near the *Nagato*. The squadron strike report vividly recounted this leader's attack: "His [the leader of the fourth Avenger section] radioman, having crawled into the exposed turret gun position, strained every nerve and muscle to track the bomb [dropped by his pilot] in its fall. He saw it plunge into the flaming hulk and brew a fresh burst of flame and smoke."[164]

The five VB-88 Helldivers that made the attack with the remainder of their air group got ahead of VT-88's Avengers, aiming for antiaircraft positions on the ship during their dives. They released their bombs from altitudes ranging from 3,500 to 3,000 feet and could easily see the *Nagato*, claiming three hits on the vessel.[165] Most of the Hellcats from VF-88 made a dive-bombing attack before the Helldivers, just behind the SB2Cs of Air Group 85, although a few were seconds late and actually dove with VB-88, some reaching almost 500 knots while screaming down on the battleship. *Yorktown's* Corsairs claimed three hits on the *Nagato*. Flak hit only one Hellcat over Yokosuka, and another on the return flight after one section of fighters strafed some small boats that put up some AA fire, but both returned home safely.[166]

Twelve Avengers and four Hellcats from Air Group 27 bombed the *Nagato* with the Hellcats also strafing during their dives. They were the last group to attack in Task Group 38.4 attack echelon, but smoke did not completely obscure the enemy vessel, so they could still see their target. The Avengers made steeper dives than usual for a glide-bombing attack because of their position at the start. From a formation described by one participant as "every man for himself," three of their 1,000-pound bombs hit the battleship, while three more struck in the water alongside, and one on the dock to which it was moored.[167]

Like the Task Group before them, 38.4 lost only one TBM, an Avenger from Air Group 27 flown by Lieutenant (jg) Harry Patterson, ARM2c Lawrence Garner, and AOM3c Carmine Marchese. None of their squadron mates saw flak hit their plane, but other pilots on the strike reported an Avenger hit during its dive that crashed into the waters of Yokosuka Harbor. This was apparently the VT-27 TBM, as all three crewmen were killed.[168]

Planes of Task Group 38.1 dove on the battleship and antiaircraft positions as the finale to the attack. Avengers from each air group had specific areas of AA positions around *Nagato* to bomb. The Avengers, escorted by fighters from VF-31 and 49, were slow to start their attack, forcing the fighters, fighter-bombers, and dive-bombers to stack up overhead, under constant heavy AA fire, while waiting for the TBMs to hit AA emplacements.[169] This is likely why the most planes shot down during the raid were from Task Group 38.1.

TBM crews from VT-49 described the intensity of the antiaircraft fire as "1/10 cumulus flak" and "thick enough for landing" as the intensity of enemy fire made it impossible for a many pilots to observe the result of their work. The lethal effect of the bombs dropped by two VT-49

Avengers was readily apparent, however. Unable to hit their briefed AA positions, they opted to bomb a large oil storage tank that immediately caught fire, belching thick black smoke.[170]

Air Group 1 considered this strike so potentially hazardous that their Avengers carried one crewman, rather than two, to reduce the potential for losses.[171] The planes dropped 260-pound fragmentation bombs on the AA positions to decimate the crews and stop the guns firing.[172] VT-1 made a glide-bombing attack, as did other Avengers, dropping their fragmentation bombs from 6,000 feet and pulling out at 3,500 to 4,000 feet above the positions.[173] Pilots reported that dropping the bombs at higher altitude reduced their accuracy considerably, as it required bomb release a mile from the target, and reported that they had seen the bombs cropped by another Avenger land several hundred feet from the AA positions targeted.[174]

Belleau Wood's Avengers engaged in violent evasive maneuvers as they dove on sixteen antiaircraft guns located in the southwest part of the harbor. Releasing their bombs at about 5,000 feet, crewmen saw all their bombs land inside the area of the guns. As they hurried from the harbor, pilots kept their planes noses down, to increase speed, to clear the harbor and enemy antiaircraft as soon as possible.[175] To counter Japanese flak, the strike included countermeasures against enemy radar-guided antiaircraft guns to throw off the aim of antiaircraft gunners. VT-49 used radio countermeasures equipment in combat for the first time on this strike, to jam enemy radar, while others dropped window to accomplish the same purpose.[176] Corsairs from Air Group 1 used newly installed tanks underneath their wings to drop window during the strike.[177]

Following the Avengers, dive-bombers, with some Corsairs and Hellcats, formed up on those from VB-6 for the attack. Some planes had difficulty seeing the *Nagato* because it was well-camouflaged and bombing by the first two waves created smoke that covered the battleship.[178] Some pilots from Air Group 1 bombed destroyers moored near *Nagato*, as they couldn't see the latter because of smoke from explosions.[179]

Pilots of VBF-6 dropped the wheels of their planes during the dive on the battleship to slow them down a bit, but their airspeed still exceeded 300 miles per hour. Pilots reported they had trouble controlling the

Corsair because of the turbulence the wheels created, but still managed to score a hit on the battleship. They flew away from the target "on the deck" to avoid the intense antiaircraft fire. Flak blew Ensign John DeAngelo off target during his dive, so he pulled up and proceeded to dive again, this time in company with another squadron.[180] One VB-6 pilot, Lieutenant George Ferguson, who led his squadron on this strike, dropped his 1,000-pound bomb from only 3,000 feet above the *Nagato* while also firing two rockets and strafing. His bomb hit the water about forty feet from the battleship, while the rockets struck it squarely. Another pilot dropped his bomb from a mere 1,500 feet and it struck the water only twenty-five feet from the *Nagato*'s hull. Three bombs dropped by VB-6 pilots hit the warship. After bombing, some pilots strafed and fired rockets at ground targets as they flew away from the harbor.[181]

When Air Group 1 attacked, VF-1 Hellcat pilots aimed their bombs for the battleship, despite the clever camouflage that made it difficult to discern where the dock ended and the ship actually began, and one of their two bombs hit it. Other pilots had too much trouble recognizing the *Nagato* during their dives and bombed destroyers and cruisers nearby, without seeing the results. Three Helldiver pilots had the same problem and dropped their bombs on the dock area next to the battleship. Seven of *Bennington*'s dive-bomber pilots could, however, aim at the *Nagato*, but only claimed one probable hit.[182]

When the planes of Air Group 94 dove on the battleship, some Hellcat pilots couldn't see the target. They dropped their bombs where they thought the ship was moored, based on their study of reconnaissance photos. Two were "off target" in their dives, however, and aimed for a cruiser and transport instead. The fighters couldn't claim any direct hits on the battleship, only three near misses, but they did score a direct hit on the transport that sank it. Helldiver pilots claimed one hit and two near misses that would have damaged the *Nagato*'s hull. VT-94 crews hit antiaircraft positions, like many of the torpedo planes on the strike, and believed they had covered their assigned targets well.[183]

The Hellcats of VF-49 began their dive on Nagato from 16,000 feet as another group of fighters and Helldivers was also beginning their attack, restricting maneuvering room during their dives, dropping their bombs from only 4,000 feet. Several landed in the water, close to the hull of the battleship near the number three turret. The bomb dropped by the commander of Air Group 49, Lieutenant Commander George Rouzee, landed only a few feet from *Nagato*'s hull. Another pilot, Ensign Miles Christensen, was unable to bomb the battleship because other aircraft spoiled his aim and bombed a nearby destroyer instead, hitting very close to the hull of the enemy vessel. Oil and debris appeared just afterward, as his bomb had done considerable damage.[184] VF-31 Hellcats also bombed the *Nagato*, but smoke prevented them from observing where their bombs struck.[185]

VB-88 Helldivers from *USS Yorktown* became separated from the remainder of Air Group 88 while forming up for the strike. Nine of them joined up with the *Bennington* air group on the way to Yokosuka and attacked as part of Task Group 38.1. When they dove on the battleship, smoke almost completely obscured it, so the pilots dropped their bombs into the smoke, scoring at least one direct hit, later confirmed by a strike photo. All these Helldiver pilots thought the flak suppression by the Avengers was "well done."[186]

As Japanese antiaircraft gunners shot down five planes during this last stage of the attack, all the crews of Task Group 38.1's air groups did not share in the "well done." Antiaircraft fire hit the VB-1 Helldiver flown by Ensign Robert Christ during his dive, but he still managed to drop his bomb, pull out of this dive, and head for the open sea as his radioman, ARM3c Joseph Pollock, threw everything he could out of the rear of the SB2C to lighten the ship. They managed to reach Sagami Wan, where Christ successfully ditched the plane near a Japanese minefield. Squadron mates saw only one man get out of the plane before it sank, but his proximity to the minefield made it impossible for any lifeguard submarine to reach him. Unfortunately, both men were later listed as killed in action.[187]

Two VT-1 Avengers went down to Japanese flak. Lieutenant William Eddin's plane was smoking as he flew away from Yokosuka. He got as far as the rally point to reform after the attack, near Suno Saki, then ditched the TBM with his radioman, ARM3c Norman Marten. Lieutenant (jg) Richard Paget also ditched his TBM, also damaged by antiaircraft fire. He and ARM2c William Heffner got into the life raft safely, as did the other crew, to await rescue. Two Helldivers from VB-6 had escorted one of the two TBMs from Yokosuka and marked the spot where they ditched with smoke to facilitate their rescue. Squadron mates alerted the lifeguard submarine nearby, *USS Galiban*, of their location with such detail that it soon rescued all four men.[188]

Air Group 94 lost two planes on the strike: a Corsair and a Helldiver. During VBF-94's dive on *Nagato*, the two wingmen flying with Lieutenant Milton Adams suddenly saw him pull out of his dive. None of the three, like other pilots, could see the battleship at this time. The wingmen were later adamant that flak had not hit Adams's Corsair. Before takeoff, he had told squadron mates that he would "hit the target whatever the cost," so they speculated he had pulled out of the dive to attack again, as DeAngelo of VBF-6 did, to get better visibility. In any event, he was not seen again, later reported as killed in action in one of the planes seen to crash in the target area.[189] Japanese antiaircraft fire also hit the VB-94 Helldiver crewed by Ensign Merle Pennington and ARM2c Melford Bendickson. The pair flew their damaged aircraft toward home but had to ditch in Sagami Wan outside Tokyo Bay. Other airmen saw one crewman get out of the SB2C and into a raft, but it was impossible for air-sea rescue aircraft, or a lifeguard submarine, to reach him. Both men were killed in action.

Japanese antiaircraft defenses were formidable, as was expected at a naval base located on Tokyo Bay. Enemy fire was intense throughout the attack, yet pilots from VB-16, who had experience at other hotly defended targets, reported that antiaircraft fire over Truk Harbor, attacked by carrier aircraft several times in late 1943 and early 1944, was more intense, as was that encountered in the Battle of the Philippine Sea in June 1944. But the impression left on VT-34 crews was that the defenses were "intense in the superlative sense of the word."[190] To counter flak, planes dropped window and rope, a lengthier version of the former, to confuse radar-guided Japanese antiaircraft guns throughout the attack.[191]

The heavy flak over the naval base at high altitude was a "barrage in depth" reaching from 6,000 to 14,000 feet[192] and a menace as planes approached the harbor and formed up for their dives. Medium and light flak greeted them once they dove on their targets. The latter came not only from the plethora of antiaircraft positions on the shore around the ships, but also from the ships themselves. *Nagato*'s medium and light antiaircraft crews, and those on other ships, joined with batteries on shore in firing at the attackers.[193] The battleship's secondary batteries were firing until several bombs hit the ship and reduced their fire.[194] In fact, by the time of the third attack wave, despite the higher losses, some crews thought Japanese fire was less directed and more random. VBF-1 pilots reported that the Japanese "appeared to be just throwing it [antiaircraft rounds] up over the target rather than concentrating on any one plane or formation." Such impressions are subjective and could reflect a momentary slackening of enemy fire in a particular portion of the sky over Yokosuka, as other groups disagreed with this assessment.[195]

Air Group 6 pilots described the antiaircraft fire as "the most intense encountered by this squadron," one adding that it looked like "stars winking the Milky Way." The air group report of the strike stated, "It is believed that the battleship *Nagato* at the Yokosuka Naval Base was protected on 18 July 1945 by the strongest antiaircraft defense ever encountered by naval aircraft. AA fire came not only from innumerable land batteries, but also from a cordon of destroyers, destroyer escorts, and one cruiser, and at least one flak ship."[196] One pilot from Air Group 27 of *USS Independence* recalled, "The flashes from the guns were so thick that the ground below seemed to be blanketed with fireflies."[197]

Obviously, the flak at Yokosuka was formidable. Besides guns near the battleship and on it, there was also a Japanese flak ship, moored close by, that contributed to the intense antiaircraft fire thrown at the attackers,[198] and pilots reported that the small island of Futtsu, bristling with antiaircraft guns in the middle of Tokyo Bay, "looked like it was on fire."[199]

Once planes began the return flight to their carriers, radio chatter was prevalent, a natural release from the tension created in attacking the main naval base in Tokyo. On the way home, the strike leader of VT-50 told his squadron to stop the radio chatter: "Remarks about Tojo would not worry the Japanese nearly as much as it would shipmates whose lives depended upon downed pilots' reporting getting through" on the radio to air-sea rescue units.[200]

The raid did not sink the *Nagato*, but certainly damaged it so much it could not have opposed any invasion that fall. Air Group 83 aptly described the mission as "the Third Fleet shot the works at the poor old *Nagato*, lying self-effacingly at Yokosuka."

—◆—

Following the strike, the Task Force moved farther off the coast to refuel and replenish and the Japanese had a short respite from attacks by naval air, but the Army Air Force continued to pound the Home Islands, as they had for months. B-29s fire-bombed smaller Japanese cities during July while very long-range fighters, P-51Ds and P-47Ns, flew strikes against airfields as far north as Tokyo from bases on Iwo Jima and Okinawa. On July 19, the 47th Fighter Squadron of the 15th Fighter Group was one of several fighter groups that struck airfields around Nagoya and Osaka. First Lieutenant Robert Worton was one of the pilots on the mission, leading "Yellow Flight," of P-51D Mustangs. He reported:

> *Moderate [flak] was encountered along the western shores of Ise-Wan Bay. At approximately 10:00 [AM] we started our run on the P.T. [primary target: Kakamigahara Airfield]. We flew with our flight line abreast, Red [the other flight of the squadron on the mission] taking the right-hand side and Yellow [Horton's flight] the left. . . . I strafed a few machine gun nests from out of range. I observed several dummies and wrecks [aircraft] in the revetments on the north side of the field.*
>
> *After breaking away from the Primary Target, I joined with Red Flight. I called in a single bogie [unidentified aircraft] high, at 3 o'clock, and started a high-speed climb after it. Apparently the Jap didn't see me, as I closed in on his tail, gave him a burst, and he blew up.*

Worton received full credit for the victory, added to his tally of two and a half enemy planes already shot down. The mission was one of the long-range fighter missions flown by the Far East Air Force to Japanese airfields in southern Japan in July and early August.[201]

Chapter Seven

A HIATUS IN STRIKES OCCURRED DURING THE NEXT FEW DAYS AS THE Task Force again refueled and surface ships continued to remind the Japanese of the enemy fleet off their coast. During the night of July 22–23, Destroyer Squadron 61 encountered a small Japanese convoy near Nojima Saki. During a one-sided engagement, the American ships sank a Japanese merchant ship and damaged another and one of their escorts, a destroyer escort. These two surface actions presaged a full day of air strikes on July 24 by American and British aircraft against the large Japanese naval base at Kure and targets in and around the Inland Sea.

On July 24, American air power continued to pummel the Home Islands. Army Air Force long-range fighters attacked enemy airfields in the Nagoya area while B-29s flew their first daylight mission in a month, bombing targets in the Osaka-Nagoya area. American carrier-based aviators made almost 1,400 flights, including 1,115 strikes against airfields from northern Kyushu to Nagoya and Kure Naval Base, while the British flew almost 300 sorties to targets along the eastern Inland Sea. The aim of the strikes was to destroy major naval units that might interfere with American convoys that would cross the northern Pacific with supplies for the invasion during the fall.[202]

The Japanese sent fighters up to oppose these attacks for the first time that month, showing the importance of the warships at Kure. American Navy flyers shot down ten aircraft over Japan and three more attempting to attack the fleet. They also destroyed about forty enemy aircraft on the ground on airfields at Nagoya and Osaka, many of them apparently ready to take off, since they burned. Of the fifty-three enemy merchant ships that went down to Navy bombs and rockets, eleven were sizeable cargo ships. Task Force 38 flyers sank the battleship-carrier *Hyuga*, heavy cruiser *Tone*, and the aircraft carrier *Amagi* in Kure Harbor and damaged more, including the heavy cruiser *Aoba*, the light cruiser *Oyodo*, two destroyers, and the old battleship *Settsu*. Balanced against the loss of four aircraft, British aviators sank a few small ships and badly damaged the escort carrier *Kaiyo*, found in a cove on the western shore of Shikoku, as well as destroying twenty-one aircraft on Japanese airfields. During three successive strikes from the three British carriers in Task Force 37, British flyers in Avengers and Corsairs, as well as British-made Firefly and Seafire fighters, attacked the carrier, scoring at least hits. The ship later sank.[203]

During the usual early morning sweeps, two Hellcats and a Corsair went down with two pilots killed. Air Group 87 lost the two F6Fs during a sweep of airfields on Shikoku and in the Hiroshima area, in preparation for the first strike on Kure later in the morning. Sixteen Hellcats, including a photo plane and its escort, took off at 4:45 AM. Finding no aircraft at their first stop, Matsuyama Airfield, the flight continued on to Hiroshima Bay, where the planes strafed and rocketed several ships, sinking a small tanker and setting a lugger on fire. A survey of more airfields and a seaplane base followed. The flight strafed and sank two large seaplanes, an Emily and a Mavis, moored off the island of Hiro and then flew to Niihama Airfield, across the Inland Sea on the west coast of Shikoku. Finding training aircraft, destined for use as *kamikazes* during the invasion, gathered on the field, the flight succeeded in setting one on fire during their strafing and rocket run. Intense antiaircraft fire, however, hit the tail of the strike leader's plane. Commander Porter Maxwell opened his parachute as he left the cockpit, and it had begun to pull him from the stricken aircraft just as it struck the sea near the field, killing him. The long duration of the flight cost another F6F when a second, unidentified pilot had to ditch near the radar picket destroyers on the flight home. One of the destroyers rescued him.[204]

VBF-6, also briefed to sweep airfields between Nagoya and Kobe, lost a Corsair. On arriving in the patrol area, the flight found the area completely covered by overcast, so they struck out for targets of opportunity along the east coast of Honshu, southeast of Kobe, where they strafed a radio station, a train, and several small vessels. As the flight began to head out to sea, the flight leader heard a report that weather to the west had improved, so the planes turned around and headed for Tokushima Airfield, where weather was perfect for an attack.

Although damaged aircraft cluttered the field, the Corsairs strafed and rocketed several aircraft in revetments, as well as hangars. Japanese antiaircraft gunners at the field were on the alert, as a flight of Army Air Force P-51s had flown past the field only minutes before the Navy planes arrived. The gunners met the attackers with "moderate," medium-caliber antiaircraft fire that hit one of the Corsairs during their attack. The plane, flown by Ensign Clifford Bausor, crashed on the enemy field, killing him. The Corsairs destroyed three Japanese planes and damaged six more planes, along with a hangar.[205]

Two more American aircraft went down to operations causes during the early morning. One was a Hellcat of Air Group 16 that had to ditch when landing, as its tail hook wouldn't go down. The pilot, Ensign George Humphries, ditched the F6F near the *Randolph*, and *USS Borie* quickly rescued him. Another unidentified pilot, from VBF-83, ditched his Corsair near the Task Force when it ran out of fuel, with the pilot also rescued.

After the opening phase of the day's operations, the first strike aircraft to attack the naval base at Kure began to take off at 7:40 AM. One hundred four Hellcats, forty Corsairs, 172 Avengers, and 107 Helldivers reached Kure for the strike. Planes from Task Group 38.1 dove on the enemy warships moored in the harbor first, followed by Task Group 38.4, with Task Group 38.3 attacking last.[206] The plan was for planes of each group to attack five minutes apart, achieving "saturation attacks."[207] The prime targets of the strike were major enemy ships anchored at Kure: battleships *Ise* and *Hyuga*, the battleship *Haruna*, the carriers *Amagi* and *Aso* (still under construction), the heavy cruisers *Tone* and *Aoba*, and the light cruisers *Oyodo* and *Juma*.[208] When it was over, the three Task Groups had lost seventeen planes in combat, with another an operational loss.

Commander Henry Miller of Air Group 6, Task Group 38.1's strike coordinator on July 18, became the strike commander for all Task Force planes, as well as for Task Group 38.1. He described the attacks by 38.1

aircraft as "deliberate, with steep dives and low pullouts" that would achieve more accurate results.[209]

The attack began with bombing of antiaircraft positions. *Belleau Wood*'s VT-31 bombed antiaircraft positions south of the harbor. The 260-pound fragmentation bombs exploded directly over the gun positions. At about the same time, VF-31 Hellcats bombed battleship *Ise*, making three near misses. On the way home, the Hellcats strafed a destroyer, luggers, and small cargo ships.[210]

Avengers from the *San Jacinto* hit AA positions south of the ships, diving through overcast at 2,000 feet, which made aiming difficult. They managed to attack through some holes in the clouds and most of them bombed the antiaircraft positions, some by dead reckoning. The bombs of one TBM hung up during this attack, so the pilot went after a destroyer firing at him, near Nishinomi Jima. Despite flak damage to four planes, the Avengers headed for home, taking time to attack shipping, as did the other attack aircraft on the strike, sinking a Sugar Dog and damaging some other small vessels. One pilot described the attack on shipping as aircraft "lining up" to attack ships in turn in the vicinity of Hiroshima and Iyo.[211]

Of the air groups aiming for warships, *Hancock* planes dove first, followed by those from the *Lexington*, *Bennington*, and *Belleau Wood*.[212] Air Group 6's primary targets were the *Ise* and *Aoba*, with the two carriers the secondary targets.[213] Most of the Avengers from VT-6 bombed the *Ise*, flying under the overcast at 6,000 feet to begin their attacks on the battleship. One division of *Hancock* Avengers, led by Lieutenant Lynn DuTemple, dropped their bombs from 2,000 feet altitude and scored two hits, followed the VB-1 Helldivers aiming at the *Amagi* through a hole in the overcast. Lieutenant John Burrus's division of TBMs circled the overcast until they found a hole, then dove on the *Ise*. Although two pilots had trouble getting on the target, bombing the cruiser *Aoba* instead, others bombed the *Ise* but didn't see the results. Burrus and another pilot went after one of the carrier hulls, the *Aso*, getting one hit on the vessel. Flak claimed the fifth pilot, Lieutenant (jg) Clarence Tiege, with radio operators ARM3c Jack Keeley and AOM3c Luther Johnson. The plane was not seen again after it began its dive.[214] The third Avenger division from

VT-6, led by Lieutenant Harold Eppler, also bombed the *Ise*, scoring two direct hits on the BB.[215]

The VB-6 Helldivers mentioned earlier also attacked both the *Ise* and *Aoba*, with three aircraft each scoring hits on these two targets. The goggles of one Helldiver pilot tore away during this dive and he couldn't get his bomb bay doors open. When he pressed the "pickle," or bomb release, nothing happened, so he strafed the *Aoba* all the way down to 1,500, then pulled out and dropped his bomb on a town on Okurokami Island. An oil line on another VB-6 SB2C parted during the dive, covering the cockpit with oil and preventing the pilot from dropping his bomb on the *Aoba*. He also later dropped his bomb on an island on the flight home.[216] Other VB-6 pilots struck the carrier *Amagi*, four of them scoring probable hits. One of them, Lieutenant John Maloney, dropped his bomb from the extremely low altitude of 900 feet.[217]

Three Hellcats of VF-6 attacked the *Ise* and *Aoba*, a fourth hit a destroyer escort across the harbor from the battleship, and three more remained at high altitude, dropping rope to confuse antiaircraft gun radar and taking photos of the strike.[218] Two bombing the *Ise* dropped their bombs at the low altitude of 2,000–3,000 feet, scoring hits, while the *Aoba*'s antagonist, Ensign Arthur Flynn, landed his bomb on the stern of the cruiser. On the return flight, as most planes strafed small ships, the photo planes encountered a Frank that blundered between the two sections of the flight. Two Hellcats, flown by Ensign John Ford and Lieutenant (jg) George Rawley, got on its tail and succeeded in hitting it in the tail as it dove for the deck. Rawley stayed with the enemy fighter, scoring hits in its engine, and then the Frank dove into the sea.[219] The Corsairs of VBF-6 had to circle Kure Harbor for fifteen minutes until it was their turn to dive on the *Ise*. Two of them got direct hits on the battleship.[220]

Air Group 94 attacked the *Ise* and *Hyuga*, as well as antiaircraft positions. Some Hellcats hit antiaircraft positions with fragmentation bombs as three more bombed one of the carriers with several fragmentation bombs. The Helldivers scored three near misses on the battleship, but the TBMs did not claim any hits.[221]

The Hellcats from Air Group 1 pushed over from 12,000 feet to bomb the battleship *Ise*. During the dive through heavy clouds, they lost sight of the battleship and bombed antiaircraft positions instead.[222] Avengers from VT-6, who also bombed AA positions, joined them.[223]

Overcast affected the attack by Corsairs of VBF-1. They had to circle the target, under intense antiaircraft fire, three times before they could dive on the enemy carriers. One section managed to bomb the *Amagi*, but couldn't observe their results as a second section attacked the *Ise*. These planes could only go into their dives from 6,000 feet because of the heavy cloud cover, but they could see their target and scored two hits on the battleship. One pilot, who couldn't line up on the *Ise* after flak hit the tail of his Corsair, chose a troop transport instead and was rewarded with a direct hit on the vessel. The third section of VBF-1 Corsairs bombed the cruiser *Aoba*, but couldn't see where their bombs landed. Although flak damaged several planes, they all flew away from Kure. Two of them would not reach the carrier.[224]

Bombing One Helldivers found antiaircraft fire to be intense, although crews described the heavy flak as inaccurate. Flak got one SB2C and damaged three more during their dives, when medium and light flak was the greatest danger. Briefed for the *Ise*, the two carriers, and the *Aoba*, one flight of Helldivers couldn't see the cruiser and bombed an old warship, the *Settsu*, instead. Lieutenant Commander Andrew Hamm, however, got a hit on the *Amagi* amidships; his two wingmen couldn't see the carrier and tried to bomb destroyers nearby, but missed. Lieutenant Francis Mulvihill got a direct hit on the *Ise*, near the bridge. Lieutenant (jg) Joyce Bardelmeier, separated from his division during the dive, chose to go after the light cruiser *Oyodo* and scored a near miss in the water that must have severely damaged the hull. During the attack, flak hit the SB2C flown by Ensign William Troyen and the plane crashed, killing Troyen and his radioman, ARM3c Robert Richards.[225]

VT-1 had experienced an unfortunate accident during takeoff, when Lieutenant (jg) George Gustafson's TBM spun in and crashed. The pilot could not get out of the plane before it sank, but the two crewmen did and a destroyer picked them up. Fourteen Avengers, however, did reach Kure and executed a glide-bombing attack on the *Hyuga* and the two carriers. Two pilots scored hits on the bow of the *Amagi* and one on the *Hyuga*. On the flight home, some planes engaged in strafing of small ships, making the squadron's rendezvous for the return flight to the *Bennington* somewhat chaotic. So much so that strafing of ground targets immediately after a strike took place in the future only when it did not interfere with assembly at the rendezvous.[226]

Hellcats of VF-49 were the last squadron from Task Group 38.1 to dive, since they had provided top cover against enemy fighters for most of the strike. Aiming for the carriers, their eight F6Fs scored two direct hits on the carrier *Katsuragi* at anchor just off Mitsuko Jima with 1,000-pound bombs, dropping their loads through holes in overcast that hung over the area.[227] During the free-for-all attacks on shipping during the flight home, Air Group 49 claimed the sinking of a small cargo ship, a lugger, and a sea truck, then reformed and headed for their carrier only to encounter Japanese fighters.

The second wave of the attack by planes of Task Group 38.4 had to circle Kure, under antiaircraft fire, until ordered in to attack. As already mentioned, Commander Sherrill coordinated the strike of the Task Group, briefed to bomb the battleship *Haruna* and the light cruiser *Oyodo*. Unfortunately, the battleship had moved from the berth since the last reconnaissance photos and a merchant ship was in its place.[228]

Assigned to suppress antiaircraft fire by bombing antiaircraft positions, Corsairs of VBF-85 and Avengers of VT-85 also hit antiaircraft guns on the *Aoba*. Among the tangle of aircraft over Kure, one *Shangri-La* Corsair pilot attacked and hit the cruiser *Tone*. Crews believed they had silenced a number of the antiaircraft batteries, although crews from Air Group 88, who followed them, did not agree, as we shall see.

Helldivers from VB-85 bombed the *Tone*, after they finally spotted a target through the heavy cloud cover over the harbor. The squadron went into the attack and scored three direct hits on the vessel, the remainder near misses. Flak hit the SB2C flown by Lieutenant (jg) Richard Mann and ARM3c Robert Hanna, setting a wing on fire at the end of their dive. Mann managed to retain control of the stricken aircraft and made a rough but successful landing in the harbor. Both men became guests of the Japanese for the few weeks remaining before the war ended.[229]

The Helldivers of VB-88 struck the cruisers *Tone* and *Oyodo*, releasing bombs at 2,800 feet and pulling out at 2,000 feet. Eleven bombers hit the *Tone*, claiming four hits with 1,000-pound bombs—three amidships—and five direct hits with fragmentation bombs. Three more Helldivers took on the *Oyodo* and one of their 1,000-pounders hit near the stack. Although no Bombing Eighty-Eight planes went down over Kure, one, flown by Lieutenant Eugene Tilton, ran out of gas while waiting to land on *Yorktown* and had to ditch in the carrier's wake. He and his radioman, who salvaged the strike camera, were quickly rescued by a destroyer.[230]

Yorktown's Avenger pilots thought the attack coordinator, Commander Miller of Air Group 6, was slow in assigning targets and when they finally began their dives, the scattered eight-tenths cloud cover made it difficult to pick out targets. When their planes broke out of the overcast, they attacked the first target that came into view. Nine Avengers dove on the heavy cruiser *Tone* and two attacked the *Oyodo*. One of the first TBMs attacking the *Tone* scored a hit. The squadron claimed a total of three hits on the heavy cruiser and two on the *Oyodo*. TBM crews didn't think there was any appreciable reduction in antiaircraft fire after the bombing of antiaircraft positions by planes of Air Group 85, but fortunately didn't lose any aircraft. During the fight home, the squadron saw "a fat Jack . . . below the TBM formation over the Bungo Strait. Quick VF [Hellcat] cover interception eliminated the Jack," an apparent reference to the air combat by *Yorktown* fighters, described later.[231]

Hellcats and Corsairs of Air Group 88 found "so many planes in the air that they over ran the target before they could push over." One Hellcat pilot, Lieutenant (jg) George Thompson, turned around and rolled into a dive to attack the light cruiser *Oyodo*. He dropped his 1,000-pound bomb from about 4,000 feet, then pulled out at 2,500 feet and saw that his bomb had hit near the bow. A VBF-88 Corsair pilot also hit the *Oyodo* squarely on the stern. Two pilots flying with Lieutenant Malcolm Cagle, Lieutenants (jg) Henry Cleland and Raymond Gonzalez, who had ditched on July 10, became separated from him. They found the *Tone* covered by smoke from previous hits, so they attacked the *Oyodo* instead. Both pilots saw their bombs hit near the stern of the cruiser, throwing debris high into the air. *Yorktown* pilots claimed five hits on the *Oyodo* and two on the

Tone, but one Corsair, piloted by Ensign Frank Ritz, went down to flak while diving on the *Oyodo*. His comrades saw him begin his dive but no one saw him pull out. He crashed near the light cruiser, killed in action. Only two pilots, the flight leader Cagle and his wingman, Lieutenant (jg) Kenneth Neyer, bombed the *Tone*; both scored hits.[232] Both men got into a dogfight on the flight back to the *Yorktown*.

Commander Miller, the strike commander, surveyed the harbor as the attack was about to start and ordered planes from Air Group 27 to attack the *Oyodo*. The Avengers of VT-27 dropped their bombs "in train" on the cruiser, claiming five hits, but without inflicting any significant damage. On their way home, a Japanese Jack fighter made a single pass at the Avengers, but did not fire at them.[233]

Flak damaged the engine of a VF-27 Hellcat assigned to photograph the strike. Early on the return flight to the *Independence*, the damage forced it to ditch at the entrance of the Bungo Strait. The pilot, Lieutenant Robert Zimmerman, made a good water landing close to a lifeguard sub, but the latter was unable to rescue him before he drowned.[234]

Also assigned to bomb the *Haruna*, Air Group 50 pilots chose to dive on the *Oyodo* and *Tone*, as the battleship had moved from its expected position. The TBMs made a fairly steep dive of 70 degrees, one more like those executed by dive-bombers, and released their bombs at 3,000 feet. One division attacked the *Oyodo* and a bomb struck the warship amidships, near the superstructure. The second division dove on the *Tone* and pilots believed they also scored one hit, also amidships. The last division of Avengers also tried to bomb the *Tone*, but found themselves out of position and attacked other targets. They had little to show for their efforts in bombing the venerable *Hosho* (the first Japanese aircraft carrier), some oil tanks, and a village near Kure.

On the trip home, the Hellcats of VF-50 spotted a Japanese Oscar pursued by a Hellcat over the Bungo Strait. The enemy fighter was eluding the American pursuer when the VF-50 pilots dove on it. The enemy plane banked sharply to escape, but Commander Raleigh Kirkpatrick got into position above one side of the Oscar, from the rear, and fired a burst at him from only 400 feet away. The enemy plane was not close to the water and immediately crashed into the sea.[235]

A separate flight of four Hellcats from VF-50 that took off from the *Cowpens* fifteen minutes later had considerable trouble reaching Kure. Two of the planes, encountering a zero ceiling and visibility of less than a quarter mile, lost the pair and returned to the carrier. The remaining two planes, piloted by Lieutenant Charles Dodson and Ensign Lee Nordgren, "went over the top" of the overcast and, after an hour, they reached Kurahashi Jima, where the Japanese carrier *Aso* was anchored. The pair of Hellcats attempted to attack the carrier, but heavy clouds thwarted them and they subsequently flew to Kure. After eyeing some bridges, the pair spotted the battleship *Ise* and pushed over to the attack. A rainbow of colored smoke greeted them in their dive, evidence of the intense antiaircraft fire the ship was firing at them. Both planes planted their 1,000-pound bombs quite near the hull, scoring near misses. As the only two American planes in the immediate vicinity at this time, they both hightailed it for home, but not before they strafed a small escort vessel, some barges, a three-masted schooner, and a factory. This escapade drew them near Matsuyama Airfield, which greeted the Navy airmen with heavy antiaircraft fire, so the intrepid duo finally turned for the *Cowpens* and safely landed with less than twenty gallons of fuel in each plane.[236]

The last planes to attack, dispatched by Task Group 38.3, also began their attack by hitting antiaircraft positions. Briefed to bomb antiaircraft positions near the *Hyuga*, also the target of Air Group 16, two Hellcats and one TBM from Air Group 47 actually bombed the battleship itself. The remaining TBMs hit the flak gun positions as briefed. Two of the fragmentation bombs dropped by the Avenger on the *Hyuga* exploded directly over the ship, instantly reducing the amount of antiaircraft fire from the ship.

After the attack, the two squadrons couldn't form up together, as there were so many other groups trying to do the same at the rendezvous point. The commander of Air Group 47 later noted that the newly introduced tail markings used for group identification, composed of two letters, were much more difficult to discern at any distance and made forming up, particularly after a strike, more difficult than the geometric markings used previously.

The VF-47 Hellcats strafed luggers and a patrol boat in the Bungo Strait. Continuing home, a flight leader, Lieutenant (jg) Robert Wallace, suddenly saw a Japanese Zero flying toward him with an American fighter in pursuit. As the Zero dived toward the water, Wallace joined in and dove as well. Quickly gaining on the enemy, he poured a burst of machine-gun fire into the Zero, then flying only 300 feet above the water. Suddenly four more American planes appeared and fired as well and the Zero immediately spun into the ocean. Wallace was credited half a victory. The other planes were not identified.[237]

Air Group 87 got off to a hard start when one Helldiver, flown by Lieutenant Albert Matteson, Jr., crashed on takeoff when a wing hit the water as the plane had difficulty gaining speed and altitude. Matteson unfortunately drowned, but his radioman, ARM2c Charles Schoonover, was rescued.

At Kure, the Hellcats of VF-87 hit the *Hyuga*, dropping fragmentation bombs on the antiaircraft batteries on the ship before the Helldivers of VB-87 began their dives. A second section of Hellcats dropped more fragmentation bombs on the warship again, before VT-87's Avengers attacked. The fragmentation bombs dropped on the secondary batteries of the *Hyuga* had some effect, as Air Group 87 pilots observed the fragmentation bombs reduced their fire noticeably.[238]

The dozen Bombing Eighty-Seven Helldivers on the strike each dropped a 1,000-pound bomb and a fragmentation bomb on the *Hyuga*, in almost vertical dives, claiming eight direct hits and three near misses. One Helldiver, flown by Ensign Epa Vaughn with ARM2c Kenneth Grout as his radioman, went down to antiaircraft fire while diving on the battleship, crashing into the water near it and killing both men. Flak damaged two more planes. Lieutenant (jg) William Timmis's bomb bay doors wouldn't close from the damage, creating drag that ate up fuel on the return flight. He had to ditch, as did another plane that also ran out of fuel, piloted by Lieutenant (jg) Harold Brehm. Destroyers fortunately rescued both crews. The radiomen on both planes saved the film of the bombing they both took, despite having to abandon their planes and float in the sea in life rafts.

The Avengers, carrying a war correspondent as a passenger, finished off Air Group 87's attack with seventeen direct hits on the battleship with 500-pound bombs. Flak damaged two TBMs, forcing one, whose crew is not recorded, to ditch near the Task Force, to be rescued by the USS *Abbott*. The consensus of the effectiveness of the raid from these Avenger crewmen was that "the attack was a spectacular illustration of carrier aircraft precision bombing and coordination. Torpedo bombers, dive-bombers, and fighters plastered the *Hyuga* from stem to stern with hits." Following the Avengers, the last section of Hellcats dropped 1,000-pound bombs, with two bombs either hitting the *Hyuga* or just missing the vessel.[239]

Air Group 34 flew with the USS *Essex* air group and attacked what crews identified only as a Kuma-Natori light cruiser (probably the *Kitakami*). Using fragmentation bombs, they scored several hits on antiaircraft guns on the ship as well as gun positions on shore nearby. When the Hellcats and Avengers began their dive, the enemy ship not did put up any antiaircraft fire, although flak did damage one Avenger, flown by Ensign William Steenberg. Pilots could not see the results of their bombing, but mistakenly assumed that the absence of antiaircraft fire continued for Air Group 16's attack that followed theirs.[240] The Japanese defenses woke up seconds after Air Group 34 left the cruiser, as Air Group 16 pilots reported intense antiaircraft fire during their attacks, as we will see shortly.

Ensign Steenberg's damaged Avenger flew away from Kure and, after he radioed his plight, several VF-34 Hellcats joined him as he flew out to sea close to the position of a lifeguard submarine, USS *Whale*. He successfully ditched the TBM as the Hellcats circled him until the sub appeared and rescued Steenberg and his crew.[241]

Air Group 16's attack began with four Hellcats dropping fragmentation bombs on the *Hyuga*, followed by the Helldivers and Avengers. Like all other crews on the strike, they found Japanese flak to be intense over the ship, beginning while the Helldivers were still five miles away. One pilot described the flak as "resembling an octopus in appearance with its many streamers." With perfect, clear bombing weather—"a dive bomber's dream; an enemy battleship at anchor" over Kure—the dive-bombers made textbook attacks with dives at an angle of 70 degrees, claiming eight direct hits, with more near misses. Flak damaged three planes during the Helldiver attack, forcing that flown by Lieutenant (jg) Dennis Herron to ditch. The engine began to smoke as the squadron flew away from the battleship, only to stop over the Bungo Strait. He managed to stay in the air until about twenty miles from a lifeguard submarine, when he made a landing in the water. Herron and his radioman, AMM2c Omar Kerouack, both got into their life raft safely. VF-16 planes circled them until more fighters from a combat air patrol relieved them. The *USS Whale* again came to the rescue in a few hours and picked up both men.[242]

The *Randolph's* Avengers followed the Helldivers during the attack, claiming more than a dozen hits on *Hyuga*. As they flew away, it was on fire, belching smoke. As VF-16's Hellcats flew away from the *Hyuga*, pilots spotted the incomplete hull of a Japanese carrier and strafed it. Once away from the harbor, they also strafed some small cargo vessels and a midget submarine, spotted on the surface, but it immediately submerged.

As the formation flew over the Bungo Strait, a Hellcat that had lagged behind spotted a Japanese George fighter, along with a Jack that was out of sight, beginning to attack the Avengers in the rear of the group's formation. The pilot, Lieutenant William Bauhof, made a pass at the enemy fighter that had fired at, and missed, the TBMs. The enemy immediately broke off the attack. As Bauhof closed for another go at the George, he had to switch fuel tanks and the enemy disappeared as he did so.[243]

The Japanese cruiser *Kitakami* was the target of Air Group 83. Some Hellcats from VF-83 preceded the bombers, hitting the secondary antiaircraft battery of the cruiser with fragmentation bombs. The Corsairs then went in, some with more fragmentation bombs, while others dropped with 1,000-pound bombs without observing results, although one hit a building on the shore near the cruiser. The Helldivers dove next, planting two bombs on the cruiser. The Avengers of VT-83 finished the attack, claiming five hits on the cruiser: two amidships, two on the stern, and one on a gun on the bow.[244]

A B-29 daylight raid was in the air over Kure at the time of the attack and some Air Group 83 pilots reported that window, dropped from high altitude from the Superfortresses, drifted among their formations during the attack.[245]

—◦—

Japanese antiaircraft fire was intense throughout the entire strike. Japanese antiaircraft bursts appeared in a rainbow of colors: red, white, blue, yellow, and purple. Impressions about the intensity of Japanese antiaircraft fire varied between air groups. Air Group 94 described it as moderate while Air Group 49 crews thought it intense.[246] Many aircraft dropped window and rope to confuse Japanese radar guiding heavy antiaircraft guns. Air Group 87 reported that antiaircraft fire as a barrage from heavy guns did not appear to be aimed a specific aircraft, an indication that window and radio countermeasures had effectively disturbed the aiming of radar-controlled guns.[247] The ships in the harbor put up medium and light flak that was much more accurate.[248]

The flight back to the Task Force was action-packed for several fighter pilots, as Japanese fighters fought with two air groups while they were still in Japanese airspace. As they flew down the Bungo Strait, pilots in Air Group 49 sighted enemy fighters and the Hellcats of VF-49 and engaged them. Three pilots who shot down the three Japanese fighters credited to VF-49 on the 24th described the fray. First, Lieutenant (jg) Jack Gibson described his shootdown of a Frank:

> We heard a call from some fighters ahead that they were jumped by enemy planes. We immediately joined up and started to their aid. As we approached the planes ahead, I noticed two planes coming toward us and I went with my wingman, Lieutenant (jg) George Williams, to investigate. The planes had wing tanks and as we approached, they dropped them and started to dive for the water. By now we could see they were Franks and we started to close on them. Our section split and I followed one, while Lieutenant (jg) Williams closed on the other. The F6F-5 had no trouble at all in closing on the Frank, with the addition of water injection. The Jap tried to turn inside me ... but every time he started a turn I would fire a short burst in front of him ... [that would bring] him back straight and level. When

I got . . . [within] effective range my first burst knocked his wheels down. I overran him and had to pull up in a wingover to drop back on his tail. He then tried skidding turns, without success. By this time I began to get my bursts in the cockpit and he commenced to smoke. He finally fell over on one wing and went straight into the water, without burning.

Williams was just as busy: "I closed rapidly on my plane which I am reasonably sure was a Frank. Just as I came into range on his tail, he executed a very tight turn, which I attempted to follow, but . . . I was not successful. Before I blacked out, I shot . . . a three-second burst and I think I killed or wounded the pilot. When I came to . . . he was falling in a tight spiral trailing a great cloud of smoke. Just before he struck the water another group of friendly fighters followed him down and fired into his plane."

A third VF-49 Hellcat pilot, Ensign Walter Yancey, recounted his action during the air battle:

I looked back and saw seven unidentified planes above and to the rear of our group. I Tally Hoed and Ensign Edward Case, leading the division [of Hellcats], made a 180 degree turn and started climbing. We started closing on a single bogey but he turned and dove away. I nosed down and saw a Jap Frank directly below. I dropped my belly tank, closed, and fired along burst. He started smoking and made a very sharp turn to starboard. I made a slight climbing turn to port and found another Frank in front of me. I closed and fired a short burst. He made a diving turn to the left. I followed him down from 8,000 feet, firing another long burst. His turn tightened and he went into the water from a steep spiral.[249]

After dispatching the second Frank, Yancey saw another enemy plane crash into the water, believing it to be the first at which he had fired.[250]

Hellcat pilots from VF-1 also tangled with enemy fighters on the way home, but had less luck. As Air Group 1 reformed after the attack, the Hellcats brought up the rear of the formation. Suddenly eight Jacks attacked the fighters from the rear and above, in pairs. Only one Hellcat pilot got a shot at the enemy planes before they disappeared.[251]

The Corsairs in the Air Group 1 formation also fought with enemy planes on the return flight when fifteen to twenty Jacks and Franks dived on the rear of the group. Two Corsairs, flown by Commander Hubert Harden and Lieutenant (jg) Charles Moxley, Jr., climbed to intercept as the remainder stayed with the bombers to protect them. An attacking Frank damaged one bomber, but the two other Corsairs saw him off. Harden and Moxley encountered one Frank that instantly disappeared, but then latched onto another pursued by a Hellcat. The Corsairs joined in and, being in a better position to hit the enemy plane, both fired at it. Harden fired a long burst, hitting the fuselage and shooting off a portion of the tail. The Frank promptly dived into the sea.[252]

Of the Corsairs that remained with the bombers, two, flown by Lieutenant Rodney Tabler and Ensign Edmund Barzyk, lost the formation during the initial Japanese attack. Barzyk ducked into some clouds and when he emerged saw a Corsair on fire, possibly Tabler's plane. The latter was shot down and killed in action. A Jack then fired at Barzyk and he dove to safety, joining a formation of Hellcats to head for home.

Two more Corsair pilots, Lieutenant (jg) Robert Applegate and Ensign Robert Speckman, became involved in a dogfight with some of the Jacks. Japanese pilots shot them both down, killing Speckman. Hellcat pilots from the *Randolph* witnessed the dogfight from a distance and saw the two shot down, although they mistakenly thought the two aircraft they saw crash into the sea were Japanese. Applegate shot down an enemy fighter during the melee before he went down. He landed in the water and got out of his aircraft before it sank. A lifeguard submarine later rescued him.[253]

Flying over the Bungo Strait, Lieutenants Cagle and Neyer of VF-88 came upon two Corsairs, apparently from Air Group 1, involved in a dogfight with about ten to twelve Jacks and Franks. Neither Cagle nor Neyer realized they were in a dogfight until they saw a plane going down in flames. Some of the Franks immediately tried to coordinate their attacks on the tails of the VF-88 Hellcats. Cagle was not able to line up on the attackers, who would break away when he was in position to fire. Neyer disappeared from Cagle's view during the melee, shot down and killed over the strait. Cagle then joined up with the Air Group 1 Corsairs, one of the three shot down in the melee described earlier. A Jack came at him head on. He fired and hit the enemy fighter between the engine and the cockpit, then got on the tail of another Jack that was shooting at the other Corsair and scoring hits. With almost no deflection, Cagle managed to shoot up the tail of the Jack and the latter's engine began to burn and smoke; then the plane spiraled down to crash into the sea. The other Corsair was still with Cagle, though damaged, as he could see bursts of smoke coming from his companion's engine, along with about six Japanese fighters. When the Americans were down to about 1,500 altitude, the other Corsair's engine stopped and the plane splashed into the sea, described by Cagle as "more of a crash than a landing." As the enemy fighters began to peel off to shoot him down, Cagle managed to fly into some clouds and lose the enemy and return to the *Yorktown*.[254]

The usual late morning and noon sweeps and strikes followed. One hundred thirty-nine Hellcats and 104 Corsairs flew twenty-two missions, most to enemy airfields to keep Japanese aircraft down in preparation of the afternoon strike. Air Group 94 had bad luck on two of these missions, losing four Corsairs from VBF-94.

The first loss was during an attempted sweep of Hamamatsu Airfield by nine Corsairs and four Hellcats from Air Group 94. Finding the field socked in, the planes turned to striking targets of opportunity north of the town, bombing several bridges and factories, seriously damaging two bridges and two factories. The attack on one bridge, however, cost them a Corsair. Although pilots thought antiaircraft opposition was generally moderate during the mission, a dedicated antiaircraft crew near the bridge shot down the Corsair flown by Ensign Ralph Boggs. His squadron mates last saw him pull out of his dive and head for the open sea. He presumably crashed soon after, as he was later listed as killed in action. One of his squadron mates bombed the flak gun before the attack was over.[255]

The second Air Group 94 strike on Hamamatsu Airfield took off shortly after noon. Despite the flak and heavy clouds over the field, the pilots still managed to strafe and rocket hangars and a radio station near it, inflicting serious damage to the latter, as well as a factory in the area. The medium- and light-caliber antiaircraft guns expected at an airfield put up fierce resistance to the raid and hit the Corsair of Lieutenant (jg) Thomas Brett, causing it to pull up sharply and then dive for the ground directly in front of another Corsair making a strafing run. One pilot thought he saw Brett in his parachute, but Brett did not survive the ordeal.

Enemy fire hit two other Corsairs during the strafing. Flak hit the engine of one F4U, flown by Ensign Hugh Donnelly, and he headed for the open sea. A section of the Corsairs led by Lieutenant (jg) Thomas Sinclair, just finished strafing, turned to escort him to the *Lexington*, but antiaircraft guns, located near a bridge, hit Sinclair's plane, damaging it as well. Both pilots flew separately and successfully ditched their aircraft, although the two were not close to each other. A lifeguard submarine later picked up both men.[256]

A SubCAP mission of Air Group 27 also lost plane that morning. As was the usual practice for pilots on these missions, after a few hours circling a lifeguard submarine, when their relief CAP arrived, they went in search of targets along the coast. The four Hellcats first attacked a small town with their rockets, coming under moderate flak as they pulled out of their dives from an unobserved warship moored in a bay. Antiaircraft rounds hit the fuselage of the flight leader's F6F, Lieutenant Burdick Burtch, severing some of the control cables. The damage forced him to ditch the plane by the nearest lifeguard submarine. He got out of the plane before it sank as his comrades circled above until the sub rescued him unharmed.[257]

Air Group 31 also lost a fighter during a photo and sweep mission that included strafing of some small cargo ships near the seaplane base at Otsu. Despite antiaircraft fire described as moderate, they sank three of the ships since pilots saw no worthwhile targets at the base itself. On the second strafing run, antiaircraft fire hit the F6F of Ensign William Hall. The plane made a wing-over, then crashed into an inlet near the seaplane base, killing him instantly. While two of his comrades circled the crash, they spotted two Pete seaplanes in another inlet and proceeded to strafe them. They hit them hard, most likely destroying them although they did not burn, before returning safely to the *Belleau Wood*.[258]

The loss of a Corsair from VBF-88 was not as tragic since the pilot was rescued. Eight of their planes joined Corsairs from VBF-85 for an attack on Himeji Airfield, facing little antiaircraft fire during the mission. Attacking the field, the Corsairs dropped fragmentation bombs on enemy planes they could see, damaging if not destroying two Betty bombers and an Oscar fighter hidden in dispersed revetments. On a second run, they strafed the field. Afterward, two *Yorktown* planes joined those from the *Shangri-La* to strafe the airfield at Miho.

Before returning to the *Yorktown*, VBF-88 strafed some small cargo ships near Takasago, sinking one Sugar Dog and damaging a few other small ships. The engine of one Corsair, flown by Ensign Edward Heck, failed just after the last strafing run and he had to ditch his plane in Osaka Bay. He made a successful ditching near Awaji Island at about 11:15 that morning. He could not inflate his life raft and floated in his Mae West for five hours until he was rescued.[259]

His saviors were Corsairs from the *Yorktown* and *Shangri-La* with a Martin Mariner Dumbo rescue aircraft. On the way to rescue Heck, the Corsairs tangled with a lone Oscar that blundered into their formation head on. Several American pilots made passes at the enemy fighter, near I Shaima Island. Lieutenant (jg) Gerald Hennesey of VBF-88 and Lieutenant (jg) Robert Bloomfield of VBF-85 shot the enemy down. Several planes made passes at the Oscar, then Bloomfield fired a long burst that set the enemy aircraft on fire. Several planes followed the Oscar down until it crashed on a beach, and Hennesey and Bloomfield both shared credit for the victory.[260]

The flight continued on, and by about 5:00 PM had neared Heck's location. The Mariner, with the VBF-85 aircraft as escort, circled the area while the *Yorktown* Corsairs tried to pinpoint Heck. After a few minutes they spotted the dye markers he had released. Swooping low, they saw him gesturing to them, with only his head and shoulders visible above the water. The pilots above spotted a Japanese lugger making its way toward him and several strafed the small vessel, leaving it smoking and dead in the water.

The Mariner arrived on the scene as a second lugger began to chug to the downed pilot from the harbor of Ei Saki. VBF-88 pilots made a second strafing attack against the ship, which defended itself with moderately accurate flak. Two strafing runs set the craft on fire, however, and forced the boat to turn back to Ei Saki.

At this point, the Mariner came in and made a perfect landing, ending up quite near Heck. The crew immediately hustled him aboard and the seaplane took off just before 6:00 PM. Two *Yorktown* Corsair pilots then engaged in strafing some more luggers encountered on the way home.[261]

—⁃⁃—

The afternoon strikes also aimed at Kure. Seventy-eight Hellcats, thirty-nine Corsairs, 123 Avengers, and seventy-eight Helldivers attacked the base. The order of attack changed from the morning, with planes from Task Groups 38.1 and 38.4 attacking before 38.3, which came last.[262]

Air Group 1, from Task Group 38.1, provided the strike commander, Commander Hubert Harden, who flew with an escort of several Corsairs from VBF-1. Five planes of the squadron dived on the *Ise*, moored on the north side of Kurahashi Island, but intense antiaircraft fire disturbed the aim of two pilots diving on the ship. One burst flipped the plane flown by Ensign Jack Jorgenson on its back, but he continued his dive and dropped his bomb. The *Bennington*'s Corsairs scored two hits on the battleship, one near the forward turret, the second just aft of it. The fifth pilot, Lieutenant Bruce Ponton, without a wingman, initially joined some Hellcats until they began to attack ships he was not briefed to attack. He turned away and soon found a suitable target, the carrier *Amagi*. He intrepidly attacked on his own, making a steep dive, but did not have the time to see where his bomb hit. He then hightailed it away from Kure, but took time to escort the damaged Helldiver from VB-1 flown by Lieutenant Kenneth Hall to the Task Force, where the latter ditched, as described later.[263]

Two other Helldivers from VB-1 were not as fortunate after they ditched from damage received during the attack. The Helldiver squadron targeted the *Ise* and the two carriers, but scored only two hits on the *Ise*. One division of Helldivers narrowly avoided a collision with Avengers in the crowded skies over Kure, throwing off their dives on their assigned targets.

Of the two damaged Helldivers, Ensign Allen Davis managed to keep his plane in the air until it was well out over the Bungo Strait. He made a good water landing and both he and his radioman, ARM1c James O'Brien, made it into the raft. The men managed to survive, and avoid capture, until a Dumbo ASR aircraft found and rescued them on July 27.

Flak had damaged the rudder of the other Helldiver, piloted by Lieutenant Hall, as he pulled out of his dive. Escorted by Lieutenant Ponton of VBF-1 to the Task Force, he made two attempts to land on the *Randolph*, but as the damaged rudder prevented full control of the aircraft, he was waved off and finally ditched the plane alongside a destroyer, *USS Black*. The *Black* soon rescued Ponton and his radioman, locating them in the gathering dusk with the aid of their whistles and lights.[264]

The Avengers of Air Group 1, armed with 500-pound bombs, attacked several ships in the harbor. One division scored a direct hit on the *Amagi*, one on the *Hyuga*, and two more on the *Ise*. The second division went after an uncompleted carrier, possibly the *Aso*, also scoring two hits. On the return flight, the TBMs engaged in the now ubiquitous pastime of strafing small ships.[265]

The Hellcats of VF-1 also scored a direct hit on the *Amagi*, amidships. One pilot, Lieutenant Francis Shea, attacked a cruiser with his wingman, whose belly tank was damaged by flak during the dive. Shea vividly and candidly described diving on an enemy ship, which he initially thought was a battleship. When his division leader signaled the Hellcats should begin their attack, he was attacking in almost the opposite direction from the target photos he had studied before the mission, adding some confusion to an already tense situation with intense flak exploding all around him. A destroyer in the middle of the harbor began to fire at his flight.

When the . . . destroyer started firing at us, the only thing I could do . . . was to divert the destroyer's AA fire and possibly lay my 1,000 lb. bomb on this target. . . . Ensign John Young and myself jinxed down from 14,000 to 9,000 feet . . . pushing over . . . in a 65 degree dive on the destroyer . . . When I started the run, I had my hand on the trigger and did not change its position. At the point of release, I caught flashes of gun fire dead ahead on the opposite side of the harbor. Realizing I could not drop my bomb with accuracy [on the destroyer] . . . I did not release, only strafed. I pulled out [to] about 1,000 feet; my speed was 400 knots, or more. I started a 40 degree climb to [the] right, violently jinxing all the way up to 7,000 feet. My speed dropped off at this point to about 180 knots and I seemed to be right over this ship that held my attention. I made a violent push over from 7,000 feet, ending up in about a 50 degree dive, on my back . . . my inverted position . . . [the] result of [the] violent pushover or a burst of flak that helped me along. I had to roll right and then left to get on target. I picked up a 45 mil lead [on his bomb sight], planning a hit at the base of the superstructure.

I dove about two points off the ship's starboard bow . . . [and] released [the bomb at] about 1,400 feet, and recovered at 800 feet. . . . The outline of the ship was all I was able to make out until I had reached an altitude of about 2,500 feet [when] the superstructure stood out like a sore thumb. My first impression of the pagoda-type structure was that if [I] hit [it] at its base (deck level), it would topple over. . . . On my retirement, I pulled away to the left, from the ship and shoreline, in the direction of the center of the harbor . . . I was looking for open water as tracers about the size of .50 caliber were all around me. I . . . [had] to alter my course a second time to avoid . . . the southwest tip of the . . . shipyard harbor.

On the way home, Shea found time to strafe a radio station on Mae Shima, then escort three bombers back to the Task Force.[266]

The pilots of Air Group 6, the second air group to attack, scored well on this strike, placing six 500-pound bomb hits on the cruiser *Aoba*, seven more 500s on the aircraft carrier *Amagi*, four 1,000-pound bombs on the *Ise*, and three 1,000-pounders on the *Hyuga*. The Avengers followed the Helldivers in their dives, protected from intense antiaircraft fire for part of the time by a thin layer of clouds, but this was not enough to save two aircraft from going down. Flak struck Lieutenant William Callon's Avenger as it dived on the *Aoba* and it crashed into the water, killing him and his two crewmen, AOCM Alton Porter and ARM3c John Scobba. Another flak-damaged Avenger managed to fly all the way to the destroyer pickets on the outer perimeter of the Task Force before Lieutenant Harry Hynd landed it safely in the water. The USS Morris quickly rescued Hynd, ARM3c James B. Gafrey, and AMM2c Orin McConnorin.

A VF-6 Hellcat, far above Kure, dropped window from a dispenser as the flak began to explode around the Air Group 6 formation, continuing to do so for about ten minutes, affecting the aim of radar-controlled guns far below as the Helldivers went into action.

The leader of Bombing Six, Lieutenant Commander Gordon Chase, experienced engine trouble from the beginning of the mission, but resolutely led the squadron to Kure, eventually landing on the Hancock with only nine gallons of fuel. He scored one of the hits on the Ise with the satisfaction of seeing "debris blossom up from his bomb." Another Helldiver pilot, rattled by the blast from his own bomb that hit the Ise amidships, found it had damaged his Helldiver. Upon landing, he discovered his wings buckled and right wing flaps extended six inches more than the left. A pilot diving on the Amagi saw five-inch guns on the vessel firing at him as he made his dive while another described his attack on the carrier as "the best dive he ever made." He scored a direct hit on the stern. Ensign Stephen DeCoste, back in action after ditching on July 18, dived on the cruiser Aoba, but as he pressed his "pickle" to drop the bomb, his wing tanks, but not the bomb, dropped off. He later succeeded in dropping his 1,000-pounder on the town of Mori and strafed fishing boats in the area. The other pilots of the air group also strafed a variety of ground targets and small vessels during the return flight to the Hancock.[267]

Air Group 31's Avengers again attacked antiaircraft positions, as they had that morning, losing one Avenger to Japanese antiaircraft fire. Hit as it was coming out of its dive, the pilot, Ensign Victor Morton, managed to stay in the air for about a mile, with flames streaming from the engine, before the TBM nosed in and crashed into the harbor. Morton and his two crewmen, ARM2c William Hall and AMM3c James Holland, were all killed instantly. Hellcats from VF-31 attacked after the Avengers, in part because they had to wait for another air group to clear the battleship Ise, their target. Of the four planes diving on the enemy vessel, two scored five hits. Air Group 31 crews later reported that they thought the strike was poorly coordinated, as Helldivers and fighters attacked before the Avengers struck antiaircraft positions.[268]

The Helldivers of Air Group 94 led the group on the afternoon strike, followed by the Hellcats and Avengers, diving through a hole in the clouds. The SB2Cs attacked one of the carriers, but did not claim any hits. The TBMs struck the unfinished carrier hull, probably the *Aso*, and the cruiser *Aoba*, hitting the former once and the cruiser three times. Another Avenger also got a hit on another, unidentified cruiser. Four Hellcats and three Avengers dove on the battleship *Ise* and the fighters made two hits on the battleship. Flak hit one Helldiver during the attack and it later ditched off the coast. Fortunately, a Dumbo rescued the pilot and radioman, Ensign Lawrence Hains and ARM3c James Thompson.[269]

San Jacinto's Air Group 49 had a rough start when an Avenger from VT-49, piloted by Ensign Claude Coffey, developed engine trouble during the flight to Japan and ditched inside the Task Force. A second Avenger circled the crew as they floated in their raft until a destroyer appeared and rescued Coffey and his crewman, then returned to the carrier. Coffey later recounted the experience of an operational ditching: "About an hour out . . . I began to experience fuel pressure trouble." After receiving permission from the flight leader to return to the *San Jacinto*, with another Avenger as escort, he "started [a] slow let down [losing altitude and] jettisoned my bombs and wing tank. . . . I was having trouble keeping the engine running [and] . . . fearing an imminent water landing, I had my crew prepare for a ditching. . . . They got out of their harnesses [and] secured all loose gear in the radio compartment. We reviewed our ditching procedure, and I was certain that they were ready in all respects before instructing my radioman [ARM2c Ewing Latimer, Jr.] to crawl up into the second cockpit [between the pilot and turret]. . . . I was able to get back to the [radar] picket [destroyers] and thence to the carrier's rendezvous sector and notify base [the *San Jacinto*] of my trouble."

Very soon, the engine began to cut in and out, then stopped completely, so he "turned into the wind, putting down my hook and flaps at about 100 feet [above the seas]. . . . I was doing slightly less than eighty knots when a big swell loomed in front of me. I pulled the stick back with both hands and we hit the water. There was only one shock. I felt water coming into the cockpit and got out immediately. From my position on the starboard wing, I could see my gunner getting out of the turret. The radioman was having trouble with his hatch; I opened it and helped him out."

The crewmen inflated the raft and the radioman hung onto it as it drifted behind the Avenger. The water was washing over the wing, so "[AOM3c James] Broderick and I inflated our Mae West . . . pushed off, reaching Latimer and the raft without difficulty . . . Broderick clambered aboard, then I deflated my life jacket was helped into the raft. The plane . . . went down just as we were settled."

The escorting Avenger circled overhead, dropping smoke lights while Coffey lit a smoke grenade to signal their position to an approaching destroyer, USS Brush, that "came along to windward of us in less than ten minutes. We were taken aboard amidships by willing and efficient hands . . . [given dry clothes and] treated to a shot of brandy, hot coffee, and cigarettes." Two days later, the Brush transferred them to the San Jacinto.[270] The remaining six TBMs led the pack for Air Group 49, aiming for antiaircraft positions. They found visibility much better than during the morning and could readily see the gun flashes from AA positions, enabling them to score hits on some of them.

The Hellcats of VF-49 provided top cover for the strike, against any enemy fighters that might make an appearance. Assigned to hit the two carriers in the port, these F6Fs were the last to bomb during the raid and scored a direct hit on one and two near misses on the Amagi.

The Hellcat assigned to take photos of the damage inflicted by the other planes made three low-level circuits over the two carriers to record damage through very intense flak that damaged the F6F on the last run, but returned safely to the San Jacinto.

Air Group 49 planes, like those of other groups, engaged in low-level attacks on shipping on the way home, claiming two Sugar Dogs seriously damaged while a Hellcat pilot shot down an enemy plane. While passing near the airfield at Seki, on Kyushu, Ensign William Henwood spotted a bogie. As the flight leader didn't see the enemy plane, he sensibly turned the flight over to Henwood, who described the successful shootdown:

The bogie was a Jap single-engined [later identified as either a Val or Sonia] two-place plane. I opened with my first burst at 1,000 feet [from the enemy plane], closing rapidly. This burst caused part to fly from the other [enemy] plane. I did not fire again until I was within fifty feet because I [had] only two guns working and they were both in the starboard wing. The Jap plane made a diving turn and I overran him. This occurred right over Seki Airfield. As the plane dove for the water, I did a hard wingover and got in a good zero defection shot, causing him to smoke and lose altitude. He soon burst into flame and crashed into the sea, about two miles east of the airfield.[271]

—— ～ ——

Aircraft from Task Group 38.4 attacked after those from 38.3, waiting thirty minutes for the strike coordinator at a rendezvous point prior to the attack. The Corsairs of VBF-88 attacked "the most attractive" target they saw, which they thought was the battleship *Haruna*. As they closed, however, it became apparent it was the old battleship *Settsu*. *Yorktown's* Helldivers and Avengers followed. The first division of VBF-88 bombed the *Settsu*, but did not hit the aging warship. The second division of Corsairs found they were diving on the cruiser *Oyodo*, pulling out with two near misses to their credit, but a midair collision prevented the last division of *Yorktown* Corsairs from attacking. The leader, Lieutenant Allyn Shefloe, collided with a Corsair from VBF-85, flown by Lieutenant (jg) Robert Reed, before the dive began. The collision bent the left wing of Shefloe's plane, which instantly went into a spin and crashed, killing him. The planes following him did not attack here, but dropped their bombs on Matsuyama Airfield. Reed's Corsair was badly damaged, but he was able to return to the *Shangri-La* and land safely. The tail of his plane separated from the rest of the fuselage as he hit the flight deck, but he was uninjured.[272]

The target of *Yorktown's* Avengers was antiaircraft positions. Once they were over the target, however, the persistent haze that interfered with attacks also bedeviled VT-88. Unable to discern the AA guns, the flight leader ordered an attack on warships and they bombed the battleship

Settsu and a destroyer, claiming seven hits on the former and three on the latter. Pilots criticized the strike coordinator after the mission, maintaining that his timing of attacks was off and directions not specific, as they had to circuit the area under antiaircraft fire while awaiting the order to commence their attack.

The Helldivers of VB-88 also dove on a battleship they initially thought was the *Haruna*, but later also was identified as the *Settsu*. Pilots got five hits without damage to any of their planes from antiaircraft fire. Circling over Kure, awaiting the attack order, they depleted their fuel and one SB2C had to ditch near the radar picket destroyers. *USS Norman Scott* rescued the pilot, Lieutenant Louis Miller, who had bombed and sealed a railroad tunnel on Hokkaido on July 15, and his radioman.[273]

The *Independence*'s contribution to the strike was eight VT-27 Avengers escorted by four VF-27 Hellcats. The planes circled the harbor, as did others, for almost an hour before the attack coordinator told them to go into the attack. When they did so, the Avengers dived on what they thought was the light cruiser *Oyodo*, but in actuality was the heavy cruiser *Tone*. Executing a glide-bomb attack, they released their bombs at 3,000 feet and scored three hits: one amidships, the second near the mainmast, and the last on the fantail. Two planes could not get into a good attack position and one bombed the *Oyodo*, scoring two direct hits. The other plane bombed an unidentified warship in the harbor. VF-27 Hellcats also attacked the *Oyodo*, making two near misses with 500-pound bombs.[274]

Air Group 85 attacked next, aiming at the cruiser *Tone*, as well as the battleship *Hyuga*. Corsair pilots scored four hits on the cruiser and three "probable" hits on the battleship. Bombing Eighty-Five, flying only eleven Helldivers because of losses and aircraft damage during the morning strike, bombed in raggedy fashion, described in the mission as "planes strung out in what could hardly be called a formation." Because of the high haze over Kure, four planes bombed the cruiser *Oyodo*, scoring two hits while another, out of position to hit it, chose the *Tone*, getting a near miss. Five more were among the few to actually locate the battleship *Haruna*, with one hitting the target squarely. Following the attack, flak hit the Helldiver piloted by Lieutenant (jg) Ralph Jones when he was over the middle of the harbor. The enemy round hit below the cockpit, slightly wounding Jones, as well as destroying his instrument panel and cutting a hydraulic line. With fluid drenching him, he flew on toward the Task Force, escorted by a squadron mate. Unable to locate the lifeguard submarine, Jones ditched his plane near a destroyer picket that rescued him and his radioman. Another Helldiver also failed to return, but the crew was less fortunate. Although Lieutenant Alfred Symonds and ARM1c Edward Hicks, his radioman, may have reached the rendezvous point, it is more likely that their plane may have been the one seen crashing in flames in Kure. Both men were killed in action.[275]

Shangri-La's Avengers also bombed the *Oyodo*, with one pilot, Lieutenant Robert Giblin, scoring two hits on the cruiser. Other pilots made two hits each on the *Tone*, the *Hosho*, and a destroyer. The old battleship *Settsu* also got attention, hit by one *Shangri-La* bomb. Pilots called the mission a "circle happy hop" to describe the extended time they had to circle in enemy airspace before they got the order to attack.[276]

In the last group to attack, three VT-50 also successfully located and bombed the *Haruna*, with one Avenger actually hitting the battleship with a 500-pound bomb. Another pilot pressed his "pickle" but the bombs failed to release. Of the other two Avengers that took off on the strike, one developed engine trouble and had turn back before reaching Kure, with another TBM escorting it home. Both planes attacked targets on the way, one bombing a factory, the other Sugar Dogs, straddling them with his load.[277]

⁓

The last attack echelon came from Task Group 38.3, which also contributed the strike coordinator for the afternoon mission, from Air Group 16.[278] This air group targeted the *Hyuga*, which displayed antiaircraft fire against its tormenters that crews described as intense. Four Corsairs attacked the battleship and scored two direct hits with 1,000-pound bombs, one by the division leader, Lieutenant Commander Charles Sawers. The two other Corsairs on the mission bombed antiaircraft positions near the ship, as ordered. Flak hit Sawers's Corsair while he dived on the *Hyuga* and his horrified comrades saw the right wing blown off the plane. It crashed, killing him.

Helldivers from Bombing Sixteen scored six hits with 1,000-pound bombs on the *Hyuga* during their attack. Pilots toward the end of the bombing queue found flak reduced as the first three planes all scored direct hits that persuaded the secondary battery AA gunners on the ship to take cover.

The *Hancock*'s Avengers followed up with 500-pound bombs and fragmentation bombs on the battleship, claiming at least eight direct hits. Crews had the satisfaction of seeing one particularly persistent antiaircraft battery on the ship go silent after a fragmentation bomb exploded above it.[279]

A division of *Ticonderoga*'s VF-87 Hellcats dove on the *Hyuga*, accompanied by seven VT-87 Avengers, dropping fragmentation bombs and firing rockets at antiaircraft guns on the ship. The second division of Hellcats and Avengers carried 1,000-pound bombs. Two F6Fs scored two hits, amidships and on bow, while the TBMs got five hits with their 500-pound bombs. More Hellcats then followed up with more fragmentation bombs. The Helldivers, followed by some of the Avengers, were late due to constant rain on flight to Kure. On their arrival at Kure, the Helldiver flight leader couldn't find the *Hyuga*, so the SB2Cs and TBMs bombed small cargo ships, scoring several hits.[280]

Air Group 83 also experienced difficulty finding targets at Kure, because of the weather. Although briefed to bomb the cruiser *Tone*, the fighters, in the lead, mistook a cargo ship for the heavy cruiser and began to attack. The Avengers and Helldivers on the strike followed them down and although many pilots immediately recognized the mistake, most continued on and bombed the cargo ship, soon determined to be already beached after an earlier attack. One Corsair pilot, Lieutenant Thomas Reidy, however, held onto his bomb, spotting the briefed target. He dived on the *Tone*, scoring a hit just forward of amidships with his 1,000-pound bomb.[281]

Air Group 34's seventeen Hellcats and Avengers, flying with Air Group 83, also joined in the mistaken attack on the cargo ship. After their safe return to the Task Force, one Helldiver from VB-83 had to ditch when its tail hook wouldn't come down. *USS Borie* soon picked up both unidentified crewmen.[282]

Air Group 47 bombed antiaircraft batteries near the *Hyuga* with 500-pound bombs. Two Hellcats dropped bombs on the ship itself and two more on antiaircraft batteries on the shore and enemy fire immediately slackened. The nine Avengers on the mission scored hits on flak batteries on the battleship, with five bombs hitting the secondary battery amidships, as others bombed batteries on the shore. One TBM pilot bombed the carrier hull *Aso*, but couldn't see the results. On the way home, two VF-47 Hellcat pilots, apparently in need of still more excitement, strafed some small cargo ships.[283]

While many crewmen on the strike thought Japanese antiaircraft fire was intense, some thought otherwise. VT-87 Avengers reported less flak than during the morning attack, but considered it to still be fairly accurate.[284] Crews from Air Group 94 also reported flak as moderate, as did those from Air Group 27, in comparison to resistance during the morning strike. Air Group 49 air crew, however, reported intense flak, both from the ships attacked and positions on the shore.

VT-88 pilots commented on the tendency of both fighter and bomber crews to strafe targets on the way home rather than form up so the fighters could protect the bombers in the event of a Japanese fighter attack. One pilot reported, "The way we left the target, fourteen TBMs could have been creamed in as many seconds."[285]

The Navy Department recognized the hazards braved by the air crews over Kure on this day by awarding them more than 110 Navy Crosses, the Navy's second highest award for bravery in the face of the enemy.

—◆—

The intense action over Kure and the airfields protecting the port was not the only excitement flyers of the Task Force had on the 24th. Fighters protecting the Task Force tangled with several enemy planes attempting to crash through and destroy American ships. The first victory fell to the guns of a VF-16 Hellcat flown by Lieutenant Donal Kenney around 9:00 AM. Task Force Fighter Control vectored two VF-16 Hellcats toward a Myrt headed for the Task Force at 29,000 feet. When the enemy saw the two Hellcats, it dived for some clouds with the two Hellcats in fast pursuit, at full power. As the Myrt was about to enter the clouds, Lieutenant (jg) William Livingston fired a burst from more than 1,000 feet away and scored some hits on the enemy's fuselage as it disappeared into the clouds.

Fighter Control told Livingston and his wingman to call off the hunt, turning it over to four more VF-16 fighters on combat air patrol. The four planes flew in two pairs, above and below the clouds, attempting to flush out the enemy plane. The two flying above the clouds saw the Myrt but could not get close enough to attack before it ducked into the clouds again. Finally the enemy flew out of the bottom of the clouds, directly in front of the two Hellcats flying underneath. Ensign Eleazer Overton fired a burst at the Myrt as it climbed back into the clouds to hide. Lieutenant Kenney pulled up into the clouds, only to find the Myrt pulling up directly in front of him. He fired a short burst and the enemy plane exploded. It burned all the way to the sea, where it crashed.[286]

An hour later, the VBF-83 Corsair flown by Lieutenant (jg) David Jeter shot down a Myrt spotted below him while cruising at 30,000 feet. Diving down on the enemy plane, Jeter shot and blew parts from the enemy plane's wing. The latter made a split-S turn and dived toward the sea. It caught fire just before it hit the water a mere five miles from the Task Force.[287]

The last enemy plane to fall to the Task Force's fighters went down before 6:00 PM. Two Hellcats from VF-16, patrolling above the radar pickets at 22,000 feet, received a vector for a bogie heading toward the Task Force from the west, slightly above them. Climbing to meet the enemy aircraft, they soon sighted a Dinah about ten miles away almost dead ahead of them. Lieutenant (jg) William Birkholm and Ensign Dean Burt came upon the Dinah from below as it began to fly in a circle. Getting inside the enemy plane's turn, Birkholm opened fire first when he was on its tail. Seconds later, Burt fired a burst that hit the right engine and wing, setting both afire. The Dinah went out of control and spun toward the sea as the second engine caught fire. It then plunged into the sea and Burt received credit for the victory.[288]

That night, destroyers and the light cruisers *Pasadena, Springfield, Astoria*, and *Wilkes-Barre* of Task Group 35.3 swept the Kii Suido. Encountering no Japanese vessels, the American ships did mistakenly attack the *USS Toro*, an American submarine on lifeguard duty, but fortunately the latter submerged before receiving any damage. The ships also bombarded the seaplane base at Kushimoto, as well as the airfield near Shionomisaki and a radar station at Uwano Hanto as Japanese shore defenses remained silent.

Air Group 91 flew Heckler missions over enemy airfields in the area that night to support the American warships. Three Avengers also took off for an anti-shipping patrol over the Inland Sea from the *Bon Homme Richard* at 6:00 PM. After circling off the coast of Shikoku for half an hour at sunset, they flew to the Inland Sea, searching for three ships reported earlier in the day. Failing to find these ships, the planes flew east, locating and attacking an armed merchant ship near Hon Shima. A rocket fired from one TBM hit the vessel amidships and a 500-pound bomb was a near miss. As the planes flew in search of more targets, the enemy ship was dead in the water. Not much later, a small troop transport came into view, anchored in cove on Hon Shima. The three planes attacked firing rockets and machine guns, scoring a direct rocket hit just behind the bridge. While both ships defended themselves with antiaircraft fire, the transport scored hits on all three Avengers. Lieutenant Ivan Witts's TBM then turned west with sparks coming from the engine, trying to reach a designated ditching position. The aircraft is presumed to have crashed in the Inland Sea, as Witt and his two crewmen, ARM3c Vawter Jones and AMM3c Donald Majesky, were all killed in action.

The remaining two planes separated in search of more targets. Both found small cargo ships that they strafed and rocketed, claiming both as slightly damaged, before they returned safely to *Bon Homme Richard*.[289]

Chapter Eight

THE NEXT DAY, THE POTSDAM CONFERENCE OF ALLIED LEADERS ISSUED the Potsdam Declaration, which spelled out the terms for a Japanese unconditional surrender. The Task Force attempted more air strikes against Kure, but poor weather reduced the number of strikes to slightly more than 500, flown in the morning. Almost all strikes planned for the afternoon were cancelled. Nine enemy vessels went down in the attacks, including a Japanese Army tanker. American flyers shot down sixteen enemy planes during the attacks, while British flyers shot down three of four Graces attempting to attack the Task Force. The number of attackers might well have been greater if the fields at Osaka and Nagoya had not been thoroughly mauled the day before.[290] Navy planes destroyed another sixty-one planes on the ground on the 25th, while the British Fleet Air Arm accounted for seven more at Tokushima Airfield. Twenty American planes went down during the day, nine lost during the early morning sweeps that preceded the morning strike on Kure.[291]

The Army Air Forces scored a coup, based on an Ultra communications intercept that revealed that 170 Japanese aircraft were crammed onto an airfield in northern Kyushu. A strike by the Far East Air Force on the 25th destroyed one-third of these aircraft.[292]

Taking off just after midnight on July 25th, VT(N)-91 flew an anti-shipping patrol over the Inland Sea with three Avengers. Two of the planes attacked ships in the Inland Sea. On the north coast of Shikoku, one TBM bombed a small tanker, firing rockets and then dropping bombs. One of the bombs exploded in the water under the ship, but the crew did not see any rockets hit home. Immediately following this attack, antiaircraft fire from a nearby unseen destroyer and shore batteries opened on the TBM. With all its ordnance gone, the TBM wisely chose to return to the *Bon Homme Richard*.

The second Avenger found a large troop transport near Nishi Shima. Dropping two bombs on the first attack run that were near misses, the TBM followed up with rockets but could not see where they hit in the darkness. Later, the same plane bombed and rocketed a lugger, also without observing the results.

American forces tracked the third plane on the mission, flown by Ensign James Williams with ARM3c Glen Weatherford and AOM3c Richard Adolphson, as it was over the Bungo Strait, heading toward its assigned patrol area at Hiroshima Bay. No further contact was ever made, with the crew all listed as killed in action.[293]

A few hours later, the first morning sweeps took to the air. Some ran into enemy planes despite the poor weather, as the Japanese rightly anticipated another strike at Kure. VBF-1 lost a Corsair at the start of a mission to sweep airfields near Nagoya. The F4U flown by Ensign Frank A. Kopf failed to reach flying speed after takeoff and plummeted into the sea. Kopf got out of the aircraft and a plane-guard destroyer picked him up shortly thereafter. The remaining ten Corsairs continued the mission, attacking airfields at Nagoya, Toyohashi, and Meiji through small holes in the mattress while encountering moderate flak. They bombed hangars and revetments, but claimed no specific damage. The flight then found five small cargo ships in Matayo Wan. During six passes on the vessels, they fired rockets and machine guns, sinking two and damaging the others.[294]

More Corsairs from VBF-6 had a similar experience during another predawn sweep. They found a hole in the clouds over Akenogahara Airfield, between Osaka and Nagoya, but the clouds closed in as they began their attack. The strike leader ordered the squadron to halt the attack, but as some were already so committed to their dives, they continued on and dropped their bombs, without seeing any damage. The flight moved on to Ueno Airfield and the four planes that held their bombs earlier dove on the field as the others stayed overhead to provide top cover. The bombs badly damaged a hangar and destroyed a Japanese fighter. During the attack Ensign Edward Dodge was shot down and killed, his plane last seen pulling out of his dive over the field. He may have been a victim of the "meager" light and medium flak put up by gunners on the field.

As this was going on, the pilots who remained at altitude as top cover spotted a Judy 33. The ensuing dogfight was described by the victor in the engagement, Ensign Robert Farnsworth. His account begins after another pilot initially located the enemy plane: "We immediately gave chase. I looked around very carefully for I thought perhaps he was a decoy for high enemy fighters. For at this time twenty miles north of us a dog fight was going on between Viking planes [from VF-31] and fifteen Franks." The flight identified the enemy plane as a Judy 3 and, as his wingman was not in a position to take a shot, Farnsworth took over. "I was clear for a shot. I waited until the Judy filled 40 mils in my [gun] sight. As I was at 6:00 o'clock I put my pipper [the center of his gun sight] in the middle of his [tail] fin and then gave [him] a four to six second burst. While I was firing I closed from about 950 to 700 feet, indicating [an air speed of] 260–280 knots. He flamed just before I lost him in the overcast. As I pulled clear, the Judy zoomed back out of the overcast and exploded."[295]

Another aerial engagement took place during a sweep by planes from the *Essex*, following an earlier sweep that cost the ship a plane. The first sweep of Hellcats of VF-83 fought the foul weather over Honshu until they found a break over the airfield at Saiki, on the east coast of Kyushu. Although pilots did not spot any enemy planes on the field, they dropped their fragmentation bombs on aircraft revetments, but had no idea of any damage they may have inflicted. The Japanese responded with accurate light and medium antiaircraft fire that hit one F6F. The plane reached the open sea at the southern end of the Bungo Strait before the unnamed pilot had to make a water landing. He exited the plane safely and soon a Dumbo rescue plane appeared and picked him up.[296]

The second sweep, flown by Corsairs of VBF-83, aimed for the same airfield, and another at Oita, but couldn't find a break in the overcast to attack either. The flight turned north to the Inland Sea in search of shipping, where they found a freighter, but just as they were about to attack, a section leader spotted two unidentified planes only 500 feet below them.

The Corsairs jettisoned the 500-pound bombs they carried and turned to investigate. They found the pair were Japanese George fighters who immediately turned together and flew towards the Corsairs. The American section leader was Lieutenant Thomas Reidy, who had scored a direct hit on the *Tone* on July 24. He fired a burst at the lead George that hit the mark. The plane began to smoke and turned over on its back, and the pilot bailed out. Ensign Franklin Comstock dove on the second George and fired at the enemy fighter, which quickly turned into him, not away as expected. Comstock immediately got on its tail and fired again, hitting a wing that caught fire. Then the plane dove into the water.

The flight rejoined the other Corsairs that, having lost the freighter in the excitement of the interception, soon located several hapless Japanese luggers. They attacked and sank one, set another on fire, and left a third dead in the water. Antiaircraft gunners on nearby Hime Shima fired at them, slightly damaging two planes, but all returned safely to the *Essex*.[297]

The tables turned, however, when VF-49 lost two Hellcats during another airfield sweep. The flight started to attack an airfield visible in the heavy overcast east of Nagoya. The dozen F6Fs made one pass with bombs and rockets that set a large building on fire before pilots noticed that extensive damage from earlier raids made expending more ordnance a waste of resources. They turned to a rail station and bridges nearby; one flight of Hellcats set two trains on fire, while the second went farther afield, bombing and rocketing two bridges over Lake Hamana that sustained serious damage. Still carrying unexpended rockets and bombs, their next stop was a factory west of the lake. All twelve Hellcats bombed, rocketed, and strafed the factory and its storage area. Three bombs and a number of rockets hit the factory, setting it on fire with several large explosions.

The Japanese crew of a medium-caliber antiaircraft gun at the factory had very accurate aim and damaged three of the attacking planes. Some rounds hit the engine of Ensign Warren Doggett's plane, starting an oil leak. They also knocked out the hydraulic system of the Hellcat of Ensign Walter Yancey, who had shot down a Frank on July 24. A third Hellcat suffered a badly damaged tail but managed to land safely on the *San*

Jacinto, but the first two had to ditch. Doggett ditched near a lifeguard submarine that soon picked him up. Yancey got a bit farther, reaching the radar picket destroyers before he made a water landing, where a destroyer rescued him.[298]

The rescue of another pilot who ditched was much more involved, as it included a flight of 200 miles across the main island of Honshu to rescue the pilot, down in the Sea of Japan after VF-85 and VF-88 teamed up to sweep airfields on Honshu. After overcast dominated all the way to Japan, the weather cleared over land and both squadrons attacked Yonago Airfield. *Yorktown* pilots bombed hangars while *Shangri-La*'s Corsairs went after aircraft revetments, both facing moderate flak. Dropping bombs, firing rockets, and strafing, VF-85 claimed thirteen planes destroyed, including a Frank and the fuel truck refueling the plane. After the first pass, VF-88 flew to Miho, while VF-85 made four more passes on Yonago.

At Miho, VF-88 made several strafing passes, then VF-85 joined them and two *Shangri-La* pilots placed two rockets squarely through the doors of a hangar that started a large fire in the building. Lieutenant (jg) Robert Bloomfield, who shared in a victory over an Oscar on July 24, and Lieutenant Donald Irgens each burned out a Betty bomber, then Bloomfield and two more *Shangri-La* pilots had the good fortune to encounter enemy aircraft in the air over the field.

Lieutenant Ralph Lester caught a Topsy just as it was taking off the field, the most vulnerable position for any fighter, and Ensign Lloyd Miller got a Frank as it was taking off, as well. Bloomfield saw a Sally bomber flying at only about 1,200 feet near Miho just after he had burned out one of the two Bettys mentioned earlier. He pulled up to gain altitude on the bomber, temporarily losing sight of it as he passed it. Turning, he suddenly found himself on the bomber's tail. He fired a burst from his machine guns that set both engines on fire, sending the bomber plunging to the ground. To follow up this victory, during the flight home, he sank a Sugar Dog with rockets. His total score for the mission was a Betty, a Frank, and a fuel truck on Miho Airfield, a Sally in the air, and a small cargo ship. The two squadrons claimed a total of eighteen planes destroyed on both fields.

During the attacks by VF-88 on Miho Airfield, flak hit the F6F of Lieutenant Howard Harrison, whom we met in chapter one, as he strafed two planes. He later commented: "I know they won't fly those planes away, although they didn't burn." Flak rounds hit the underside of the engine of his Hellcat and his wingman told him there were two large holes in the engine, which was quickly losing oil. Harrison flew north, to the Sea of Japan, "pouring on the coal" until he reached a point about fifteen miles off the small port of Jizu Suki. Jettisoning the cockpit hood, he ditched in a stall with no flaps, stepped out of the cockpit and onto a wing, inflated his life raft, and jumped in to await rescue. His squadron mates circled him until their fuel ran low and they had to return to the *Yorktown*. As they left they noticed a Japanese destroyer escort about ten miles from Harrison's raft, but fortunately the enemy ship did not observe them orbiting his position and made no attempt to capture him.[299]

Harrison's location in the Sea of Japan made any rescue problematic, as rescue planes would have to fly more than 300 miles across Honshu to reach him. Successful rescues in this area were few, up to this time.

When his squadron mates landed on the *Yorktown*, two pilots, Lieutenants (jg) Maurice Procter and Joseph Sahloff, whom we met in chapter one and who had collided with his squadron commander on July 15, made the unusual request that they immediately take off and guide a Dumbo air-sea rescue to Harrison's location. Permission granted, they took off and rendezvoused with a PBM Mariner that had already been in the air for more than twelve hours and was now very low on fuel, with a radio that worked only intermittently.

The Hellcat pair stationed themselves off the wings of the PBM, establishing through hand signals that the latter should respond to messages from the fighters by rocking its wings to signal yes or zooming up to answer no. Eight more Hellcats from VF(N)-91 from *USS Bon Homme Richard* soon joined them.

Upon reaching the mainland of Japan, the flight found the overcast to extend up to 17,000 feet. As the ceiling of the PBM was 5,000 feet lower, the rescue flight had to proceed through the overcast and hope that by dead reckoning and the grace of above they would reach Harrison's raft. Inside the overcast, visibility was limited to about thirty feet. The radio on the PBM was working at this time and the pilot asked Proctor and Sahloff if they could find the right location flying through the soup. During the two-hour flight through the dense mist, the Hellcat pilots' conversations, on another frequency, revealed the tenuous nature of their enterprise: Sahloff asked Proctor, who took the lead on navigation, "Do you know where we are?" Proctor responded, "No, but let's keep going," then told the PBM pilot, "Just five minutes more, dead ahead." To reinforce the impression that they were right on course, Sahloff flew close to the PBM and waved his plotting board while puffing on a cigar.

When they finally flew out of the overcast, they were directly over Miho Airfield, which they had attacked only a few hours earlier. The antiaircraft crews were ready after the morning attack and fired at the planes as they passed overhead, but failed to hit them. The Mariner pilot was unfamiliar with the established policy of jinking to avoid flak, so the fighter pilots showed him how.

A short time later, the flight reached Harrison on his raft. Sahloff zoomed down to pinpoint his position for the PBM while Proctor patrolled the area. The PBM landed and picked up Harrison just as Proctor located a *Shangri-La* pilot shot down earlier in the day only a few miles away. He circled the raft and radioed the PBM: "If you taxi over here, you can pick up this other guy." The "other guy" is believed to have been Ensign Cecil W. Moore of VF-85. He had assisted in the rescue of a squadron mate on July 1, but now required a rescue himself. Flak had hit his Corsair during a midmorning attack and he had ditched off Jizu Suki, too. The PBM with the two survivors returned to the Task Force and landed close to a destroyer, as its fuel was practically exhausted and it could not take off again. The destroyer shelled the Mariner and sank it after the crew and fighter pilots were safely aboard.[300]

Moore's plane had gone down during another joint VF-85/VF-88 attack on Yonago a few hours after the first attack already described. Flak hit Moore's engine after his second pass on the field so he, like Harrison, flew north, ditching close to Harrison's raft.

Like the earlier attack, the planes on this second attack found Yonago open and dropped fragmentation bombs on their first pass as antiaircraft gunners went into action again. One division of VF-85 Hellcats remained high overhead as top cover and located and reported antiaircraft positions to the planes attacking the field. On the first pass, *Yorktown* pilots bombed hangars and strafed the planes they could see on the field.

After the first pass, the flight went after some small ships seen a short way down the coast. *Shangri-La* pilots shot up a small cargo vessel, while *Yorktown* pilots attacked an armed transport. The VF-88 fight leader, Lieutenant Malcolm Cagle, whom we met in chapter seven, told the flight leader of the Corsairs: "We'll race you to see which squadron can sink their ship first."

Shangri-La Corsairs made several rocket and strafing runs on the cargo ship, hitting a lifeboat filled with men who had already abandoned ship. It slowly began to sink by the stern as the crew jumped over the side. A few VF-88 Hellcats strafed the decks to suppress antiaircraft fire for the follow-up planes that fired rockets that hit the stern. On the second pass, they fired more rockets that hit the bridge; one traveled completely through the ship and came out the other side. The flyers saw many dead Japanese sailors on the decks as they left the scene. The ship later sank, as American planes that passed over the spot later in the day saw only an oil slick.

Both squadrons then returned to Yonago Airfield. *Yorktown* pilots flew "at deck level" and found four camouflaged fighters—a Topsy, two Tonys, and a Tojo—that they set on fire. VF-85 claimed three destroyed on the field, with many more damaged.[301]

Another early morning mission that accounted for more Japanese planes, both on the ground and in the air, was an encounter between ten Hellcats of VF-31 and fifteen Japanese Franks. The mission began with a dawn takeoff at 4:30 AM. The F6Fs headed for several airfields near Nagoya, but found all completely covered by overcast. Eventually the planes found a hole in the clouds over the town of Hikone. The flight divided into two sections, attacking a marshalling yard and factories near the town, then reformed over Lake Biwa and struck out for Yokaichi Airfield, southwest of Nagoya, found in the clear. Six Hellcats stayed at altitude and four attacked the field. Although wrecks from previous raids and straw, dummy aircraft cover the field, they managed to set two Nicks on fire and riddle two more single-engine fighters while pilots encountered very little flak.

About ten minutes into the attack, the strike leader told most of the attacking planes to climb and reform, sending two other planes to continue strafing the enemy field. An enemy fighter suddenly made an attack pass at him, immediately followed by a second enemy plane. As he called "tallyho," more Japanese fighters began to appear through the clouds, diving from 12,000 feet. Five chose to head for deck while the others remained and fought it out with the Hellcats. Following each pass at the American fighters, they would then pull up to entice a Hellcat to follow them into the clouds; other Japanese fighters were lying in wait above the clouds to shoot them down. Fortunately, the speed advantage of the Japanese fighters, from their dive, made it almost impossible for the American planes to follow them, but as the fight continued the Hellcats slowly gained altitude until they reached about 5,000 feet. In the melee, Ensign Edwin White collided with a Frank that was firing at him head on. Both planes disintegrated in the air. The flyers last saw Ensign Herbert Law as he climbed into the clouds to gain altitude. He was shot down, but survived to become a prisoner of war.

None of the Franks attacked the Hellcats in a group, but singly, making their attacks less effective, as the F6Fs were able to evade them. This was a graphic example of the inexperience of the enemy pilots flying these machines, not uncommon for Japanese pilots in 1945.

The Americans shot down eight Japanese fighters, seven Franks, and one Tony by dogfighting with individual Japanese planes, out-flying them, and then shooting them down. Lieutenant Cornelius Nooy shot down four Franks. Lieutenant James Stewart and Lieutenant (jg) Charles Robison each shot down a Frank, while Ensign Clayton Egil shot down the Tony. The Frank that collided with White was, of course, credited to him and three more enemy fighters were listed as probably shot down. After the dogfight, the nine remaining planes returned to the *Belleau Wood*, six damaged in the fray. The two sent down to strafe just before the melee returned on their own.[302]

Besides the losses on strikes, sweeps, and aerial dogfights, operational losses were a normal part of carrier routine. As the morning strikes were about to take off, a VF-16 Hellcat catapulted from *USS Randolph* and crashed into the sea. The destroyer *USS Bullard* promptly picked up the pilot, Lieutenant Glydol Pace, and soon rescued another airman from VB-16, a Helldiver radioman.

Another pilot from Air Group 16 was one of the fighter pilots on combat air patrol near the Task Force who also shot down enemy planes that morning. The first Japanese victim, shot down by Ensign Joe Watts of VF-16, had been chased by four Hellcats after the bogie was reported at 30,000 feet. The planes began to climb to intercept, but one had a mechanical problem, forcing it to return to the carrier with a second as escort. The two remaining Hellcats, flown by Lieutenant Ralph Reid and his wingman, Ensign Watts, flew out of overcast, into the clear, and saw the bogie directly overhead. The enemy plane began to fly away as they climbed until they were also at 30,000 feet. The pair closed quickly, moving into position to attack with one on each side. At this point, the enemy plane, a Myrt reconnaissance job, began to evade them, anticipating an attack. It suddenly dived to port and Reid fired a burst, but couldn't see any hits. The plane then turned toward Watts and he got on its tail and fired. Three bursts entered the enemy's engine, cockpit, and wing root. The Myrt caught fire at the wing root and spun toward the overcast, then the sea, out of control.[303]

A second Myrt went down to American guns only a few minutes later, close to the Task Force, shot down by Lieutenant Robert White of VF-6. Flying at 10,000 feet about ten miles west of the Task Force, the four-plane combat air patrol received the order to fly due west and climb. One plane dropped out with engine trouble, but the other three continued to climb. When the trio had reached 22,000 feet, White spotted two planes that turned out to be Corsairs. Then fighter controllers told them to fly east, at 30,000 feet, and shortly thereafter the flight leader, Lieutenant Harry Wachser, tallyhoed a bogie about eight miles away, off to the left. They gave chase and closed slowly. As they neared the enemy plane, the third member of the flight, Lieutenant (jg) George Rutledge, made an attack run on it. He overran the enemy plane and White had his chance:

Rutledge over ran [the Myrt] going by on the left side with the Jap in a right, diving turn. The red Japanese circles were prominent as I came in. My run was slightly from above [the Myrt] and as I closed

I was [at] about four o'clock from him. I saw [my] tracers hitting the fuselage, but my point of aim was sliding back. I ceased firing, banked a little more, and pulled my point of aim . . . forward. Then I gave him another burst. This time pieces flew, and fire leaped, from the right side of the plane. Then smoke poured out, he rolled on his back, and plunged into the sea. . . . directly over our group of ships. He crashed about a mile from the [Task] Force . . . one parachute opened and appeared headed for the ships.[304]

Bad weather severely hampered the morning strike, briefed to bomb the battleship *Ise* and the cruiser *Aoba* at Kure. Despite this, a handful of planes did manage to bomb ships in Kure after the Task Force target coordinator ordered all planes on the strike to attack targets of opportunity, which most did. Only one American plane went down on these missions, ditched near destroyers with the pilot rescued.[305]

Some groups, however, never reached a target. Air Group 83 turned back because of the bad weather, but not before they had lost a plane. A Helldiver flown by Ensign Thomas Dimitri had crashed on takeoff. The unidentified radioman, mentioned earlier in this chapter, was rescued by *USS Bullard.* Unfortunately, Dimitri drowned.

Four Hellcats and seven Avengers from Air Group 50 found the going tough, flying at between fifty and one hundred feet to reach Japan. The Avengers eventually tried to attack the port of Susaki, but the low ceiling prevented this and they returned to base, as did two of the Hellcats. The other two F6Fs, flown by the flight leader, Lieutenant Charles Dodson, and his wingman, Ensign Lee Nordgren, persevered, as they had the previous day. Turning back once, they tried again and penetrated the heavy clouds on the second attempt by flying over it. The pair continued on to Kure, where they broke into the clear, near Kurahashi Jima, shortly after 10:00 AM. Spotting the carrier *Aso* moored near the island, they began to dive from 18,000 feet, but cloud cover increased as they lost altitude, so they halted the dive and looked for a better target, eventually spotting the battleship *Ise* directly below them. They dove on the battleship in an 80-degree dive through heavy antiaircraft fire to score near misses on the vessel, throwing water over the decks that obscured it for a few seconds. As the only two American planes over the harbor at that moment, they then sped for home, taking time to strafe some barges and a patrol boat near Haka Shima, and later a schooner.[306]

The intrepid duo from VF-50 were not the only planes to reach Kure and attack warships anchored there. A few minutes after they attacked, four Hellcats from *Hancock*'s VF-6, carrying 1,000-pound bombs, made it to Kure, followed by two more Hellcats from *San Jacinto*'s VF-49. The *Hancock* planes also found a hole in the clouds over the naval base and three Hellcats dove on the *Ise*, led by Lieutenant Commander Roland Schumann, Jr. Although Schumann's bomb fell short, the other two pilots scored hits on the battleship. The fourth VF-50 Hellcat, separated from the others, could not line up on the *Ise* and instead bombed a small cargo ship also anchored in the harbor.

Some minutes later, the VF-49 Hellcats dove after Schumann's flight and met heavier flak, as the surprised Japanese antiaircraft gunners got to work. Smoke from antiaircraft bursts made it harder for them to see the battleship and only one pilot, Lieutenant (jg) Nelson Goodson, could release his bomb, but it was a direct hit, amidships. The bomb release of the other VF-49 Hellcat failed over the *Ise*, so the pilot later bombed a factory on Shikoku.

Four other VF-6 Hellcats on the strike reached the Inland Sea with VT-6 Avengers. With three of the Avengers, the fighters bombed an armed merchant ship anchored in a cove on the southern shore of Shikoku. One bomb, dropped by a Hellcat, hit the superstructure of the enemy vessel, causing it to explode and sink. The other three TBMs bombed a smelting plant across the Bungo Strait on Kyushu. Several Helldivers from VB-6, also thwarted in their attempt to reach Kure, settled for bombing buildings in the seaplane base at Ususuki on Shikoku.[307]

The *San Jacinto*'s TBMs of VT-49 chose several factories and a bridge on Shikoku as their alternate targets. The VF-49 Hellcats that didn't reach Kure bombed hangars at Uwajima Seaplane Base, as well as the town, and two harbors.[308]

Air Group 31 lost the other groups after leaving the radar pickets behind and proceeded to Japan. The Avengers reached the vicinity of Kure on their own, but did not attack without their fighter escort. Soon after their arrival, the Task Force target coordinator told all groups to attack targets of opportunity. Most of the Hellcats jettisoned their bombs, but three bombed a smelting factory in Saganoseki, destroying a portion of the main plant building. The Avengers bombed revetments on the airfield at Niihama, but didn't observe any result. Neither attack drew any resistance.[309]

Alternate targets also occupied Air Groups 94 and 27, where little or no flak greeted them. The *Lexington*'s Avengers and Hellcats bombed sundry targets on Shikoku. The *Independence*'s Hellcats and Avengers chose the town of Heki, on Honshu, bombing buildings in the town and ships in the harbor, sinking a Sugar Dog.[310]

Air Group 1 lost a Hellcat during the forays on targets of opportunity after the target coordinator called off the Kure strike. The F6Fs began by bombing a large factory on the southern coast of Shikoku. Then, they turned to a lighthouse, and while strafing it spotted a destroyer escort anchored in a cove nearby that was shooting at them at the same time flak guns located by the lighthouse fired at them, too. The Hellcats went after the latter and flak hit Ensign Charles Stetler's F6F in the engine during the attack. The flight turned for home, but about ten miles from the radar picket destroyers, Stetler's engine overheated from the damage and he had to ditch. After a good water landing, he opened his seat pack with his life raft, inflated it, and jumped aboard. His comrades zoomed down, over his position, to mark it for an approaching destroyer that rescued him within ten minutes.[311]

The Corsairs of VBF-1 bombed a railroad bridge near Tano on Shikoku, then strafed and destroyed two locomotives. *Bennington*'s Helldivers attacked bridges, a factory, a breakwater, and small ships, sinking several fishing boats and Sugar Dogs. The Avengers attacked a rail bridge, a small marshalling yard, a roundhouse, and the station in the town of Tanabe. None of the places *Bennington* flyers visited offered any opposition.[312]

The Corsairs of VBF-88 bombed aircraft revetments at Niihama Airfield and small ships and bridges on the coast of Shikoku. Air Group

88 Avengers bombed a factory and a roundhouse on the same island, at Susake. The TBM pilots had the unusual experience of seeing what they later reported were civilians, perhaps members of the newly raised home defense forces, manning an antiaircraft gun during the attack, but flak was "meager," at best.[313]

Besides the second sweep to Yonago Airfield, described earlier, seventeen more late morning sweeps and strikes took off by noon when the Task Force cancelled most air operations because of the abominable weather over the main islands of Japan. One, flown by Air Group 16, aimed for the airfields of Iwakuni and Matsuyama. Taking off at 11:45 AM, fifteen Hellcats from VF-16 found both fields totally covered by overcast. As an alternative, they chose to attack ships reported, and attacked, by their squadron mates near Nagashima Island earlier that day. The earlier mission, which took off at 5:30 AM, also targeted shipping when the assigned airfields were socked in. They bombed and strafed a lighthouse and small cargo ships near Misaki, a Sugar Dog near Iyo-Nada, and a merchant ship near Nagashima Island.

When the late morning flight reached Nagashima, they found the merchant ship attacked that morning beached. The Hellcats attacked again, inflicting additional damage, but encountered heavy antiaircraft fire from two destroyer escorts nearby. Flak hit two of the Hellcats, damaging both so much that they ditched before reaching the carrier, as will be recounted shortly.

During the flight home, the Hellcats had the unusual experience of encountering two midget submarines. They bombed one that was underway, causing it to submerge, then strafed a second, beached near two Japanese floatplanes. The F6Fs then destroyed the latter.

The two damaged Hellcats were unable to stay with the flight very long, and both ditched about twenty-five miles apart, in the Inland Sea. A Dumbo rescue plane picked up Ensign Calvin Yoder, but Ensign John Hantschel had a different fate. He made a successful water landing and got into his raft as a squadron mate, Ensign Knute Lee, orbited above him. Eventually Lee ran low on fuel and began to return to the *Randolph*, but ran out of fuel in the Bungo Strait. He ditched near a lifeguard submarine that picked him up, safe and sound. Hantschel, however, was not rescued. The plane that picked up Yoder conducted an unsuccessful search for him and he was later listed as killed in action.[314]

—— ◆ ——

Although strikes had been called off for the afternoon, several missions still took to the air. One was a relief flight for the VF(N)-91 Hellcats that escorted the Mariner to rescue Lieutenant Howard Harrison of VF-88, mentioned earlier. Four night-fighter Hellcats took off after 4:00 PM and met the Dumbo and its fighter escort returning with the rescued Harrison off the coast of Shikoku. Alerted about another Dumbo heading into the Inland Sea for another rescue, the pilots volunteered to accompany the rescue plane. Their search was successful, as they located the pilot in his raft south of Kure. It was Ensign Yoder, whom we also met earlier.

At this point, two of these Hellcats, flown by Ensigns Kenneth Baldwin and J. C. Stires, ran low on fuel and had to leave the mission early. On their way back to the *Bon Homme Richard*, they found two Japanese Willows over the Bungo Strait, flying only 500 feet off the ocean. Stires made the first pass at one Willow, followed by Baldwin. Stires's burst shot some pieces off the enemy plane, and then Baldwin administered the coup de grace burst that caused the plane to glide toward the sea, then crash.

The other Willow tried to escape by turning toward Kyushu, so both Hellcats followed in pursuit, easily overtaking the much slower Japanese plane, firing at it as they shot past it. Pieces flew off the enemy plane during each pass, but the enemy plane stayed in the air until it had reached Kyushu. Their fuel running even lower, the Hellcats left the Willow still in the air but flying erratically. The pilot was slumped forward in the cockpit, obviously wounded. Both pilots returned safely to the carrier, but the two that had stayed with the Mariner while it picked up Ensign Yoder did not.

The two pilots, Lieutenant Warren Smith and Ensign John Selway, left the Mariner as it started for home with Yoder aboard, after sundown. Their fuel was low and the Mariner was safe from interception by Japanese fighters in the darkness. Low fuel stymied the fighters' flight home, compounded by a weather front that confronted them south of the Bungo Strait. They turned back toward Shikoku, intent on ditching near the southernmost tip of the island. They radioed a lifeguard submarine that told them simply to "wait," something they couldn't do in the circumstances. Then the pilot of the Mariner they had escorted to pick up Yoder, Lieutenant (jg) Kenneth Lee of VH-3, came on the air. They explained their plight and asked him to pick them up at the location where they would ditch, a short distance from Okino Saki. All three planes landed pretty much at the same time, with the moon to light their way, in heavy swells. The Hellcats each came in on either side of the Mariner and struck the water first, followed by the PBM. Selway got out of his F6F and into the water, displaying a blinking light on his Mae West that enabled the Mariner to locate him and pick him up. Smith had gotten into his raft, but the light on his Mae West made the second pickup just as easy. The Mariner then took to the air with both men and headed to its base on the island Okinawa. When it landed, it had very little fuel left, but had successfully rescued three American fighter pilots. A good day's work by any standard.[315]

The last action of the day took place during a dusk combat air patrol. Four night-fighter Hellcats of VF(N)-91 were flying a patrol at 10,000 feet near the Task Force when fighter controllers on *USS Yorktown* vectored them to a bogie at 20,000 feet. Only three climbed to intercept, as one was unable to keep up with the rest. Soon four enemy planes came into view, a Grace and three fighters flying in a circle. The four enemy planes immediately turned east toward Japan when they saw the Hellcats approaching, two ahead of the Grace and one behind, losing altitude to increase their speed to escape the American fighters closing on them. The Hellcat flight leader, Lieutenant (jg) Robert Kloze, leveled out at 16,000 feet, then boosted his power and rapidly closed in on the enemy fighters. The last enemy fighter turned away and Kloze concentrated on the Grace as it released something that looked like window. Kloze dodged it, then continued to press closer, but reduced his throttle to avoid overrunning the enemy plane. He then fired one burst, followed by a second, now close enough that as the Grace began to burn, the flames streamed back onto his Hellcat and Kloze could feel the heat in his cockpit. The enemy plane then suddenly rolled to the left and spun down into the ocean, striking the water close to several American destroyers. When he looked around, Kloze found that the three fighters had escaped.[316]

That was the end of combat operations for the day. The Task Force then sailed south to refuel, turning north again to launch more strikes on July 28.

Chapter Nine

JULY 28 PROVED AS ACTION-PACKED AS THE 24TH, WITH IMPROVED weather allowing American flyers to fly almost 1,200 strike sorties to enemy airfields located in northern Kyushu and southern Honshu. *USS Wasp* had joined Task Group 38.4 on July 26 and her air group flew strikes for the first time on the 28th, when the naval base at Kure was again the target. Flyers sank twenty-eight enemy ships, including the battleships *Ise* and *Haruna*, the cruisers *Oyodo* and *Aoba*, a destroyer, a submarine, and two old heavy cruisers, *Iwate* and *Izumo*. Japanese fighters rose to oppose the strikes and twenty-one enemy planes went down to American guns in aerial combat with another 115 destroyed on the ground.[317]

The British flew more than 225 sorties to enemy airfields along the eastern side of the Inland Sea, as well as shipping in the sea itself, sinking two frigates and several merchant ships, as well as destroying eight aircraft on Japanese airfields.[318] Although not assigned to the Task Force, *kamikazes* sank their last American ship, the destroyer *USS Callaghan*, off Okinawa on the 28th.

Army Air Force long-range fighters were again in action in southern Honshu, attacking Tokyo airfields.

The Japanese government released an initial reply to the Potsdam Declaration that basically ignored it. The Japanese leadership believed that accepting peace was not necessary at this moment.[319]

The usual dawn sweeps took off in the hour before 6:00 AM as 191 Hellcats and seventy-one Corsairs flew missions to airfields to impede Japanese fighter defense during the last raids on Kure Naval Base, but

Japanese fighters were in the air again and several aerial dogfights took place that morning.

Three fighter squadrons, VF-85, VF-86, and VF-88, swept the airfields at Yonago and Miho, where antiaircraft gunners greeted them with a spirited defense. At Miho, VF-85 pilots made two passes, firing all their rockets into aircraft revetments as an enterprising pilot, Lieutenant (jg) Joseph Huber, found a dozen Japanese planes hidden in a grove of trees some distance from the main airfield. He made several runs on the planes, destroying five of them. A total of nine were claimed as destroyed on the airfield. Eight *Yorktown* F6Fs followed up, bombing hangars and knocking out an antiaircraft gun. Turning to Yonago, *Yorktown*'s Hellcats strafed antiaircraft positions and hangars, but pilots couldn't readily assess the results as VF-85 also strafed the field, destroying four more planes.

The *Wasp* planes made their first pass on enemy planes on Yonago Airfield and had the luck to find some Franks taxiing, ready to take off. Ensign Clifford Gunn, Jr., destroyed one and also hit some parked two-engine aircraft. Lieutenant Armind Holderman saw a Frank approaching the field from the sea and gave chase at low altitude. He fired many rounds at the enemy plane, which eventually blew up.

On the second attack run, *Wasp* planes strafed targets on Miho Airfield, burning one Frances on the ground. Japanese antiaircraft fire was intense, however, and evened the score. Rounds hit Lieutenant (jg) Thomas Morton's Corsair and the engine began to flame, only 900 feet above the airfield. The plane then rolled over, out of control, nosed down, and crashed into the sea, killing Morton.[320]

Japanese pilots had the same fate soon after when thirteen Hellcats of VF-16 arrived at the airfield at Ozuki just as some Franks were taking off, no doubt scrambled to oppose another anticipated attack on Kure. One section of four Hellcats, which had remained at high altitude as the others began to dive on the field, saw seven Franks climbing from Ozuki. Taking advantage of the altitude advantage, the section leader, Lieutenant Cleveland Null, "tallyhoed" his flight and dived on three of the enemy already at 2,000 feet. He came in on the tail of one Frank and fired a burst from his machine guns from about 300 feet, hitting the enemy plane, which immediately caught fire, then exploded. As the other two Franks climbed above him, one of the remaining four began a head-on pass toward him. Null pulled up over the fighter, made a split-S turn as the Frank dove for the ground, and followed him down. With several turns he got within firing range, and then poured a burst into the Frank's fuselage. The enemy went into a spin as the pilot bailed out.

While Null was dispatching this enemy fighter, his wingman, Ensign Keith Meyers, had spotted the four other Franks trailing the first three only one hundred feet above him. He pulled up and fired at one, and the enemy pilot bailed out.

As Meyers took care of his first Frank, Null had climbed to regain altitude to find yet another Frank beginning an attack on him from two o'clock. He again pulled up over the enemy plane and made a sharp diving turn, positioning himself on the enemy's tail. As the latter began to pull up and climb, Null got on his tail and "walked" machine-gun rounds from the tail up the fuselage to the wing. The right wing caught fire; then the Frank spun to the ground and crashed.

After this victory, Null wasn't done yet. He spotted a fourth potential victim "on the deck" below him. He dove on it, chasing it through some valleys as the Frank hugged the ground in a vain attempt to get away from the superior American pilot. Null fired a burst from long range, without any result. In the meantime, Ensign Meyers had spotted the long-range pursuit from above, dove, and caught up with the Frank as it reached the coast. He fired at the Frank from behind, observing some of his rounds hitting the cockpit. The plane began to smoke, and then made a three-quarter turn as two other pilots, Lieutenant Ithiel Hatch and his wingman, Ensign Vernon Hood, whom we will meet shortly, appeared and fired a burst just before the plane crashed into a hill.

A third member of Null's flight, Ensign George Humphries, who had ditched on July 24, followed Null on his first attack. As Null shot down his first victim, Humphries saw a Frank near him and fired a burst at it. The enemy fighter burst into flames and crashed. He then saw two more Franks attempting to flee by hugging the ground through valleys below. He dived on the pair, closed, then fired at the trailing plane, then flying at about 500 feet. This Frank began to smoke and crashed into the ground. The other Frank was caught by Meyers as described earlier.

Some of the pilots who had dived on the field also got into the fray. As he pulled out of his attack dive, Ensign Cletus Schwartz spotted a Frank and chased it close to the ground until he got into position to fire. Several bursts caused the enemy to do a split-S turn, then crash.

Another member of the attack force, Lieutenant Hatch, destroyed two Franks. Spotting one at 5,000 feet north of the enemy field, he struck from above and behind. One burst set the enemy on fire and a second made it explode just in front of him. He pulled up to evade the debris, as his wingman, Ensign Vernon Hood, fired at another Frank that began to smoke and was later credited as shot down. Hatch had also fired a burst at this plane, then circled around and found yet another Frank snaking its way through valleys below. Hatch, with Hood on his wing, dove and followed the enemy pilot through a small valley, firing several bursts. As both planes turned around a hill, Hatch got into position and fired again, hitting the wing and fuselage, which caught fire. The Frank crashed into another hill as the enemy pilot tried, unsuccessfully, to bail out just before the crash.

More VF-16 Hellcats that strafed the field also had victories that morning. When several of the attack sections reached the rendezvous point after the attack, four Franks attacked them. Lieutenant John Bartol turned to meet two of them, but spun out. After he recovered, a Frank made a pass at him, but overshot and missed his Hellcat. Bartol got on the enemy's tail and fired a burst that set the Frank on fire. It promptly crashed into the sea. At the same time, two more Franks made an unsuccessful attack on two Hellcats, one flown by Lieutenant James McPherson. The two Americans attempted to catch the enemy planes but could not, so they returned to the rendezvous point. As they arrived, another enemy fighter, this time a George, made a pass at McPherson's F6F. Macpherson turned the tables and got on the enemy's tail, shooting it down. The total score for VF-16 in the melee was thirteen enemy planes destroyed.[321]

Two of the Scouting Six Dauntless dive bombers in flight during the fall of 1941. The plane nearest the camera, marked 6S14, is the Dauntless flown by Ensign Edward Deacon that ditched near Hickam Field after American antiaircraft fire mistakenly shot it down during the attack on Pearl Harbor.

The pyre of the Dauntless dive bomber flown by Lieutenant Clarence Dickinson after Japanese fighters shot it down on December 7, 1941.

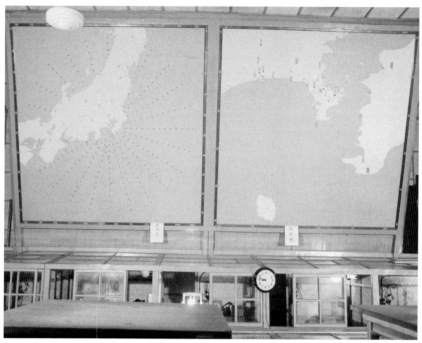

The Japanese Navy's Air Defense Control Room at Yokosuka Naval Base, near Tokyo. Controllers used the board at left to track American aircraft.

An Avenger, nicknamed "Turkey" by navy aviators, of VT-6 flying over Japan during the summer of 1945.

A bomb bursts close to two Japanese luggers in a small port on northern Honshu, July 15, 1945.

A F6F Hellcat of VF-88, carrying a drop tank to extend its range, flies over the Task Force in August 1945. The two-letter tail marking, part of the system adopted in late July, identifies it as an aircraft of Air Group 88, base on *USS Yorktown*.

A Curtiss Helldiver of VB-6 in flight off the coast of Japan in July 1945.

The port of Kushiro, Hokkaido, on fire after the American attack by several air groups on the afternoon of July 14, 1945.

Avengers of Air Group 83, with Avengers of Torpedo Squadron 34, drop 500 pound bombs on Hakodate, Hokkaido, during the July 14 strike.

Crewman aboard the battleship USS Missouri observe the shelling of the port of Kaimaishi on northern Honshu during the first bombardment of the Home Islands on July 14, 1945.

The battleship *USS South Dakota* fires a broadside at Kaimaishi during the bombardment of July 14.

The aircraft carrier *USS Shangri-La* off the coast of Japan, just after the Japanese surrender in August 1945.

Misawa Airfield on northern Honshu under attack by American Naval aircraft on July 14. Both Air Groups 16 and 34 attacked the field that day.

A close-up view of Misawa Airfield during the attack of July 14, showing Japanese bombers burning in revetments after bombing and strafing attacks by American planes.

A VF-16 Hellcat takes off from *USS Randolph* for a mission to Japan in July 1945.

One of the Japanese ferries sunk near the port of Aomori, 14 July 1945.

Before a strike on Japan, pilots received instructions in the briefing room of an aircraft carrier, 1945.

Planes from Air Groups 85 and 88 attack a Japanese destroyer escort in Muroran Bay on July 14, 1945.

Helldiver pilots of VB-83 on the flight deck of *USS Essex*, summer 1945.

Crewmen of an American lifeguard submarine help an American aviator aboard from his life raft off the coast of Japan, July 1945.

A British aircraft carrier of Task Force 37, believed to the *HMS Formidable*, steams off the coast of Japan just after the Japanese surrender in August 1945.

A Japanese seaplane, code-named Mavis by the Americans, heads for the sea, shot down off the coast of Japan in July 1945.

A Curtiss Helldiver of VB "Bombing" Sixteen takes off from the flight deck of the carrier *Randolph* for a strike on the Home Islands in July 1945.

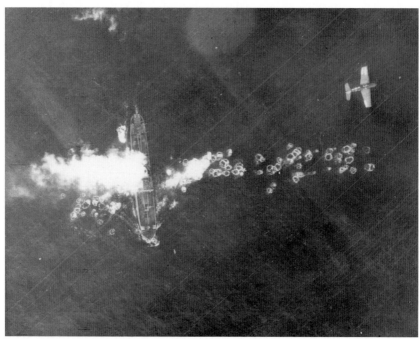

A Hellcat flies over a Japanese freighter under attack in the Tsugaru Strait in mid July 1945.

Following the Japanese surrender, American sailors fill the decks of two Japanese submarines of the same class as the I-13. American planes and destroyer escorts sank the submarine off the coast of Japan on July 16, 1945.

An aviation ordnanceman on *USS Yorktown* loads ammunition on an aircraft, July 1945.

An Avenger of VT-16 wings over in flight, July 1945.

Two, small Japanese cargo vessels, code-named "Sugar Dogs" by American intelligence, under a strafing attack by Navy planes off a small town on the east coast of Japan, July 1945.

A Japanese "Tony" fighter in the sights of an American fighter just before it went down over Japan during the summer of 1945.

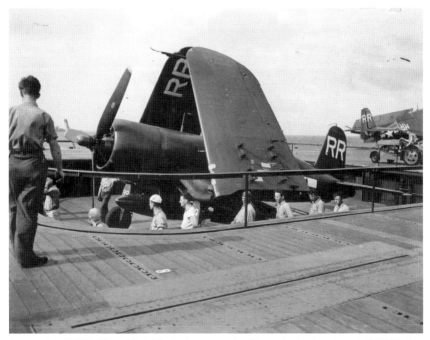

A Corsair of VBF-88, with folded wings, on the flight deck elevator of *USS Yorktown* during the strikes on Kure on 24 July.

The American destroyer *USS John D. Weeks* off the coast of Japan during the summer of 1945. The vessel rescued several American airmen who ditched that summer.

Dock facilities at Yokosuka Naval Base under the bombs of American planes during the attack on the battleship *Nagato* moored in the harbor on July 18, 1945.

More Japanese planes went down to American guns in a swift, uncontested aerial engagement during a sweep and photo mission flown by VF-31. On the way to their targets, the Hellcats ran into four Pete single-engine floatplanes. The enemy planes were flying straight and level, in formation. The Hellcats attacked, taking the enemy completely by surprise, shooting down all four planes quickly as five Japanese crewmen managed to parachute to safety. The squadron's report of the short episode concluded, "[Enemy] pilots were not strafed in 'chutes." After this slight interruption, the eleven F6Fs continued on their mission and bombed factories in the town of Nikone. As their assigned airfields were socked in, the planes also strafed a rail yard near the town, hitting a locomotive, freight cars, and a roundhouse. After this, they finally found an airfield, at Yokaichi, that was in the clear. The Hellcats made two rocket and strafing runs on aircraft revetments, claiming two aircraft destroyed and six damaged, and also found time to fire rockets at a small train near the airfield. Continuing their sojourn, the planes were able to photograph the airfield at Ogura, near Kyoto, finishing up with the strafing of four small cargo ships near the coast on their way home. The four pilots credited with the Petes were Lieutenant Reilly Raffman, Lieutenant (jg) Jerome Wolf, Jr., and Ensigns James O'Brien and Howard Wicker.[322]

The tables turned on Navy flyers, however, during a mission that morning that took photographs to update the status of potential targets and assess damage already done at Kure, flown by Hellcats from VF-87. Unknown to the Americans that morning, the *Tone* was on the bottom, but the cruiser's antiaircraft gunners still managed to fire their guns fairly accurately, continuing to do so throughout the day.

After taking photos over Kure, the planes attacked Matsuyama West Airfield, bombing, rocketing, and strafing aircraft revetments and antiaircraft positions. The latter responded in kind with intense flak, and antiaircraft fire shot down one of the Hellcats, which crashed on the field, killing the pilot, Ensign Cyrus Walker. The attackers went back for a second run, turned to strafe a train stopped in a station nearby, hitting the engine, then returned to Matsuyama again for a third strafing attack. While heading for home, they strafed a few Sugar Dogs before returning to the *Shangri-La*.[323]

Airfields as far afield as those near Nagoya also came in for attention that morning, from Hellcats and Corsairs of Air Group 1 as overcast at some potential target fields didn't deter them. The flight leader took the thirteen planes under the overcast at Okazaki Airfield. Despite light- and medium-caliber flak, they made several attacks, bombing a hangar, setting a plane on fire, and damaging other aircraft. Then, the flight turned to Kowa Seaplane Base, where they bombed and strafed several floatplanes until it became apparent these were wrecks from earlier attacks. At their third target, Toyohashi Airfield, they destroyed one plane and damaged eight others during two strafing runs on the field. Japanese gunners were silent during the first run but woke up for the second, firing a short barrage as the planes began their dives, slightly damaging one plane. On the way home, they strafed a lone Sugar Dog, then discovered that some planes were very low on fuel, as their auxiliary gas tanks were malfunctioning. Ensign John Lundgren ran out of gas before he could land on the *Bennington*, and had to ditch near the carrier. The *USS Harrison* quickly rescued him.[324]

The *Essex*'s Hellcats came home unscathed from an airfield sweep that morning after shooting down three Japanese planes. After circling over several enemy airfields with no reaction, VF-83 encountered enemy planes at a fourth. Over Metatsubara Airfield, the airmen saw three Tony fighters taking off and several Hellcats dove on the enemy planes. Two Hellcats pursued one Tony for several miles before Ensign Clyde Clark got in a burst that hit the right wing and fuselage, shooting it down. Two more pilots, working in tandem, accounted for the other two Tonys. They were "quickly dispatched to their ancestors by the teamwork" of Lieutenants (jg) Hugh Batten, who had ditched while landing only a few days earlier, and Samuel Brocato. Following these shootdowns, the flight bombed the airfield through moderate flak, setting five enemy planes on fire.[325]

Planes assigned to the morning strike on Kure began to take off from their carriers about an hour after VF-83's engagement. Upon reaching Kure, aircraft from Task Group 38.3 attacked first, as they were in the best position to do so, followed by planes from 38.1 as 38.4 brought up the rear.[326,327] The plane of the target coordinator, Commander Wallace Sherrill from Air Group 85, who also had coordinated the Task Group 38.4 attack on July 24, had a mechanical problem during the flight to the target and his bomb dropped prematurely. He still made an important contribution to the mission as target coordinator,[328] however, although the mission did not go completely smoothly. Air Group 86 air crew, flying their first strike of the campaign, complained that attacking aircraft had "stacked up" under constant antiaircraft fire while waiting to make their dives.[329]

From Task Group 38.3, Air Group 34 Avengers were the first planes to attack, aiming for the *Tone*, nicknamed "old four turrets forward and a ski slide aft" by American flyers, and its antiaircraft batteries. After jockeying for position, the Avengers dove, pulling out of their dives at the low altitude of only 500–800 feet. Their dedication paid off with eight direct hits with 500-pound bombs.

The *Monterey*'s Hellcats couldn't attack the *Tone* with the TBMs. Two of the four VF-34 Hellcats on the strike bombed the *Oyodo*, but the cruiser was so heavily enveloped in smoke, they couldn't see if their 1,000-pound bombs did any damage. A third F6F bombed a large troop transport, while the fourth attacked a beached tanker at Okurokami Shima. All planes returned to the *Monterey*, but one, an Avenger flown by Lieutenant Lester Lampman with radioman ARM3c Victor Larison, crashed over the side of the carrier while landing. A Task Force plane guard vessel promptly rescued both men.[330]

Air Group 47 also attacked the *Tone*. The four Hellcats on the mission bombed antiaircraft positions on the shore near the ship, while seven TBMs made a glide-bombing attack on the cruiser. Pilots "laddered down" and reached almost 400 knots airspeed during their dives. They released their bombs at 3,500 feet and made at least eight direct hits on the vessel.[331]

Air Group 87 had a difficult start to the mission when engine trouble forced the Helldiver flown by Lieutenant Ralph Pucci to turn back, escorted by two Hellcats, only to ditch near the radar picket destroyers that rescued Pucci and his radioman. The remaining planes continued on to Kure, but soon another fell out of formation. Ensign Paul Stephens's TBM went into a spin and crashed into the sea. Stephens and his crew, ARM3c Robert Pierpaoli and ARM3c Eugene Egumnoff, were all killed in the crash.

The Hellcats of VBF-87 from the *Ticonderoga* carried fragmentation bombs and a few 1,000-pounders. They attacked antiaircraft positions on the shore that displayed spirited opposition to their strike, as well as AA guns on the *Tone* itself. Crews from Air Group 47 noticed the heavy flak that greeted the *Ticonderoga* air group.[332] Flak shot down the Hellcat of Lieutenant Thomas Schaeffer as the planes made their attack and it crashed into the bay. Following the bombing of the *Tone*, little flak came from the ship, although shore batteries kept up heavy fire. The F6Fs of VF-87 armed with 1,000-pound bombs attacked last, after the torpedo planes, but could not observe the results in their haste to exit the scene and the intense antiaircraft fire.[333]

The eleven Helldivers from Bombing Eighty-Seven then came in on the cruiser. Although the first bombs missed, four dropped by Lieutenant Hugh Dunkum, Jr., and Lieutenant (jg) Curtis Cameron hit the vessel squarely. Heavy antiaircraft fire struck Lieutenant (jg) Raymond Porter's plane but he made the group rendezvous for the flight home with his engine smoking. The Helldiver couldn't stay in the air, however, and Porter soon ditched in the Inland Sea. Porter and his radioman, ARM3c Raymond Brisette, both got into their life raft. Planes detailed for the afternoon strike spotted the two men in their raft, but a rescue was not in the cards. Porter is listed as killed in action and Brisette became a prisoner of war. Held at Hiroshima during the first atomic bomb attack on the city two weeks later, he later succumbed to the effects of the atom blast.

The eleven *Ticonderoga* Avenger crews who attacked the *Tone* after the Helldivers observed antiaircraft fire coming from the old battleship *Settsu*, as well as from batteries on the shore and a destroyer. Their fire damaged two TBMs, but the Avengers made a good attack and struck the ship with ten 500-pound bombs, some consolation for the loss of three planes by the group on the strike.[334]

Briefed to attack the battleship *Hyuga*, now reported sunk, Air Group 16's target changed to three submarines seen in a cove on Kurahashi Island just before the *Randolph* launched its aircraft. The subs were identified as two RO-57 class and one larger I-9 class, moored next to each other. The Helldivers, carrying 1,000-pound bombs intended for the battleship, dove on the cove first, with four Hellcats. None of the planes scored any direct hits, but they did claim two near misses on one sub, as antiaircraft fire from the flak positions protecting the subs was formidable. Flak hit one of the last three SB2Cs to attack, crewed by Lieutenant Garland Trussel and ARM3c Franklin Miller, just before it went into its dive. The SB2C went into an uncontrollable spin and their squadron mates thought the plane lost with both men. Fortunately, the crew survived the ordeal to become prisoners of war.

Antiaircraft fire also hit a second Helldiver, flown by Lieutenant Clair Williams and radioman ARM3c Clay Darling, coming out of its dive. It crashed into the water, killing both men.

The TBMs of VT-16 attacked after the Helldivers, accompanied by four more Hellcats. Crews later reported that the submarines "made a beautiful glide-bombing target." Most of the Avengers missed hitting the subs, but two pilots, Ensigns Leo McNally and William Parker, scored hits on the large submarine, later declared as sunk. The target coordinator for the attack later reported that "the torpedo bombers are the boys that did the damage this morning."[335]

The last group from 38.4 had a rough start to the mission, as Air Group 83 lost a Helldiver soon after takeoff. Lieutenant James A. Riner had engine trouble and ditched the plane near a destroyer, *USS Walker*, which quickly rescued him and his radioman. On their arrival at Kure, a change of target also greeted the group. Diverted from their original target, the *Hyuga*, the planes struck three camouflaged ships seen inside the harbor on July 24, believed to be either destroyers or light cruisers. Hellcats covered the Avengers during their attack then went in themselves, dropping fragmentation bombs, and got one hit on a ship. The Corsairs of VBF-83 split into two divisions, one diving with the Avengers, the other with the Helldivers. The latter misidentified the target cove and struck a cargo ship by mistake, scoring one direct hit and a near miss. The

Avengers, however, found the destroyers and claimed eight hits on one, as did the Hellcats. The TBMs got three hits on a second destroyer, as did the Corsairs.[336]

———

Task Group 38.1 made the second attack. Planes of Air Group 6 attacked first, followed by Air Groups 1, 31, 94, and 49 all targeting the battleship *Ise* and cruiser *Aoba*.[337] As the first group to attack, VT-6's Avengers bombed antiaircraft positions in the shipyard and near the port, as well as the *Aoba*.

The fighters of VF-6 bombed the cruiser with two direct hits to their credit, one hitting squarely amidships. During the dive, the premature explosion of a fragmentation bomb rocked Lieutenant Joseph Redding's plane violently, forcing it into an almost vertical dive. Seemingly unfazed by this close call, he continued his dive and planted his bomb on the cruiser's bow. Another pilot spotted a destroyer and surfaced submarine as he began to fly away from the *Aoba* and calmly proceeded to strafe both ships, although in his natural haste to get away from the continuous antiaircraft fire, he did not have the time to observe any damage inflicted.

The four VBF-6 Corsairs detailed for the strike dived just after the Helldivers, with wheels lowered and dive brakes on full to reduce their diving speed. Three of them made hits on the *Ise*'s bow. On the way home, the air group commander gave them permission to strafe shipping on the Bungo Strait. They set a schooner on fire and forced a powerboat to beach.

The Helldivers of Air Group 6 scored six direct hits on the *Ise*, and then strafed ships in Kure Harbor. The squadron leader, Lieutenant Commander Gordon Chase, fired rockets and his machine guns during the dive, then released his bomb from the extremely low altitude of 1,600 feet, pulling out at only 900 feet. His reward was a hit on the bow of the battleship with his 1,000-pounder. A few aviators reported that they saw the main batteries of the battleship firing during their dives, clear evidence of the desperation of Japanese sailors, as the likelihood of a sixteen-inch shell hitting a diving aircraft was astronomically low.[338]

The Corsairs of VBF-1 divided their flight into two divisions, to strike the *Aoba* and *Ise*. Despite intense antiaircraft fire, they claimed two hits on the *Aoba* and one on the *Ise*. The TBMs also attacked the *Aoba* and seven planes claimed eleven hits with 500-pound bombs. One Avenger, flown by Lieutenant (jg) Frederick Snyder, lost the other planes during the attack and joined up with planes from Air Group 88, striking buildings on the naval base. His bombs caused a major explosion that threw debris almost 1,000 feet into the air. The Avenger crews considered this strike as "the best that VT-1 has flown" up to that time. Flak damaged the Avenger of Lieutenant Lynn DuTemple, who had scored two hits on the *Ise* on July 24, forcing him to ditch near the radar picket destroyers on the flight home. Fortunately, he and his two crewmen, ARM2c Richard Gentzkow and AOM1c Mark Hardisty, were soon rescued.

One of the VT-1 TBMs flew as a small-scale Dumbo rescue plane on this strike, carrying one large and one small life raft, with survival gear, in the bomb bay of their Avenger. Despite a faulty radio, the crew spotted some airmen in the water of the Bungo Strait and dropped the large raft to them. Continuing the search for more downed aviators, they soon located a second group of survivors near the island of Kurahashi Jima and dropped the remaining small raft to them before returning to the *Bennington*.[339]

The Helldivers of VB-1 also attacked the *Ise*, scoring four hits with 1,000-pounders: "Hits came with such regularity that the battleship deck spouted smoke and flames at intervals of only a few seconds." Antiaircraft fire was intense and fairly accurate, coming close enough to rock some planes, but not close enough to shoot any down. The first pilots bombed the *Ise*'s secondary battery, reducing the volume of antiaircraft fire for the planes that followed them. One pilot, Ensign Henry Collins, released his bomb at only 1,000 feet, then pulled the large number of eight Gs during his pullout.[340]

The planes of Air Group 31, seven Hellcats and seven Avengers, also targeted these two warships. The fighters claimed seven hits on the *Ise* while the Avengers claimed four hits on the *Aoba*. Crews reported seeing phosphorus streamers in the air over Kure and, in a report of the strike, complimented the target coordinator for a well-organized strike, a totally different assessment from that of Air Group 86, mentioned earlier. The disparity in these impressions underlines the controlled chaos of the strike, during which hundreds of planes dove on targets in harbor within a very short time.[341]

Air Group 94 did not mention the degree of coordination during the strike, but they certainly had a tough time on the strike, losing four aircraft. Bombing Ninety-Four led the group in their dives and made three hits with 1,000-pounders on the *Ise*, while a Corsair from VBF-94 scored another. Torpedo 94 attacked the *Aoba*, scoring seven hits with 500-pound bombs, while one TBM got a hit on the *Oyodo*. Of the four planes lost, Ensign Norton Sims's Avenger was shot down, as was a Helldiver. Sims and the radioman, ARM3c Clarence May, were both killed, but the turret gunner, AMM3c Oliver Horn, managed to bail out to become a prisoner of war. The Helldiver's crew, Lieutenant Joseph Costigan and ARM3c Warren Collins, also perished. A second Avenger ditched, as did a Corsair, but fortunately all crewmen survived. A Dumbo rescued the crew of the Avenger, Lieutenant Orrin Larson, AMM3c David Gay, and CAC John Young, as well as the pilot of the Corsair, Ensign Edward Bell.[342]

Air Group 49's eight Hellcats were the last to dive on the battleship, after flying top cover for all the planes in the Task Group for most of their attack. The leader of the squadron for this strike, Lieutenant Commander George Rouzee, whom we met bombing the *Nagato* in chapter six, also acted as the strike coordinator for all the planes from 38.1. The Hellcats made a day of it, pulling out of their dives at the dangerously low altitude of only 500 feet, but only one plane claimed a direct hit that caused a large explosion on board the *Ise*. So much smoke covered the battleship after the attacks of previous groups, however, that it was impossible for pilots to observe the results of their bombing, but they could see the guns of the battleship's main battery firing during the attack.[343]

                —◦—

As the last wave to attack, Task Group 38.4's target was the *Haruna*. From Air Group 85, VT-85, briefed to suppress antiaircraft fire with general purpose 100-pound bombs, dropped them on the *Tone* and *Oyodo*, destroyers, and shore batteries. Two 100-pound bombs hit the *Tone* while ten hit the *Oyodo*, doubtless reducing the heavy antiaircraft fire that had already struck the Avenger flown by Lieutenant Guy Brown over Kure, disintegrating the TBM in midair. Brown and his crew, AOM2c Charles Smith and ARM2c William Winn, were killed.[344]

VBF-85 dove on the *Haruna* itself, placing six 1,000-pound bombs directly onto the battleship. The Corsairs made very steep dives, and one pilot remarked on a Christmas tree–like effect from the multi-colored flak bursts seen during his dive. As the Corsairs neared the ship, pilots could see the main, 16-inch guns firing at planes diving on the *Oyodo*.[345] The Helldivers from Bombing Eighty-Five placed four 1,000-pound bombs on the battleship. The group returned to the carrier, flying over the island of Shikoku rather than the Bungo Strait to avoid enemy fighters.[346]

VT-50 also had the *Haruna* as its primary target, diving after Air Group 85. The Avenger pilots "put every bomb so close together to the target that the water was a churning maelstrom around it," and six of them were direct hits. Flak was intense and accurate and damaged the TBM of Ensign William McGuire, who had scored one of the hits. The engine caught fire and, within seconds, enveloped the underside of the fuselage. The plane then crashed, but one crewman, believed to be McGuire, was seen to jump from the plane and land on Nishinomi Jima. He and his crew, ARM3c James Daniel and AMM3c Gerald Coon, however, were killed.

Flak also bracketed Ensign Dana Overman Jr.'s Avenger soon after it left the *Haruna*. Hit in the underside of the fuselage, a 25mm round wounded the radioman, ARM2c Clarence Mortensen, fracturing his left arm. Pieces of shrapnel also hit the turret gunner, AOM3c James Helms, but he quickly applied a tourniquet and bandaged Mortensen's wound, which, in the opinion of the Air Group 50 flight surgeon, saved his life.[347]

Planes of Air Group 86 were assigned to bomb the battleship *Haruna* and the cruiser *Oyodo*. The Corsairs of VBF-86 split into three groups, one diving with the Helldivers that attacked first, the second group diving with the Avengers who followed up. The third group attacked only after flying as top cover in case Japanese fighters appeared.

The first Corsairs to dive couldn't see the *Haruna* because of smoke from earlier attacks and chose to bomb an old cruiser nearby. The second division, diving with the Avengers, aimed for some of the persistent anti-aircraft batteries on shore, while the last two groups bombed the *Haruna* but could not see the results.

The Helldivers made two hits on the battleship, but flak fire seriously damaged an SB2C. The aircraft, crewed by Lieutenant Commander William Bush and ARM1c Charles Bougan, was smoking as it left the target. Unable to reach the *Wasp*, the craft ditched near Ikino Shima, where a lifeguard submarine rescued both men. A second Helldiver also went down to flak damage on the return flight as four planes strafed buildings and small vessels in the islands south of Kure. Antiaircraft fire struck the Helldiver flown by Lieutenant (jg) T. E. Jensen, with ARM2c Robert Sayre as radioman, as they strafed a small cargo ship moored at Hon Ura. The plane did a slow roll and squadron mates saw two parachutes begin to open just as the plane crashed into the sea, killing both men.

At this point in the attack, antiaircraft gunners on the *Tone* were very evident to the *Wasp*'s TBM crews, so much so that they wondered if the ship was even under attack. It was, as we have seen. They split their attack with eight diving on the *Haruna* and seven on the *Oyodo*, but crewmen could not observe the results. With the *Oyodo* covered by smoke, none of the crews could see where their bombs landed, nor could the crews who attacked the *Haruna*. Flak hit one TBM during the attack on the *Haruna*, shooting off an elevator. The TBM, flown by Ensign Clarence Johnson with ARM3c David Hancock and AOM3c William Hemenway, spun in and crashed into the water.[348]

Air Group 88 had to delay its attack on *Haruna* while Air Group 86, ahead of them, made a wide circle before their attack. Briefed to attack the cruiser *Oyodo* before takeoff, over Kure, the strike coordinator, Commander Sherrill, told the *Yorktown*'s Helldivers and Avengers to attack the *Haruna* instead, probably as other groups had already seriously damaged the light cruiser. The Helldivers dropped their bombs 2,500 feet above the battleship, enveloped in a rainbow of flak bursts during their dives. Three of their bombs were direct hits, two hitting the superstructure. The Avengers of VT-88 followed, diving on the battleship. Although some bombs on three planes hung up, the squadron still scored four direct hits.

Ten of VF-88's Hellcats dove on the *Oyodo*, as originally briefed, since Commander Sherrill thought it necessary to reduce the intense antiaircraft fire coming from the cruiser. Flak damaged one *Yorktown* Hellcat during their attack, but the fighter pilots did well, as five of their 500-pound bombs hit the cruiser.[349]

The cruiser *Oyodo* also received attention from Air Group 27, also at the order of Commander Sherrill. Following the bombing attack on the cruiser by VF-88 Hellcats, VT-27 Avengers approached the ship from the stern as its antiaircraft gunners poured shells at them. Four 500-pound bombs hit the ship, one squarely amidships, and immediately started fires that enveloped the ship aft of the bridge.[350] This was the last action that morning over Kure. The consensus of crews returning from the mission was that Japanese resistance was intense, particularly from the cruisers *Tone* and *Oyodo*, with some groups on the receiving end of more antiaircraft fire than others. An interesting observation reported by some men on the mission was the difference in the color of flak bursts, dependent on the location of the battery. Flak fired from guns on the shore was black, while the multi-colored bursts came from the ships.[351]

⸺

Between the morning and afternoon strikes on Kure, more sweeps targeted airfields to dissuade Japanese fighters from interfering with the strike. The *Lexington* launched ten Corsairs from VBF-94 just after noon, detailed to attack Oi Airfield. Here, the flight made two attack runs, claiming the destruction of at least two fighters and damage to about a dozen more. Following the first strafing run, Ensign Robert Cunningham was missing from the flight. Last seen diving with the other planes, on the second pass his squadron mates saw his plane burning on the edge of the enemy field, the unlucky victim of light antiaircraft fire that other pilots described as moderate.[352]

Most of these sweeps went to airfields, but a squadron from one group, VBF-1, changed their target to shipping in flight, not an uncommon occurrence, as intelligence on enemy airfields and shipping was constantly updated. Fighters from VF-6 had located three warships at Owashi Wan while returning from a sweep on Akenogahara Airfield a bit earlier, where they destroyed a Betty and some hangars. The *Hancock*'s planes had fired most of their ammunition before they found these ships, but attacked an armed merchant ship anchored with the warships anyway, missing it. They then circled the scene until the Corsairs of VBF-1 arrived, and helped to coordinate the latter's attack. On arrival at Owashi Wan, the *Bennington*'s flyers found six ships: four destroyer escorts and two armed merchant ships. The enemy ships fired accurately at the attackers as six Corsairs attacked the southernmost warship, a destroyer escort, and scored one hit with a 500-pound bomb and another near miss that would have damaged the hull. Directed by the *Hancock* planes to the northernmost destroyer escort, they then dropped the one bomb they had left and fired two dozen rockets at the enemy ship. Two rockets scored direct hits, setting the destroyer escort on fire. It immediately beached itself to prevent it from sinking.

The antiaircraft defense from the ships, although not intense, hit the engine of the Corsair flown by Ensign Oron Fisher. Leaking oil, he headed for the *Bennington*, escorted by a squadron mate. By the time the pair reached the carrier, oil covered Fisher's canopy. After receiving a wave-off on his first landing attempt, he began to circle for another attempt but his plane suddenly rolled over on its back and crashed into the ocean. Fisher went down with the plane. The remainder of the flight strafed a train on their way back to the carrier, forcing it to seek safety in a tunnel; then they flew to the *Bennington*.[353]

The afternoon strike found the cruiser *Oyodo* turned over on its side, one sign of the successful efforts of the morning strike. Air Group 27 described the scene: "The once proud little cruiser, the darling of the Jap fleet in the battle of the Philippine Sea, had gone over on its side and lay stark and still in the soft mud of Kure Harbor."[354] Planes from only two Task Groups took part in the second Kure strike of the day. Weather delayed the rendezvous of Task Group 38.3's group, so Task Force strike coordinator, Commander Seth Searcy of Air Group 88, whom we first met in chapter three,[355] told them to hit targets of opportunity, although Air Group 86 still went to Kure.[356]

All four squadrons of Air Group 1 took part in the afternoon strike on Kure. Five Hellcats attacked the battleship *Ise* and one of their 1,000-pound bombs hit the battleship. Just after the successful pilot, Ensign

Robert Bausinger, released his bomb, flak hit his plane, damaging it so he had to make a flaps-up landing on the *Yorktown*.[357] Five Corsairs bombed the aircraft carrier *Amagi* in a 70-degree dive, scoring one square hit amidships. Two planes, however, lost the remainder of the flight at the rendezvous point and bombed the unfinished carrier *Katsuragi*, moored at Mitsuko Island. They also scored one hit.[358]

Bombing One also went after the *Amagi*, as well as the *Ise*. Three planes bombed the carrier, but couldn't see where their bombs landed. Four, including the squadron commander, Lieutenant Commander Andrew Hamm, attacked the *Ise*. Hamm scored one of the two hits on the vessel, but flak hit the left wing of his Helldiver during his pullout from the dive. As the plane flew over Nishinomi Jima to begin the journey home, a hole in the wing grew larger and the Helldiver began to lose altitude. The radioman, ACRM George Rumrill, bailed out when the plane was still at about 800 feet and landed on the island to become a prisoner of war. Just after he bailed out, the SB2C crashed into the water, killing Hamm.

Commander Hamm's wingman, Lieutenant (jg) John Wagner, narrowly avoided the same fate. Antiaircraft fire hit his plane just as he released his bomb on the *Ise*. The explosion threw the Helldiver onto its back, but Wagner pushed the control stick forward with both hands and regained control. A review of the aircraft's condition revealed that flak had shot away one of the horizontal stabilizers on the tail, holed the rudder, and wounded the radioman, ARM2c Marvin Bradshaw. Wagner couldn't remove his hands from the controls for even a second during the fight to the *Bennington*, so he couldn't hold his plotting board to figure the correct course. Fortunately, a squadron mate, Ensign Howard Meyer, found him and guided him back to the carrier. Upon their arrival, Wagner then discovered that his tail hook wouldn't come down. With a wounded gunner, he couldn't risk a water landing, so he made a perilous but successful wheels-up landing on the flight deck, screeching to a halt before the first plane barrier.[359]

The Avengers of Air Group 1 attacked antiaircraft positions on shore, near the *Ise*. Eleven TBMs dropped 500-pound bombs that crewmen saw explode directly over the antiaircraft gun positions. The mission also saw the use of a Dumbo Avenger again. This plane, like the one used on the morning strike, dropped a large life raft to two airmen in the water only ten miles from Nishinomi Jima and the smaller raft to two more men in the Bungo Strait.[360]

A crew from Air Group 6's four squadrons also ended up in a raft after the mission to Kure. During the attack, two Corsair pilots from VBF-6 scored two hits with their 1,000-pound bombs on the battleship *Ise*.[361] Six of the eleven Helldivers from VB-6 that dived on the battleship also scored hits. The other planes experienced mechanical problems that either prevented them from dropping on the battleship or caused them to miss it. One had oil spray over the front of his canopy at the beginning of this dive, just as flak buffeted his plane, so the pilot dropped his bomb on one of the islands in the harbor. Another opened his landing flaps, instead of dive flaps, when he began his dive, flipping the Helldiver onto its back. By the time he had recovered control, he was out of position to bomb the *Ise* and attacked the *Aoba* instead, but did not see his bomb strike the cruiser.[362]

The Avengers aimed for the *Aoba*. Ten TBMs made a high-speed run on the cruiser, scoring four direct hits, through the heavy flak that faced all airmen at Kure that afternoon. Antiaircraft fire damaged the TBM flown by Lieutenant Lynn DuTemple. He began the flight eastward, joined by an Avenger from VT-49 that escorted him as far as the radar picket destroyers. DuTemple made a good water landing and a destroyer rescued him and his crew.[363]

The Hellcats of VF-6 consisted of a team to record damage done during the raid and another section that dropped window during much of the time groups were attacking their targets. The strike was over by the time the window dropping ended, and the seven F6Fs sensibly sought targets elsewhere, rather than hazard the formidable flak defenses of Kure by themselves. While returning to the carrier, they strafed a small coastal freighter outside Kure Harbor, then bombed a smelting plant at Saganoseki on Shikoku Island, starting a large fire, but without inflicting any obvious damage to it.[364]

Twenty-five aircraft of Air Group 94 took part in the afternoon strike. The Task Group strike coordinator flew one of the Hellcats, with two more F6Fs as his escort. All the F6Fs bombed the town of Kochi, on the way to Kure, so they could reach the target in time for the coordinator to get to work. A fourth Hellcat, separated from the other three in heavy clouds, joined another flight that bombed the carrier *Katsuragi* at Kure.

The Helldivers preceded the Avengers, who had three Corsairs as escort, flying with them in diving on their target, the *Ise*. They succeeded in scoring three hits on the vessel. The torpedo planes, with the Corsairs, detailed to attack the cruiser *Aoba*, did so at the same time the dive-bombers attacked the battleship. Of the ten planes attacking the ship, nine claimed to have made hits with the 1,000-pound bombs they carried.[365]

Air Group 49 also dove on the *Ise*. Each Hellcat carried one 1,000-pound bomb and of the three hits they claimed, one hit directly on the number two turret holding sixteen-inch guns. All the hits scored started fires, and crews saw smoke envelop the ship as they started for home.[366] As the Avengers of VT-49 began their dives, this smoke caused the pilots some difficulty in aiming their bombs, but two managed to get direct hits on the cruiser *Aoba*.[367]

Fifteen Hellcats and fourteen Avengers from *USS Belleau Wood*'s Air Group 31 attacked both the *Ise* and the *Aoba*, both targets putting up formidable flak. Twelve of the F6Fs got hits on the *Ise* and eight of the Avengers dove on the *Aoba*, claiming five direct hits. The other TBMs found the smoke over the cruiser too thick and bombed warehouses and dry docks in the harbor, but could not see the results of their efforts.

When planes from Task Group 38.4 went in to attack, aircraft from the carriers *Yorktown*, *Wasp*, and *Independence* attacked simultaneously, followed by those from the *Shangri-La* and *Cowpens*.[368]

Air Group 88 was the first to attack, briefed for the *Haruna* and anti-aircraft positions on shore, since the *Oyodo* was partially submerged when the group arrived over Kure. The Corsairs reached speeds of 450 knots during their dives and all planes met heavy flak barrage at about 3,000–4,000 feet, just about where they would pull out of their dives. Scattered clouds prevented all these planes from aiming at the *Haruna* and they missed the battleship. But one pilot dived on the *Tone* and claimed a hit.

Bombing Eighty-Eight's Helldivers scored two hits on the battleship, but lost a plane flown by Lieutenant (jg) Perry Mitchell, with ARM1c Louis Fenton, hit by flak during its dive. As the plane crashed near the *Haruna*, crews in other planes saw one crewman parachute from the stricken plane over Eta Shima, but, unfortunately, both men were killed.

VT-88 had the usual job for Avengers, bombing antiaircraft positions on the *Haruna* and on Eta Shima. They dropped eighty fragmentation bombs, most on the *Haruna* and some shore batteries. When the flight returned to the *Yorktown*, the ship was at General Quarters. While waiting to land, a pilot who had flown the morning strike announced over the radio: "If they haven't yet got me today, they ain't never gonna get me today."[369]

Air Group 86 had a near tragedy before the group reached Kure. The Helldiver flown by Lieutenant (jg) Edward Hanson, Jr., and ARM3c Charles Coleman crashed into the sea when it hit the slipstream of another plane. Fortunately, *USS Norman Scott* quickly rescued both men. The group continued on to Kure, where they attacked just after the planes from the *Yorktown*. One flight of Corsairs of VBF-86 bombed the *Haruna*, a second antiaircraft positions in the area, and a third group a large troop transport. Pilots could not see if they did any damage to the *Haruna*, but did make one hit on the transport. The *Wasp*'s Helldivers dove on the *Haruna* and the cruiser *Oyodo*, getting one hit and a near miss on the battleship and two near misses on the cruiser. Japanese antiaircraft fire was intense from ships and shore batteries and it hit the SB2C flown by Lieutenant (jg) Joseph Brown as he pulled out of his dive. The plane spewed white smoke and began to lose altitude until it ditched between Nino Shima and Eta Shima. Fortunately, Brown and his radioman, ARM2c Frederick Lockett, both survived to become prisoners of war.

The Avengers of VT-86 split into two groups, one diving on the *Haruna*, scoring two direct hits. The other section bombed the cruiser *Tone*, also scoring two direct hits and sharply reducing the volume of antiaircraft fire it displayed. As the group returned to the *Wasp*, the Avengers strafed lighthouses, mills, and small boats.[370]

The four Hellcats and eight Avengers from Air Group 27 were, like some other groups, originally assigned to hit the *Oyodo*, but the cruiser's sinking condition led them to attack the *Haruna*. The VF-27 Hellcats went in first, getting a near miss on the battleship, before the TBM pilots dove and scored three direct hits. One Avenger pilot, Lieutenant (jg) Clement Street, did hear the order to switch targets and ended up bombing the cruiser *Tone*, scoring at least one hit just above the waterline. After his dive on the *Haruna*, another pilot discovered one bomb had not released, so he also dropped it on the *Tone*.[371]

The twenty-nine planes dispatched by the *Shangri-La* then took their turn at the warships in the harbor, losing three planes during the attack. Four Corsairs that reached Kure dived on the *Ise*, scoring two hits with 1,000-pound bombs. But one of the successful pilots, Lieutenant (jg) Joseph Hjelstrom, did not return home. Flak must have hit his plane after he dropped his bomb, as he was last seen by his wingman during their dive.

VB-85 also scored one hit on *Haruna* while encountering vicious, accurate flak. The strike report later recorded that the antiaircraft gunners on the battleship "by this time must have had a great deal of practice [in firing] on retiring planes." Antiaircraft fire hit Lieutenant Edward Gibson's Helldiver after he pulled out of his dive, as he crossed the island of Nishinomi. The plane burst into flames and crashed into the water near the island. Gibson and his radioman, ARM3c Charles Linsz, were both killed instantly. Lieutenant (jg) Maynard J. Mitchell was flying just behind Gibson and flak from the same battery struck his SB2C as well, wounding his radioman, ARM2c William C. Pinkerton. Mitchell flew toward the southern tip of Shikoku, but the engine failed when the plane was between the southern tip of Shikoku and Kyushu, so he had to ditch. He got out of the plane, readied the life raft, and then helped Pinkerton into the raft just before the Helldiver sank. He put several tourniquets on his gunner and the two men awaited rescue, which appeared later in the form of a Dumbo that picked them up. *Shangri-La*'s Avengers did well during their dives on the battleship, making almost a dozen hits on or quite near the *Haruna* with 500-pound bombs.[372]

The last planes to attack, three Avengers from VT-50, scored one hit on the *Haruna*. Two others had turned back, one with engine trouble escorted by another, but both planes bombed a factory and some small cargo ships on their way home.[373]

As mentioned earlier, antiaircraft fire was intense over Kure. Some crews, however, reported that antiaircraft fire was heavier as they left Kure than during their dives, perhaps indicating that the morning attacks, and the first bombing during the afternoon, reduced the number of guns close to the target ships still able to fire.[374]

Coordination of attacking groups for this strike was good, unlike the morning strike, so none had to loiter over Kure before they attacked.[375] The strike report by Air Group 31 complemented the target coordinator, Commander Searcy of Air Group 88, for doing a good job.

⌁

After the strike coordinator told the groups of Task Group 38.3 to hit other targets, planes went in search of prey along the coast of the Inland Sea. One of the highlights of their search for targets was the location of a transport ship near Tokuyama, about 50 miles southwest of Kure. Helldivers found a medium-sized vessel and started to attack it. One pilot from VB-16, however, thought it brandished a white cross that identified a hospital ship, and thus bombed a dockyard nearby. Another could not see the marking and dropped his bomb, which fortunately missed.[376] *Essex*'s Helldivers and Hellcats and Air Group 47 also found the same ship, but the flight leader called off an attack as he also saw the hospital marking on the ship, which the group later identified as the *Baikal Maru*.[377]

The search for targets led other groups to strafe, rocket, and bomb a wide variety of small craft, including patrol boats, small cargo vessels, and luggers in the Inland Sea and its ports. The Hellcats from VBF-16 dive-bombed a cargo ship, scoring one direct hit and several near misses that left the vessel low in the water. VT-16 found a large cargo ship in Ube Harbor. Dropping more than thirty-five bombs, they holed the hull in the bow and stern.[378] Air Group 34 finally found a 5,000-ton cargo ship after searching for a target for some time. Hellcats attacked the hapless vessel first, scoring one direct hit with a 500-pound bomb amidships that threw debris high into the air. The Avengers followed up with bombs that landed in the water all around the ship, leaving it seriously damaged.[379]

Corsairs from VBF-87 found two destroyers near Tokuyama and bombed one, planting their bombs so near the warship that it rocked violently, while others attacked a merchant ship. Heavy flak from Tokuyama damaged Ensign William Stanley's Hellcat, forcing him to ditch. Regrettably, he was unable to get out of the plane before it sank, and he drowned. The Helldivers of VB-87 bombed a coastal tanker anchored in a cove on the island of Iwai Shima. Four 1,000-pound bombs hit the ship and it promptly blew up and sank.[380]

Planes from Air Group 47 spotted a large cargo ship in a cove on the same island. Four Hellcats attacked it first, followed closely by six Avengers. Crews couldn't see the results of the fighter attack, but the TBMs scored six hits on the cargo vessel. Two bombs split the keel and the superstructure disappeared, then the ship immediately sank.[381]

VT-83 managed to find some small cargo ships also near Tokuyama. One pilot bombed some storage tanks on the shore, setting two on fire, while two more pilots bombed the ships, making a direct hit with a 500-pound bomb and two near misses with 1,000-pound bombs that exploded under the stern. Although crews did not see the ship sink before they turned for home, it was on fire.[382]

⁓

As evening approached, the usual Japanese "snoopers" approached the Task Force. At 5:00 PM, fighter controllers vectored four Hellcats from VF-87 combat air patrol to a bogie approaching the fleet. The weather was poor, with heavy clouds and rain showers. Approaching the enemy plane, the patrol few under a rain squall and when it emerged into the clear, found the enemy, identified as a Jill torpedo bomber, in front them, flying toward the Task Force. Lieutenant William Petersen, leading the flight of Hellcats, instantly "whipped around" and got on the Jill's tail. With the other three planes behind him, he closed with the Jill as it fishtailed to avoid what was coming as the rear gunner fired at the Hellcats. When Petersen was only 300 feet from the torpedo bomber, he opened fire. The Jill exploded instantly.[383]

Only a short time later, two VBF-83 Corsairs, flying another combat air patrol, were vectored to another bogie flying close to the water near the

Task Force. They closed and intercepted what they found to be another Jill, carrying a torpedo intended for a ship of the Task Force. Lieutenant William Harris fired a burst from his .50 caliber machine guns that hit the port wing of the enemy bomber. It caught on fire and crashed into the sea, only five miles from the outer screen of the Task Force.[384]

Chapter Ten

THE USUAL FLEET WITHDRAWAL OCCURRED AFTER THE STRIKES ON July 28, to refuel destroyers, before air strikes resumed on the 30th. Late on the night of the 29th, the American battleships *USS South Dakota*, *Indiana*, and *Massachusetts*, joined by *HMS King George V*, again bombarded the Japanese mainland at Hamamatsu for almost an hour, striking a railroad factory, a propeller plant, a military barracks, and other structures in the town. Japanese shore defenses did not retaliate.[385]

As the Japanese announced their refusal to accept the terms of the Potsdam Declaration, the Task Force returned to airfield, transportation, and shipping strikes on July 30, having put paid to the remnants of the Imperial Fleet at Kure. More than 1,400 sorties by American and British aviators struck airfields from the eastern Inland Sea to the Tokyo area, as well as any ships in the area. American planes sank a minelayer and twenty enemy merchant ships, including three fair-sized cargo ships, and destroyed another 115 enemy planes on enemy airfields. British flyers sank a destroyer and a transport ship, along with a few smaller ships as well as seven planes on enemy airfields.[386]

Before the early dawn sweeps took off, three night-prowling Avengers from VT(N)-91 were still in the air, having flown since midnight. Their main mission was to carry gun spotters for night bombardment of Hamamatsu. Each TBM flew at a different altitude and used a different radio frequency to correct the fall of shot from the warships. The weather was clear, so flares were not necessary for the spotters to recognize the targets and adjust the fire of the warships. One technique to adjust fire was for the Avenger to drop an incendiary bomb on the target just before the bombardment started. The spotter used this as a reference point to adjust the fire from the warships.

Only a few antiaircraft guns fired at the Avengers, but they did not score any hits. A radar-controlled searchlight did locate one Avenger, but a salvo of shells caused it to go out almost immediately. When the bombardment was over, the three planes went in search of targets of opportunity. All of them dropped butterfly bombs on the airfields at Mikatagahara, Hamamatsu, and Tenryu. Two of them dropped a few incendiary bombs on small towns, and three bombed a railroad bridge over the Tenryu River. Despite the clear conditions that night, crews observed little of the damage they inflicted on the targets. There was no report of Japanese opposition to the Avengers' harassment.[387]

Nineteen missions took to the air in the hour after dawn. The earliest mission by Air Group 16, flown by VBF-16, ran into an enemy plane, the only encounter with enemy aircraft on the 30th. Most of their assigned targets, enemy airfields, were inaccessible because of overcast, but a hole near Kiryu Airfield permitted the flight to bomb the town of Ashikaga, where they set some factories on fire and destroyed a rail terminal as well as rail cars in the rail yard. As the attack finished, Lieutenant Anthony Fizalkowski spotted a Japanese Nell twin-engine bomber. He set out in pursuit with the three pilots of his division. As they drew within a few miles of the enemy bomber, it turned around to land at Kiryu Airfield, less than ten miles from Ashikaga, setting up Fizalkowski to shoot it down. As antiaircraft gunners shot at him, he fired a few bursts as the Nell drew near at lower altitude and hit the fuselage and left wing, setting the port engine on fire. The propeller then began to windmill as two members of Fizalkowski's flight also fired bursts at the plane, but with no apparent effect. As Fizalkowski turned for another pass, the Nell dove into a fog bank from about 500 feet altitude, with little chance it could recover and land safely, only a probable victory.[388]

VF-94 left the *Lexington* for a sweep to Yaizu Airfield, on the coast southwest of Tokyo, at 4:30 AM: twelve Corsairs armed with bombs and four without to take photos of several airfields in the area. The attack aircraft divided into two sections, some bombing hangars and others the antiaircraft positions defending the airfield, which put up a spirited defense, while a third stayed overhead as top cover. Following the first two divisions, the last group then bombed shops on the field, but flak damaged Lieutenant Charles Brock Jr.'s Hellcat during his dive. Of fourteen enemy fighters found at Yaizu, pilots claimed eleven as destroyed. During the search for planes hidden off the field, the flyers found a train and strafed it, destroying the locomotive. All in all, the Corsairs spent about two hours in the vicinity of the airfield before they headed for home. During the flight home, Brock had to ditch off the coast, inside a minefield that prevented an immediate rescue by a lifeguard submarine. After twelve long hours in his life raft, a Catalina from Rescue Squadron 4 landed and picked him up.

The four photo planes took good pictures of several fields in the area. One of these pilots, Lieutenant Lawton Bayliss, strafed an area in which he had noticed some well-hidden Japanese planes during a mission on July 25. His strafing started a fire in some trees, so the other three pilots came in to strafe as well and set several more planes on fire, hitting hidden aircraft, identified as Bettys and Oscars. When they finished strafing, ready to fly back to the *Lexington*, Bayliss was no longer with them. They searched the area for signs of his Hellcat until their fuel gauges told them it was time to return to the carrier, but without success, and he was later listed as killed in action. One of the planes was so low on fuel when it landed on the *Lexington* that it ran out of gas as it taxied onto an elevator. Although the circumstances of his loss are unknown, it is likely Bayliss was a victim of antiaircraft fire during one of the strafing runs.[389]

Air Group 6 had no losses when a dozen Hellcats and twelve Helldivers attacked Itami Airfield near Osaka. The Helldivers dropped 500-pound bombs, fired rockets, and strafed during their dives, destroying a twin-engine plane and damaging more than a dozen more in aircraft revetments. One bomb made a direct hit on an antiaircraft gun, one of the guns firing at the attacking planes, and another exploded a hangar in front of a diving SB2C. The Hellcats dropped bombs on hangars, destroying two and damaging four more.

After their passes on Itami, four fighters escorted the Helldivers back to the carrier while the remaining fighters moved on to two more airfields. At Ogura, the F6Fs fired rockets and strafed aircraft on the field, damaging two and also damaging four more hangars. At their last stop, Tambaichi Airfield, they found a number of planes in the open that they damaged with rockets and machine-gun fire. During the sweep, pilots over Itami noticed the outline of a large plane, resembling a B-29, painted on the runway, most likely intended as a lure for American bombs.[390]

———

The second sweep flown by Air Group 16 took off an hour after the mission to Itami, again Hellcats escorting Helldivers. Their mission was also a sweep of three airfields, near Tokyo, but all were covered by overcast. The fighters eventually found a hole in the mattress over the town of Honjo, north of Tokyo, where they bombed factories and warehouses as the Japanese fought back with "meager" flak. The Helldivers found an opening in the clouds at the town of Takasaki and most of the thirteen planes on the strike attacked a rail bridge and a highway bridge, scoring a direct hit on one bridge. Two SB2Cs were able to locate the airfield near the town and dropped their 500-pound bombs in the runway. The planes finished the briefed mission by strafing some more factories; then the flight began their return to the *Randolph*. On the way home, the Helldivers indulged in more strafing: the airfield at Fuji, trains, and more factories.[391]

The poor weather that morning did not prevent twelve Hellcats of VF-49 from striking Himeji Airfield, where pilots described the flak as "meager." One four-plane flight bombed and rocketed hangars on the field, then strafed while the other two flights remained overhead as top cover. Moving on to two other airfields close by, the planes that had already expended their bombs and rockets stayed overhead while the other two flights struck Kakogawa and Akashi. With no planes seen on the former, the Hellcats bombed hangars and strafed revetments, but the damage inflicted on earlier raids made an assessment of the utility of this mission difficult. At Akashi, the raiders caught an enemy fighter on the ground and "burned" it. Two rockets fired by one Hellcat set a supply depot on fire.

Before returning to the carrier, the flight struck another airfield, at Minato, this time adding antiaircraft positions to the usual menu of hangars and aircraft revetments. On the flight home, the Americans made a stop at I Shima and, finding no obvious military targets, expended their remaining rockets on fishing boats docked on the island.[392]

The poor weather experienced by all air groups that morning stymied a mission by elements of three air groups to strike the airfield at Kisarazu. Thick overcast clouds covered the entire area when the planes arrived, so the strike leader, Commander Sherrill of Air Group 85, already strike leader and coordinator several times, took the sixteen Hellcats, thirty-two Corsairs, and twenty-nine Avengers in search of a break in the clouds for a target. The area southwest of Tokyo was in the clear, so the groups attacked several factories. VBF-85 and VB-85, as well as VBF-88 and VB-88, bombed the International Aircraft Factory, a second factory near in it, and some bridges, all near Fujisawa. A "spectacular" explosion occurred during the bombing of the second factory, taken by crews to be ammunition exploding. Lieutenant William White of VB-88 was in his dive when this occurred and his plane was surrounded by exploding tracers that reached up to 6,000 feet. Fortunately, his plane made it through the maelstrom undamaged. The bombs at the aircraft factory were well-aimed, with a number of hits that caused serious damage to the plant. The defenders put up moderate to intense antiaircraft fire that severely damaged a *Shangri-La* Corsair flown by Lieutenant Richard Schaeffer. The planes from *USS Wasp* targeted another factory a few miles away, believed to be the Japanese Gas Engine Factory. The Corsairs and Helldivers of Air Group 86 made the attack together through accurate, light antiaircraft fire. One flight of Corsairs and the SB2Cs hit the main plant, while the second flight of Corsairs hit another factory, the latter left smoking. Fighter and dive-bomber pilots scored a number of hits on the engine factory, inflicting serious damage. On the return flight, VBF-85 and VBF-88 Corsairs strafed several torpedo boats, sinking one. Lieutenant Richard Schaeffer, of VBF-85, made it partway to the safety of the *Shangri-La*, but the damage to his plane was so severe that he was forced to ditch off the coast. Unfortunately, he did not get out of the plane before it sank, and he drowned.[393]

Two more Corsairs were lost on a sweep to Oi Airfield and a second visit to Yaizu Airfield, early that morning. Twenty-four planes of Air Group 94 took off an hour after the first mission described earlier. Repeated strafing and rocket attacks destroyed seven enemy planes hidden in revetments and along roads near the field. Japanese camouflage of their aircraft was so good, however, that flyers had to make their strafing runs at 200 feet, or less, to spot the enemy planes. Such extremely low altitudes made the Corsairs vulnerable to the light flak that shot down two planes. Ensign Edd Garrison crashed on Oi Airfield, while Ensign Alfred Morris was last seen over the field. Both men were later classified as killed in action.[394]

At 7:30 AM, the usual strikes took off from their carriers, seventeen in all. Air Group 1 sent ten Hellcats and eleven Avengers to strike Kowa Seaplane Base, near the town of Mihama on the Chita Peninsula. The planes flew past the base, giving the impression they were headed to another target, then quickly turned and dove on the installation. The fighters concentrated on antiaircraft positions, hangars, and revetments while the Avengers bombed the main hangars, warehouses, shops, and administration buildings. Resistance was light, in part because the sudden turn had surprised the defenders. Partial overcast also provided cover for the attackers during the approach and reassembly afterward. After the first pass, four fighters formed up with the Avengers to return to the *Bennington* while six others made another attack pass. Two Hellcats took time to strafe a factory in Toyohashi before the fighters went back to strafe aircraft dispersals at the seaplane base twice more. Then, as the flight flew back to the *Bennington*, some Hellcats strafed another factory in Toba, across the bay from Toyohashi. The total score at the main target was four planes claimed as destroyed and eleven damaged by the Hellcats, along with three flak batteries silenced. The Avengers inflicted serious damage to hangars, warehouses, repair shops, and the main building.[395]

Planes from Air Group 6 had a bit more trouble during their raid on three airfields: Tambaichi, Itami, and Sano around Osaka. Two Hellcats, four Corsairs, and eleven Avengers made the attacks, beginning at Itami, where the Japanese responded with heavy antiaircraft fire. Two F6Fs dived first, followed by the TBMs with four F4Us covering them. The Hellcats dropped their bombs on a repair shop and a hangar; the shop exploded. The Avengers bombed aircraft revetments, repair shops, and hangars and claimed serious damage to these structures. The Corsairs hit the same buildings, as well as the only plane seen on field, which they damaged with a near miss. Antiaircraft fire hit Ensign Norman Bitzegaio's TBM during the dive, blowing off the right wing. The plane crashed on field, killing him and his two crewmen, ARM3c John Vehaun and AOM1c John Street.

After the flight reformed, the Corsairs and Avengers with the Hellcats visited Tambaichi Airfield, strafing and rocketing aircraft in revetments and a flak gun, without observing the results, then moved on to more revetments at Sano Airfield, where they strafed a George fighter in a revetment and a plane on the runway, but could claim only damage to the two, as neither aircraft burned.[396]

Air Groups 34 and 83 teamed up to hit the major airfield at Atsugi, near Tokyo: eight Hellcats from each group, four *Essex* Corsairs, seven VT-34 Avengers, and fourteen *Essex* Helldivers.

The Hellcats bombed and rocketed antiaircraft positions, dropping fragmentation bombs on the gun crews who initially put up an intense barrage, but whose fire slackened, not surprisingly, after American planes bombed them. Several Hellcats stayed overhead with one that experienced mechanical problems near the field, but after the main attack, these also got into the act, attacking several factories in towns near Atsugi, destroying a locomotive in a marshalling yard.

Most of the Avengers, and the Corsairs, bombed up to fifty enemy fighters: several twin-engine and even some four-engine aircraft, although most were later believed to be either dummies or previously damaged or destroyed "duds." They did set a few planes on fire and claimed at least one as destroyed, as most of their fragmentation bombs exploded directly over revetments. A few VT-83 Avengers may have gotten more substantial results, as they dropped their 500-pound bombs along a road identified as having planes lining it on an earlier raid. These bombs started several fires that may well have been aircraft burning.[397]

A larger effort, by aircraft from four air groups, visited Mineyama Airfield and ships in the harbor at nearby Maizuru. Avengers from VT-27, VT-50, and VT-86 with Hellcats from VF-50 and VF-86 took part. Shortly before the planes took off at 7:30 AM, new orders redirected *Yorktown* planes, briefed for these targets, too, to attack shipping at Tsugaru. *Shangri-La's* aircraft were redirected to the search for shipping east of Maizuru.

The main strike went in with four VF-86 Hellcats leading the Avengers as four more provided top cover. The former attacked a destroyer on their first run and two freighters, setting the latter on fire. The *Wasp's* TBMs stuck warehouses and an area under construction, as well as an enemy ship of unidentified type that suffered serious damage. Avengers from the *Independence* scored direct hits amidships on a large troop transport that exploded. VT-50 pilots scored one hit and a few near misses on an armed merchant ship. One VT-27 pilot bombed ships in the naval base, hitting a patrol craft. Photos taken during the raid showed an Italian liner, the *Costa Verde*, moored in the harbor; it became the target of a raid later that day.

Japanese ships and shore batteries fired at the attackers when they appeared over the harbor. Crews later described the effort as "extremely accurate" as it claimed one Avenger from the *Independence*. Flak rounds hit the TBM piloted by Ensign Daniel Berardinelli during its dive and it crashed into the harbor, killing him and his crewmen: AOM3c Michael Nagy and ARM3c Harold Gibson. As the remaining planes cleared the harbor, a flak ship was particularly persistent in firing at them.

After the Avengers had left the harbor, the *Wasp's* Hellcats strafed and rocketed some Sugar Dogs in a cove, leaving two burning. The four Hellcats acting as top cover went in after the Avengers, bombing buildings in the harbor, scoring a direct hit on a transport, firing rockets at two freighters that caught fire, and bombing a harbor tug that sank.[398]

At the same time, VF-50 made one bombing run on Mineyama Airfield, destroying two airplanes. Japanese gunners put up a moderate barrage against them, but failed to hit any American planes. The flight then strafed small vessels at Ima Saki, destroying a Sugar Dog.[399]

Air Group 85 Corsairs and Avengers looked for ships near Maizuru, finding a freighter, Sugar Dogs, and luggers at Obama Wan. Although there was hardly any opposition, their bombs missed the ships, but strafing found the mark and set the cargo vessel ablaze while rockets set two Sugar Dogs alight.[400]

Yorktown's ten Hellcats and fourteen Avengers struck at ships at Tsugaru, where the target coordinator told them to take a look at some ships about forty miles east of Maizuru. Arriving at the small port, the TBMs divided into three sections. Because of difficult radio communication, only one section dived on two armed merchant ships, scoring a hit on one, while the others bombed a marshalling yard, a factory, and a rail tunnel in the town. One bomb entered the tunnel entrance before exploding, while others tore up tracks in the yard. As with some other missions that morning, *Yorktown's* Avenger pilots met little opposition. The Hellcat pilots met more determined, moderate antiaircraft fire while they bombed and strafed another armed merchant ship and a submarine in the harbor. Several bombs hit the ship and it began to sink, and another bomb may have hit the submarine.[401]

After planes from the early morning missions landed, the midmorning strikes, nineteen in all, took off for the two hours before noon. One of these was a second strike on Maizuru, aimed at hitting the Italian liner *Costa Verde.* The liner was obscured by clouds when the planes arrived at the harbor, however, so Air Groups 85, 86, and 88 split up, dividing the visible shipping in the harbor between them. Antiaircraft gunners put up determined resistance.

Air Group 85 went for ships at the naval base. VB-85 Helldivers bombed a cargo ship, as did some *Shangri-La* Corsairs that also attacked a destroyer with "undetermined" results. Five of the latter found more enticing prey, a light cruiser, believed to be the *Kashima,* in a cove north of the port. They dive-bombed it, scoring one direct hit.[402]

Yorktown's planes attacked ships in the center of the harbor. Some Corsairs led the attack, followed by the Helldivers and remainder of the F4Us. The strike coordinator, Commander Searcy, made a direct hit on an armed merchant ship that sank in only a few minutes. The Helldivers got a direct hit on a tanker that began to sink, and also damaged a merchant ship and dock facilities. Three pilots attacked a large ship they thought might be the liner, but lingering to confirm this was not possible in their haste to escape the antiaircraft fire lacing the air above the harbor.[403]

Coming out of the harbor, the *Yorktown*'s Corsairs went in search of a destroyer reported by *Shangri-La* pilots, but couldn't locate it. They did, however, come upon several armed merchant ships in a cove near Maizuru and attacked them, scoring a direct hit on one despite enemy flak. Several pilots found a few luggers in another cove and attacked them, as well. Antiaircraft fire hit Lieutenant (jg) Donald Penn's Corsair as he was pulling out of his dive, and the plane began to quickly lose altitude. A water landing became necessary, so he jettisoned the canopy of the fighter, dropped his belly tanks, and ditched the plane about ten miles off the coast. Penn got safely out of the aircraft and about four and a half hours later, a Dumbo rescue plane picked him up, as we shall see.[404]

The *Wasp* Corsairs dived through flak to score direct hits on a Teratsuki-class destroyer with fragmentation bombs, scoring hits near the bridge and the aft turret as rockets struck the stern and amidships. Pilots then strafed a large transport north of the main harbor. Most of the Helldivers of VB-86 bombed repair shops in the naval base, since clouds prevented them from attacking ships, but two still managed to hit a gunboat in the harbor. The flak was intense, particularly as they left the harbor, like the earlier strike that morning. Again, a flak ship, now identified as a partially sunken warship, put up considerable ordnance.[405]

The only other aircraft lost on a strike that morning came from VF-49. The eight Hellcats and nine Avengers from *USS San Jacinto* aimed to rough up Himeji and Minato Airfields, west of Osaka. The Hellcats and Avengers bombed revetments, hangars, and repair shops, claiming damage that included a hangar that caught fire and one plane destroyed in a revetment. Antiaircraft fire was accurate and slightly damaged two TBMs. One Avenger that couldn't open its bomb bay doors during the attack later dropped its bomb load on an airframe factory in Kakogawa, starting a fire. As the TBMs rendezvoused to begin the flight home, Ensign Claude Coffey, who had ditched on the 24th, spotted a merchant ship anchored off I Shima, in the Kii Strait, and strafed it. The ship caught fire and was still burning later in the day when another flight of VF-49 Hellcats attacked it again.

After the first attack, the fighters split into two groups. One rocketed the Harima Arsenal as the others struck Minato Airfield, where they bombed a repair shop while rocketing and strafing revetments and building, facing no opposition. Only one aircraft, a twin-engine fighter, was in view and two rockets landed near it.

As the planes left Himeji, antiaircraft fire hit Ensign Byron Box's Hellcat. He not only stayed in the air, but managed to expend his rockets, to lighten his ship, on the same merchant ship strafed by Ensign Coffey. His plane couldn't make it all the way home, however, and he had to ditch near the radar picket destroyers. One of them picked him up, unharmed.[406]

Japanese merchant ships, such as those attacked by VF-49, were not the only targets of Navy flyers that morning. During a sweep that had already destroyed a locomotive and damaged a factory and several small cargo vessels, four *Shangri-La* Hellcats received orders to investigate several submarines reported anchored at Ajiro Ko. They found six midget submarines and two small cargo vessels at anchor and immediately attacked with rockets and machine-gun fire. Making several passes, they damaged the submarines, possibly sinking some. Then, they flew up the coast searching for more targets and found three larger submarines and more midget submarines in a cove at Shimoda Ko. They strafed these as well, seriously damaging at least one large sub. After antiaircraft guns on the shore fired at them, several planes dropped fragmentation bombs and strafed these positions, silencing them.[407]

The early afternoon strikes, fifteen in total, took off from their carriers without incident at 2:00 PM, destined for enemy airfields. A highlight of the action was a fighter strike by Hellcats and Corsairs from five air groups to the airfields at Utsunomiya. The distance the thirty-nine Hellcats and four Corsairs from VF-27, VF-50, VBF-85, VF-86, and VF-88 had to fly to reach the airfield would not allow a course with any deviations to confuse the enemy as to their target. This, combined with the poor weather met throughout the flight, induced "nervous strain" for the pilots, as the strike report from VBF-85 put it.

After a Corsair dropped out with engine trouble and another joined it as escort back to the *Shangri-La*, four VBF-85 F4Us made it to Utsunomiya Airfield and bombed, rocketed, and strafed aircraft revetments. One pilot later commented that the heavy antiaircraft fire from gun positions near the town of Utsunomiya "was right where they were supposed to be," a tribute to accurate intelligence during the briefing. The *Shangri-La* pilots claimed three aircraft destroyed. VF-50 Hellcats also attacked the field, dropping 500-pound bombs on their first pass. Returning to strafe twice more, they claimed a hangar destroyed and six enemy planes "probably" destroyed.

VF-86 F6Fs dropped fragmentation bombs and strafed on their first pass, then used rockets and machine guns on subsequent passes, hitting hangars, as few enemy planes were visible. As the attack began, flak hit a VF-86 Hellcat flown by Ensign Leo Ahern, heavy-caliber fire later described as "intense." His flight leader, Lieutenant George Harlan, described what occurred:

> *We made our first run from south to north between two fields—Utsunomiya South and Utsunomiya. AA was heavy and intense. Ensign Leo Ahern was hit here about 12,000 feet up. A burst [of flak] in front of us forced me to make a right turn. The next cluster hit aft in my section and I saw it burst near Ahern's plane. The plane then fell out of formation, trailing a light stream of smoke, but it did not appear to be out of control. I made S turns to see how badly Ahern was hit and tried to reach him by radio, but received no answer. AA was so intense [I] could not remain circling. After my first run, I returned to the area, but found no trace of [the] plane or sight of [a] parachute, either in [the] air or on [the] ground.*

Unfortunately, Ahern's Hellcat crashed near Utsunomiya and he was killed. After Ahern disappeared, Harlan spotted a train near the field and attacked it with rockets. The train caught fire and the locomotive exploded. VBF-85 Corsairs from *Shangri-La* also destroyed another locomotive near Naha Minato.[408]

VF-88 concentrated on antiaircraft positions on their first pass at Utsunomiya, dropping 500-pound bombs, but pilots reported that many of the positions had no guns, although they still found enemy antiaircraft fire to be moderate. They returned for two more passes, firing rockets at hangars and then strafing aircraft revetments. The five enemy planes destroyed fell victim to pilots searching hard for aircraft and making solo strafing runs, as most visible on the field were either dummies or wrecks.

Besides contributing eight Hellcats to the attack phase, *Yorktown* sent four more planes,: the photo plane and its escort. They took photos of Utsunomiya Airfield before, and after, the attack to allow accurate assessment of the damage inflicted during the raid.

Although pilots saw up to forty possible aircraft on the field, at least half were dummies and many of the remainder of "questionable status," meaning mostly likely wrecks from previous attacks. The dearth of operational aircraft at Utsunomiya made the score of aircraft destroyed low, given the number of American aircraft involved in the attack. Pilots could claim eight enemy planes destroyed on the field, all by *Yorktown* and *Shangri-La* aircraft.

This low score led some pilots, besides Lieutenant Harlan of VF-86, to go in search of more fruitful targets. *Independence* pilots attacked two trains, steaming in opposite directions near the field, with rockets that stopped them both, firing their engines, and hitting some rail cars with rockets. Following these final actions, the Navy fighters returned home "with more peace of mind than in the approach," particularly given the straight-arrow course taken to reach the field.[409]

Another afternoon raid to Kakamigahara netted twice the number of enemy aircraft destroyed on the ground than at Utsunomiya, all claimed by only six Hellcats of VF-31. The experienced pilots looked for enemy planes in less obvious places, off the airfield, so they ran up a higher score. The planes attacked with bombs first, five hitting aircraft revetments containing more than one plane. One pilot hit a revetment holding four planes, another three, with five of the enemy aircraft claimed as destroyed.

The Hellcats then visited two other fields, Komaki and Kiyosu, also briefed as targets, but found no planes on either, so they returned to Kakamigahara. On a subsequent pass at this airfield, ten of twenty-three rockets fired found the mark and destroyed another five aircraft. A total of twelve strafing runs on still more revetments, and roads near the field, netted six more planes destroyed. Some planes disintegrated when hit by machine-gun rounds. Pilots described the camouflage netting employed to conceal planes on the field as unconvincing, with obvious splotches of camouflage that stood out from their surroundings. Other camouflage techniques used by the wily Japanese were impressive, however, forcing pilots search intently to find more enemy planes. Some were located in huts off the field, along roads or even footpaths, as well as inside wooden shacks.

Although fortunately no planes were lost on the raid, several were damaged by light flak—namely, 13.2mm machine guns that could be deadly to American aircraft often flying only several hundred feet from the ground, a tactic necessary to locate these hidden enemy planes.[410]

—◆—

Besides the daily sweeps and strikes that made up many of the sorties flown by the Task Force flyers that summer, some missions were rescue escort operations, warding off Japanese ships from capturing pilots down in the sea and protecting rescue aircraft from Japanese fighters. Pilots flew two such missions on the 30th, the last taking off at 3:45 PM. Four night-fighter equipped Hellcats left USS Yorktown to help in the rescue of Lieutenant (jg) Donald Penn of VBF-88, who was then floating in the sea north of Maizuru after he was shot down that morning, as described earlier in this chapter. While the Hellcats were on the way to the scene, after rendezvousing with the Dumbo from the Army Air Force's Rescue Squadron 4 with call sign "Playmate 29," they received word that fighters then circling Penn had to leave, as they were low on fuel. Two pilots, Lieutenant (jg) Edward Chamberlin, whom we met in chapter five, and Lieutenant Henry O'Meara, sped ahead of the others to reach the downed pilot as soon as possible. On the way, they took a few minutes to strafe an electric train, three steam locomotives, and buildings on an airfield that were directly on their flight path.

When the pair reached the bay north of Maizuru, a Japanese destroyer escort fired at them as they searched for Penn. They sighted a Japanese freighter on fire that the departing fighters had told them was near Penn, but not the man himself. He was difficult to spot, as he had pulled a green poncho over himself in his life raft when a Japanese floatplane circled overhead, searching for him.

Then the following two Hellcats, led by Lieutenant Fred Sueyres, whom we met during another rescue in chapter five, arrived with the Mariner and began to search for Penn, with the Catalina flying close to the water. One of the Hellcats fired machine guns at the burning Japanese freighter, to discourage any antiaircraft gunners that might be aboard. During this search, Sueyres looked over some launches in the area to see if they had already captured Penn. One made the mistake of firing at Sueyres and he retaliated with his .50 caliber machine guns, which promptly forced the enemy gunner to shut up as the boat raced for some rocks and cover. As this was going on, the Catalina sighted Penn, who was flashing a mirror to signal his location in his raft. As the Catalina pilot, 1st Lieutenant John Rairagh, got into position to land in the sea, Sueyres's wingman, Ensign Hollis Eldridge, whom we met in chapter five, spotted a Japanese destroyer escort heading out of Maizuru Harbor toward the raft. Eldridge remained circling over Penn while Sueyres raced toward the enemy ship.

In the meantime, Chamberlin saw a seaplane landing in the bay. Investigation proved it to be a Japanese Jake, possibly intent on capturing Penn. Chamberlin promptly strafed the plane, "burning" the enemy craft. He then located more Japanese aircraft, a four-engine Mavis seaplane and another Jake, and strafed them as well. His wingman, Lieutenant O'Meara, found another Pete floatplane and destroyed it, but flak, firing at the flyers the whole time, damaged his F6F.

As the strafing ended, Sueyres radioed Chamberlin and O'Meara to join him in attacking the Japanese destroyer escort, then steaming hard toward Penn and the Catalina, which had, by this time, landed in the bay. Sueyres, still by himself, initially drew the enemy ship's fire from the Catalina by circling it as he zigged and zagged to avoid being hit. He followed up with an attack run on the enemy vessel, drawing more fire from the Mariner and Penn that were, by now, close off the enemy vessel's port bow.

Lieutenant Rairagh, pilot of the Catalina, described some of the action from his vantage point: "After a few sweeps, the copilot [1st Lieutenant Thaddeus Zelasko] spotted a mirror flash … and we headed for the spot. A Jap destroyer which had been lying off the west about three miles opened fire on us with her AA guns … Her fire was heavy, but inaccurate, due to our constant changing of direction, air speed, and altitude. The destroyer started toward us as we came in for a landing. We landed close to the man [Penn] and the navigator and surgical technician were able to pull him into the blister on the first pass. Our fighters came in and strafed the destroyer" but it was "within 40mm range and as we took off, 40mm shells were dropping around us." About five minutes later, after "breathing a sigh of relief … one of your fighters … said he was in trouble with low oil pressure and would have to ditch."

This pilot of the plane in trouble was O'Meara. To complicate matters, the flak damage to his engine caused a catastrophic loss of power that required an immediate water landing. He did so, as far from the enemy destroyer escort as possible as Chamberlin circled above him.

The Catalina headed for him, with Ensign Eldridge, who had seen O'Meara ditch, as escort. The Japanese warship changed course to intercept the new rescue. The sun had set by this time, but Sueyres continued to harass the enemy vessel, drawing its fire, and attention, from the new man in a raft and the planes rushing to his rescue.

The Dumbo first spotted Chamberlin circling O'Meara, the man in the water. With this news, Chamberlin and Eldridge joined Sueyres in attacking the destroyer escort, making repeated runs against it. Their attacks knocked out the forward guns and caused an explosion on the stern of the vessel that slowed it down, billowing steam and smoke.

While the three Hellcats mauled the enemy DE, the Mariner landed and picked up O'Meara. Rairagh again described the scene: "We got down to about thirty feet [from the water], made a skidding turn about a quarter of a mile from our man and landed. Here the opposition was rough. Our first destroyer was closing in, using rapid 40 and 20mm cannon plus 50 caliber with a second destroyer coming out from shore to cut us off." During the first attempt to pick him up, O'Meara lost hold of the rope, so the Catalina made a second pass. "The navigator went out on the wing with one end of the rope, draped it from the blister with the surgical technician holding the other end. This time we were successful in getting the man alongside. He was worn out and half drowned so we had quite a time getting him aboard. We took off and started climbing." As the Catalina started to fly away, the three Hellcats broke off their attack on the destroyer escort, as only one plane had any ammunition left, and that only for one machine gun.

The fighters escorted the Catalina all the way over Honshu, through the dark of night, their journey highlighted by Japanese searchlights that tried to illuminate them near Nagoya. The three Hellcats landed on the *Yorktown* at 8:10 PM and the Catalina landed in the water near the Task Force screen of destroyers. A boat from the *USS Norman Scott* came alongside the Catalina and took the crew and rescued passengers aboard, a successful end to two daring rescues.[411]

Beginning at 10:00 that night, Destroyer Squadron 25 made a shipping sweep off Suruga Wan, sinking a picket boat and possibly sinking an FTC with torpedoes. The warships also shelled an aluminum factory and the marshalling yards in the town of Shimizu, without encountering any opposition. Air Group 91 again flew Heckler missions over airfields in the vicinity to support the surface ships.

The effect of air strikes on Japanese airfields and aerial combat during July was considerable. Navy and Army Air Force flyers destroyed approximately 800 Japanese planes during the month, excellent preparation for the invasion of Kyushu that was still, at that time, in the offing.

Chapter Eleven

DURING THE TEN DAYS BEFORE THE TASK FORCE AGAIN ATTACKED THE Home Islands, several significant events signaled the rapidly waning fortunes of the Japanese Empire. On August 3, Japanese resistance in Burma effectively ended. Three days later, the first combat use of an atomic bomb obliterated the Japanese city of Hiroshima, only about fifteen miles northwest of the port of Kure. Two days later, on August 8, the Soviet Union declared war on Japan, three months after the end of the war in Europe as agreed in January at the Yalta Conference.

As the Task Force withdrew to refuel after the raids of July 30, a typhoon moved into the area and the ships spent two days maneuvering to avoid the storm. When the Task Force returned nearer Japan for air strikes planned for August 5, the Commander in Chief, Pacific Fleet (CINCPAC) cancelled them, as the 20th Air Force would strike the same area, and ordered the Task Force northward to attack northern Honshu for a second time.

The notoriously poor Japanese summer weather intervened once again, delaying the strikes from August 8 until the next day. On the 8th, however, weather conditions caused a false radar report of enemy warships approaching the fleet. American ships sent to engage them found nothing. Strategic bombing had continued after the bombing of Hiroshima, with the last B-29s lost in combat going down on the 8th.

As Soviet forces began the invasion of Manchuria, Navy strikes resumed on August 9, just as suicide aircraft attacks on the Task Force increased sharply, an indication that the Japanese military was not yet prepared to surrender, despite two atomic bomb attacks. About twenty enemy aircraft did attempt to attack the Task Force on the afternoon of the 9th, the first such large-scale attacks since operations began on

July 10. None reached the carriers, as the combat air patrols and destroyers in picket station, code-named "Tomcat 2," shot them all down. But not before one crashed the destroyer *USS Borie*, the last successful suicide attack on an American warship operating off the main Japanese islands.

The destruction of Japanese planes trying to crash the Task Force began with a "snooper" that fell to the guns of a VBF-86 Corsair in the morning of August 8. Four *Wasp* Corsairs flying a combat air patrol near the Task Force were vectored to an unidentified plane seventy-five miles from the Task Force, around noon. The quartet intercepted the enemy plane, identified as a twin-engine Nick, in about twenty minutes, but almost immediately lost the enemy plane in clouds. Circling to starboard, one pilot, Lieutenant Lilburn Edmonson, located the plane attempting to flee westward, toward Japan. Using fuel injection to gain speed, he chased the enemy plane and soon overtook it. He attacked from one side while the gunner shot tracers at him. His rounds hit home and started a fire in a wing root. Flames soon engulfed the Nick and it went into a vertical dive, crashing into the sea.[412]

Four hours later, another Corsair pilot scored another victory. Lieutenant James Rowney of VBF-88 shot down a Dinah also "snooping" the Task Force. While flying a combat air patrol, the fighter director sent one section of *Yorktown* planes to investigate a bogie. He told Rowney and the other two pilots with him to "take it easy" and climb to 30,000 feet. After flying about thirty miles, the pilots sighted the enemy plane. Rowney dove on the enemy with the sun behind him as the other two pilots followed him. He approached it from the side, as had Edmonson that morning, and fired a burst 1,000 feet from the Dinah that "smoked" its right engine. His second burst, fired from 500 feet, hit the right wing. His companions also fired some bursts into the Dinah before it caught fire and began a slow spiral down to the ocean below. At about 10,000 feet the plane burst into flames, then exploded into several pieces that fell into the sea. Despite the assist from his comrades, Rowney received full credit for the kill.[413]

Air strikes resumed on August 9, with more than 1,450 sorties flown by the Americans and British flyers to airfields in northern Honshu. There was no enemy air opposition to the strikes, designed to destroy Japanese aircraft assembled on some airfields and believed to transport Army troops to the Marianas for a raid (code-named "Ken-Go" by the Japanese and "Damocles" by the Americans) to stop B-29 raids on Japan.[414] The highlight of the day, of course, was the second atomic bomb attack on a Japanese city, Nagasaki on the island of Kyushu. The attack took place at 11:02 that morning, shortly before Navy planes took off from their carries on the second wave of strikes, south of the fog line.

During these strikes and sweeps, American Navy flyers destroyed 189 Japanese aircraft on enemy airfields, sank five patrol boats, and shot down seven enemy planes in air combat. The British accounted for several small escort vessels, while both American and British flyers attacked and sank two destroyer escorts and an old destroyer.[415]

The action started when a dozen sweeps took off from their carriers just after 4:00 AM, to hit airfields, shipping, and factories on northern Honshu. The inclusion of dive-bombers on these dawn sweeps was an innovation that was not popular with fighter crews. The former were slower, with more limited range than fighters, and required fighter escort, reducing the number of planes that could dive on a target at the beginning of a strike. In addition, there was often limited current intelligence about targets for dawn missions. Fighters often had to search for airfields that were in the clear and offered suitable targets, all of which took time. The inclusion of shorter-range Helldivers limited the time they had to do so, and SB2Cs couldn't make as many strafing runs as fighters, reducing the impact of a strike.

Overcast over some targets led to attacks on alternates. Briefed to strike the naval base at Ominato, sixteen Corsairs and fourteen Helldivers from *USS Shangri-La* hit Misawa Airfield instead because of unsuitable weather and the distance to the target. Misawa Airfield was on the list of those targets "to be flattened."

The mission had a rough start when one Helldiver, with an unidentified crew, had trouble with turbulence from the slipstream of the plane ahead and spun into the sea just after takeoff. The destroyer *USS Ault* was on hand, fortunately, and picked up the crew.

Although overcast covered most of Misawa Airfield, *Shangri-La's* aircraft found a hole through which to attack. The Corsairs dropped fragmentation bombs on aircraft revetments, but many of the planes seen in them were dummies, so pilots did not claim any enemy planes as destroyed. The dive-bombers used 500-pound bombs on hangars, shops, and buildings, hitting an ammunition dump that blew up. The moderate flak reported fortunately did not damage any aircraft.[416]

The *Hancock* sent eight fighters, four Hellcats, and four Corsairs to another airfield that had better pickings to offer. Four Hellcats from VF-94 joined them for the strike, minus one Hellcat lost soon after takeoff. An oil line burst in the engine of Lieutenant Robert McAboo's Hellcat, forcing him to ditch near the Task Force. He got out of the plane and a destroyer, *USS McGee*, soon rescued him.

Pilots found many enemy planes, not dummies, at Jimmachi Airfield: single-engine fighters, twin-engine Nell bombers, and training planes no doubt intended for *kamikaze* attacks on the fleet. Here there were minimal clouds covering the field as the planes began their dives, so pilots could see the results of their efforts.

Not only were there operational aircraft in the usual aircraft revetments, but some were on the airfield itself, runways, and open parking areas. After bombing the main field, where they destroyed Nells and fighters, the Corsairs found many training planes parked near a landing strip a few miles from the two main Jimmachi landing strips. Strafing, they destroyed a total of nine Japanese planes that would not take to the skies again after the Corsair attack. The Hellcats dropped their bombs from only 800–1,000 feet, pulling out of their dives only a few hundred feet from the ground. One pilot, Lieutenant Herschel Pahl, remarked after the mission: "I saw so many planes that I wanted to get rid of my bombs and start to work on them with rockets and .50 cal. bullets."

There was little, light antiaircraft fire from the field, so the pilots began to leisurely strafe after dropping their bombs. Pilots formed a traffic circle, taking turns to strafe individual enemy planes, setting them on fire, then pulling out to come around again to strafe again. Pahl reported later: "We must have made twenty passes at planes. . . . All of them seemed to be gassed up and ready for takeoff. They burned easily." He himself "burned" five planes during the strike: a Zeke, a Jill, and three trainers. The total score for the four Hellcat pilots was twenty-one planes destroyed.[417]

The *Lexington*'s Hellcats soon joined in the attack, hitting a separate part of Jimmachi Airfield. Spotting fifteen enemy planes clustered on one landing strip, two F6Fs dived and dropped their 500-pound bombs, destroying four planes. Without any Japanese antiaircraft fire here, the four planes also formed a traffic circle and leisurely made repeated strafing and rocket attacks on individual aircraft located in several parts of the airfield. Several planes also found the satellite field loaded with training planes, mentioned earlier, and attacked them as well. The total score for the four VF-94 Hellcats was twenty-two planes destroyed, totaling forty-three for Air Groups 6 and 94.[418]

Bennington's aircraft made three visits to Matsushima Airfield on the 9th. The first was a 4:00 AM sweep by sixteen Hellcats from VF-1 that targeted antiaircraft positions around the field, in preparation for the strikes that followed. Dropping 500-pound bombs on the guns that fired intensely, they reduced the volume of fire, but not enough to ensure that all planes would return safely.

Following the bombing, the Hellcats flew to Sendai, where they attacked docks facilities and strafed a cargo ship. One flight took a swipe at the airfields at Sendai and Matsuda while another strafed a factory in the area, before returning to Matsushima for a second attack. The Hellcats made six strafing runs on the field this time, netting ten twin-engine aircraft destroyed. The antiaircraft guns still in action exacted a price, however. On the last attack pass, flak hit the Hellcat of Ensign Charles Stetler, who had ditched from flak damage on July 25. He pulled out of his dive and recovered while the plane was on its back. Then it suddenly dived into the water about a mile offshore, killing him instantly. Flak also hit the plane of the strike commander, Lieutenant Commander Melvin Hoffman, blowing off the tail hook. Since he would be unable to land on the carrier without it, Hoffman ditched his plane at the radar picket destroyers, where the *USS Harrison* rescued him.[419] An hour after this attack, more *Bennington* planes, informed of the good pickings at Matsushima by the first strike, arrived at the airfield: a dozen Corsairs and fourteen Helldivers. The remaining antiaircraft batteries were ready for them, offering moderate fire against the attackers, but failed to down any.

American pilots found about sixty Japanese aircraft on the field, most twin-engine Nicks, Bettys, and Helens, in revetments and in the open. Most appeared to be fueled and ready to take off, providing a new experience for the Corsair pilots in strafing Japanese aircraft that would burn when hit.

The attack began with bombing of hangars by some Corsairs and Helldivers as other Corsairs bombed aircraft revetments while a few stayed overhead as top cover. The result was three hangars and the associated workshops set afire and destroyed. Following this, two enterprising SB2C pilots made a strafing run on aircraft in revetments, but none of the planes they hit burned. The fighters made six strafing runs on different parts of the field, with better results. Each pilot would fix on one enemy aircraft and concentrate on it, not pulling out until they were quite close to "the deck." Their bombs and rockets blew up six planes and set fifteen twin-engine and two single-engine planes on fire. Some of these planes were in the open, as the Japanese were in the process of moving them to safer locations after the first attack an hour before.[420]

At about the same time, three air groups struck another airfield, at Yabuki, after another Helldiver crashed just after taking off from the *Wasp*. The plane spun in just after leaving the flight deck and crashed into the sea. Lieutenant (jg) John Naughton and his radioman, ARM2c Chester Warchol, both escaped and were rescued by *USS Wadleigh*.

Thirty-nine Corsairs and thirty-nine Helldivers from Air Groups 85, 86, and 88 took part, with two Hellcats that took photographs. *Wasp*'s planes were the first to dive, followed by planes from *USS Shangri-La*, then those from the *Yorktown*. With no planes visible on the field, VBF-86 and VB-86 concentrated on hangars and other buildings, as did Air Group 85. Following the bombing, the VBF-86 Corsairs fired at a few trains in the station near the airfield, destroying one locomotive, stopped in the station, and leaving two more steaming.

VBF-85 Corsairs attacked before the *Shangri-La*'s dive-bombers, destroying eight planes on the ground, as well as some hangars. The dive-bombers hit hangars and shops, and also bombed aircraft revetments. While pilots saw some fires around the revetments, they could not note specific damage. The Corsair pilots also took out two more locomotives during the mission.

Bombing Eighty-Eight hit aircraft revetments, as they did not see any enemy planes on the field and did not claim any as destroyed, or damaged. The *Yorktown*'s Corsairs dove before the Helldivers, also bombing several hangars and an antiaircraft position, destroying the latter. The only resistance to the mission was machine-gun fire and two ineffective flak bursts after the bombing.

Following their attack at Yabuki, VBF-88 still had rockets and machine-gun ammunition to expend, so they turned to nearby Iwaki Airfield. The Japanese responded with light flak from only one gun, so American flyers made a total of eight passes on the field, firing rockets into hangars and machine-gun rounds at aircraft that were plainly visible on the airfield, destroying sixteen. Many of these were single-engine trainers, capable of flying one-way *kamikaze* missions. During one pass, a Corsair strafed the lone antiaircraft gun, manned by two gunners. When he was done, both men were sprawled near the gun.[421]

Members of the crew of a small coastal freighter had the same fate as the flak gunners at Iwaki. Two Hellcats of VF-34 went in search of targets after being relieved from a two-hour patrol over a lifeguard submarine, early that morning. Flying along the coast, they spotted a coastal cargo ship near the coastal town of Kuji. As they looked the ship over before attacking, the crew mistook the flyers for Japanese and waved. This mistake was immediately evident, however, when the pair of F6Fs fired rockets at the vessel and strafed it with machine-gun fire. The first two rockets fired were short, but on the second pass, two more hit the ship's superstructure, starting a fire. Crew members still uninjured jumped overboard as the two F6Fs made more strafing passes, for about twenty minutes. At the beginning of the attack, the ship started to head for shore, and by the time the attackers' ammunition was low it had beached on the shore, leaking oil and on fire. Later in the day, American pilots observed the ship still beached and on fire, from stem to stern.[422]

During the morning strikes, more than 300 planes from fifteen air groups attacked more airfields in northern Honshu. One strike involved elements of five air groups that teamed up for a visit to Koriyama Airfield, where they destroyed and damaged buildings on the airfield, as few aircraft were evident, encountering little antiaircraft fire. The attacking force totaled thirty-two Hellcats, twenty-two Corsairs, and fifty-six Avengers.

Planes from USS *Cowpens* and *Shangri-La* led the attack. Most of VT-50's TBMs bombed barracks, destroying at least two of them, but one pilot dropped his fragmentation bombs on an area where earlier photos had shown many aircraft parked, although smoke made it difficult to determine if any planes were, in fact, damaged or destroyed.

The *Shangri-La* contributed a dozen Corsairs and fifteen Avengers to the Koriyama raid. Also targeting hangars, their planes dropped their bombs in this area, claiming five aircraft destroyed. Pilots reported some machine-gun fire aimed at them from the hangars, but it ceased once their bombs began to land. One Corsair had a fuel leak on the way to the airfield and turned back with another as escort. To expend their ordnance before reaching their carrier, both planes rocketed a power plant in a factory in the town of Taira and believed they destroyed it.

The Hellcats from USS *Wasp* waited for their first groups to attack before they turned to hangars on the field, leaving four destroyed. They also strafed some training planes on the field, but these didn't burn. Lack of time prevented any follow-up passes, so the Hellcats quickly rocketed and strafed some locomotives in a nearby rail yard. The TBMs of VT-86 also bombed hangars, hoping to catch any enemy planes parked near them. *Wasp* pilots thought the raid was well organized and executed, with one group attacking after the other, without confusion. The consensus of pilots who had flown a number of missions was that the raid was "one of the most orderly and effective combat attacks of this nature [on an airfield] that they had witnessed."[423]

Air Groups 27 and 88 were the last groups to bomb the airfield. The *Independence* Avengers, with some of the Hellcats, bombed hangars, aircraft dispersal areas, and other buildings. Other F6Fs, aiming for antiaircraft positions, switched to aircraft revetments after they discovered that antiaircraft fire was minimal, but the few aircraft seen by *Independence* pilots were dummies. Some of the TBM pilots experienced the not uncommon problem of bombs that hung up during their dive. One with five bombs that wouldn't drop on the airfield dumped them on the town of Koriyama, while two Hellcat pilots who couldn't line up their targets properly during the attack dive chose to bomb the town of Miharu.

Yorktown's Corsairs dived before their Avengers, aiming for antiaircraft positions that offered minimal resistance. The TBMs followed up and placed their bombs "squarely" on the hangars at which they aimed. One radioman on an Avenger joked that he saw a Japanese soldier sitting on a toilet, reading a translation of the popular American comic strip *Dick Tracy*, as his TBM dove on the enemy airfield. Bombs hit some training planes and single-engine fighters, and a gigantic explosion in the hangar area delayed an estimate of the damage inflicted for about twenty minutes. One TBM pilot couldn't dislodge his bomb no matter how hard he pulled the bomb release and had to land on the *Yorktown* with the bomb still in the bomb bay. Jarred loose during the landing, it fell out of its shackle onto the doors of the bomb bay, but fortunately remained inert. Before they returned to the *Yorktown*, two VBF-88 pilots scooted over to Iwaki Airfield and strafed hangars with rockets and machine-gun fire, leaving many hangars on the field on fire.[424]

The report of Torpedo Squadron 85 for the Koriyama strike reveals the reaction of pilots to the clever means the Japanese used to conceal their aircraft, after the news of the atom bomb attack on Hiroshima, on August 6, reached them. The early morning mission to bomb the airfield yielded few tangible results as, like other missions that day, pilots reported the few enemy planes visible during their attack were training biplanes, with fighters and bombers more expertly camouflaged: "The Japanese are concealing their air force very successfully. The atomic bomb may be a means of winning the war, but its effect on the morale of carrier pilots, dropping one-hundred-pound general purpose bombs on targets they can't see, is bad."[425]

Tragedy struck Air Group 83 before its Hellcats (taking photos), Corsairs, and Avengers reached Hachinhoe Airfield that morning. On the flight to the target, Lieutenant William Harris, who had shot down a Jill on July 28, met a tragic end when the 1,000-pound bomb carried by his Corsair accidently exploded over the sea. Only pieces of the wings and engine were visible after the explosion. When the remaining aircraft arrived at Hachinhoe, the Corsairs bombed antiaircraft positions and little fire came from these positions around the field after that. The Avengers split into four divisions, with one bombing hangars and other buildings and the others aircraft revetments where enemy planes were parked. Crews, however, saw little tangible effect from their fragmentation bombs and turned to targets off the coast as potentially more satisfactory. The fighters found and strafed a small cargo ship and a lugger. The lugger beached itself after the attack while the cargo ship, obviously damaged from earlier attacks, was on fire.

On the flight back to the *Essex*, one Avenger experienced a sudden engine failure and had to ditch about fifty miles from the Task Force, near the radar picket destroyers. Lieutenant (jg) Dewey LeClair, and his two crewmen abandoned the aircraft safely and got into their life raft. Several Hellcats circled above as others searched for, and found, a destroyer that they led to the survivors. The warship then picked them up. A Hellcat also ditched, after it ran dangerously low on fuel. Unable to reach the *Essex*, Ensign Hugh Batten tried to land on another carrier, but had to ditch before the carrier could turn into the wind to land him. A plane-guard destroyer quickly picked him up.[426]

Unlike at Koriyama and Hachinhoe Airfields, enemy aircraft were plentiful when three air groups struck Matsushima Airfield. Pilots of VT-49 thought this airfield "a more satisfactory type of aircraft target for the Avenger pilot than previous assignments, where often no plane could be spotted in the target glide" and "were unanimous in stating that they had never hit an enemy airfield with so many planes." Besides the usual dummies and wrecks, there were also operational planes camouflaged to look like wrecks.

Twenty-two Corsairs and Avengers from Air Group 1 dived first, followed by nine TBMs from VT-31, with *San Jacinto*'s eight Hellcats and eight Avengers finishing the strike. Japanese resistance was "meager," at best, throughout the raid.

VBF-1 and VT-1 aimed their bombs at aircraft revetments and the few buildings still standing at Matsushima on the first pass, and then fired rockets on the second and their machine guns on the third. Five aircraft destroyed and hangars and buildings on fire was the result. One Avenger, whose bomb failed to drop on the first dive, went around and made a second dive, setting a sixth aircraft on fire. While waiting for the fighters to finish more strafing runs on the airfield, the *Bennington's* Avengers found some small cargo ships to strafe near the airfield.

VT-31's Avengers bombed hangars, too, but the bombs hung up on three planes and the target coordinator ordered them to bomb aircraft revetments on their second dive, since the hangars were by now in flames from the efforts of Air Group 1 and the other *Belleau Wood* Avengers.

The last planes to dive, Hellcats and Avengers of Air Group 49, went after aircraft revetments in various parts of the airfield. The TBMs dropped 250-pound bombs that started fires, indicating they had hit some planes that caught fire. One enemy aircraft was literally blown out of a revetment. After releasing their bombs, the Avengers followed up with more strafing runs and the Hellcats made a single-line-abreast attack on aircraft dispersal areas and taxi strips. After the photo planes had taken pictures of the carnage, they spotted some untouched Japanese planes under trees and rocketed and strafed them, too. Before turning for home, Hellcat pilots found, and strafed, a destroyer escort near the seaplane base at Yamada. For the strike, *San Jacinto's* pilots claimed a total of thirteen enemy planes destroyed, with more damaged.

After leaving Matsushima wrecked, the seven remaining Corsairs of VBF-1 made a rocket attack on a destroyer and two destroyer escorts anchored at Onagawa Wan, about thirty miles from the enemy airfield. The enemy ships put up intense antiaircraft fire while two F4Us bombed the destroyer and five attacked the destroyer escorts. One rocket hit amidships on the destroyer and three rockets hit a DE.

Unfortunately, the intense antiaircraft fire from the warships hit Ensign Vincent Landau's Corsair just after he fired his rockets, which hit a destroyer escort. The plane exploded in midair, killing him instantly, and the wreckage crashed near the enemy vessel. But as the planes turned for home, the destroyer escort hit by rockets turned partially onto its side with the stern low in the water. Later, British planes found and attacked two more destroyer escorts, the *Amakusa* and *Inagi*, sinking both. A Canadian naval aviator won the Victoria Cross, the equivalent of the Medal of Honor, during this attack. While diving on one of the enemy vessels, flak hit his Corsair. Although it was on fire, he still managed to score a direct hit with a bomb, sinking the ship.[427]

About two hours after the raid by Air Groups 1, 31, and 49, Hellcats from two more air groups reached Matsushima to continue their work. More F6Fs from VF-49 found antiaircraft fire still minimal and spotted a number of twin-engine Bettys and Helens on the field when they arrived. Although some overcast hung over the field, they attacked anyway, rewarded with a bag of thirteen planes destroyed. The enemy planes were scattered around the airfield and well-camouflaged, but the pilots scoured the area, firing rockets at the enemy bombers on a number of passes. Lieutenant (jg) George Williams, who had shot down a Frank on July 24, fired five rockets into a revetment holding three enemy bombers. All three disintegrated in the blast. He then "burned" another Betty on a runway with his machine guns as Japanese flak gunners made feeble efforts to fire back at the Hellcats, but didn't hit any of them.

Hellcats from VF-94 also struck Matsushima, after they found their assigned airfields covered by overcast. They arrived after VF-49 and found the antiaircraft gunners a bit more accurate, as flak damaged two planes that managed to return to the carrier. Pilots dropped their bombs on hangars and barracks, destroying at least two barracks. They found it difficult to distinguish operational aircraft from wrecks, but during their four rocket and strafing runs nevertheless netted another seven enemy bombers destroyed.[428]

As mentioned at the beginning of this chapter, the second atomic bomb exploded over the city of Nagasaki at 11:02 that morning, shortly before the second wave of strikes began to take off from their carriers. Two air groups flying on these strikes weren't as lucky as the Hellcats of VF-94; three of their aircraft failed to return and Air Group 83 lost two more planes, making a total of five lost by the group since the first take-off at dawn. Air Group 16 lost a Corsair during a raid on the naval base at Ominato that led to another daring rescue the next day. These losses, compared to those at the airfields, attest to the accuracy and determination of Japanese shipboard gunners when attempting to repel American air attacks.

These gunners displayed an intense antiaircraft barrage as planes from the *Randolph* attacked Ominato Harbor first, with VBF-16's Corsairs bombing antiaircraft positions on the shore with fragmentation bombs. They also hit a destroyer or destroyer escort in the harbor, but without any dramatic results, pilots also strafed the dock area and rocketed a railroad bridge in the town.

Bombing Sixteen attacked the largest ship in the harbor, an old cruiser converted into a minelayer of the Pekiwa class, and although bombs landed close to the vessel, there were no direct hits. Some rounds of the intense flak from ships hit one of the last SB2Cs to dive, flown by Lieutenant Ernest Porusky. After pulling out of the dive, his squadron mates were horrified to see the Helldiver roll over twice, then crash into the harbor, killing Porusky and his radioman, ARM3c Richard Raymond. Intense flak over the harbor also destroyed the tail hook of Ensign John McNamara's plane. Since it couldn't land on a carrier without this vital piece of equipment, he ditched his plane near a destroyer inside the Task Force, but fortunately McNamara and his radioman, AOM3c Edward Alexander, were quickly rescued within five minutes of landing in the water.

The Corsairs and Helldivers of Air Group 83 attacked after the *Randolph*'s planes. Two Corsair pilots scored hits on the minelayer that started a fire amidships; then they attacked a few destroyers in the harbor with rockets, without results. As they flew out of the harbor, antiaircraft fire hit the Corsair flown by Lieutenant (jg) Vernon Coumbe, but he managed to keep the plane in the air for a few miles before ditching about five miles south of the harbor entrance.

The Helldivers of VB-83 followed the F4Us and also targeted the minelayer. Three of their bombs hit the vessel, all amidships, and one pilot felt the shock of the explosion as it rocked his Helldiver. Antiaircraft fire hit one of the SB2Cs, flown by Ensign Paul Bacci, whose bomb hit the enemy ship. He pulled out of his dive and flew south from the harbor, his plane streaming smoke, but after a few miles of flight, the plane suddenly rolled over and dove into the sea, killing Bacci and radioman ARM3c William Driscoll.

After he ditched the Corsair, Coumbe got into his raft to await a Dumbo rescue plane to appear, but his rescue did not happen until the next day. After fighting the current that drew him close to shore during the night, he found himself only a mile offshore of a fishing village the next morning. His story will continue in the next chapter.[429]

— ‿ —

The usual early afternoon strikes took off from their carriers after 1:00 PM, fifteen missions to strike airfields again, as well as shipping. Air Group 6 flew another mission, alone, to Matsushima Airfield since it was rich in aircraft targets. At takeoff, a Helldiver lost engine power and had to ditch near the carrier, but a plane-guard destroyer, USS Ringgold, picked up the pilot, Ensign Howard Harrison and crewman, ARM3c Raymond Predmore.

The remainder of the strike—four Hellcats, eight Corsairs, nine Avengers, and nine Helldivers—reached Matsushima, and the four Hellcats opened the attack by dropping 500-pound bombs that destroyed an enemy bomber in a revetment. A subsequent strafing run set another on fire. Flak, described as moderate, hit two of the Hellcats, but both returned safely to the carrier.

The Helldivers attacked next, aiming for more aircraft revetments. Some of the SB2C pilots fired rockets during their dives, then dropped their 500-pound bombs on revetments, planes parked on runways, and even a radio station on the field. Their Helldivers returned for a second pass and strafed two Betty bombers and a piloted Baka suicide bomb. The Corsairs and Avengers followed, with the Corsairs making three runs on the field, firing bombs and rockets. The TBMs hit revetments, too, and runways before flying out to sea to wait for the Helldivers and Corsairs to finish their strafing before all aircraft returned to the carrier. The total of enemy planes destroyed by the group was fourteen.

Unfortunately, one Helldiver didn't make it back to the Hancock. Antiaircraft fire hit the underside of the Helldiver flown by Lieutenant John Freeman, wounding his radioman, ARM3c Robert Mileston, and knocking out the hydraulic system, radio, and ailerons. A VF-94 Hellcat, from another strike, suddenly appeared and notified the Air Group 6 commander of Freeman's plight. With a Corsair detailed as escort, he headed back to the *Hancock*, flying at only 300 feet off the water. Leaking both gas and oil, the stricken SB2C finally reached the radar picket destroyer screen for the Task Force and made a successful water landing. Both men got safely into their life raft and the *USS Harrison* appeared within ten minutes and picked them up.[430]

One more plane was a combat loss during an afternoon airfield strike. The three air groups based on *USS Randolph*, *Monterey*, and *Bataan* flew another strike to Misawa Airfield, already hit four times earlier that day. It was the third attack of the day on Misawa for Air Group 16 and the second for Air Groups 34 and 47. Thirty-six Hellcats and twenty-nine Avengers pummeled the field this time, but they destroyed fewer aircraft than earlier raids since there were now fewer operational aircraft to attack. Air Group 16 destroyed three, Air Group 34 four, and Air Group 47 at least two enemy planes on the ground.

Flak was a bit heavier than on earlier missions, but some pilots speculated this was because the Japanese may have used more tracer ammunition to oppose this raid than the earlier raids. Airmen could plainly see tracers that gave the impression of more rounds in the air. In conjunction with smoke from antiaircraft gun bursts, it gave the appearance of more ordnance coming their way.

Air Group 16 Corsairs and Avengers attacked together, most aiming for buildings and hangars. Two VBF-16 Corsair pilots, however, bombed antiaircraft positions during their dives. This was prescient since when the raid was over one of their number was missing. Ensign William Rogers, whom we first met strafing locomotives on July 15, was last seen diving on the airfield, where he apparently crashed; he was later listed as killed in action. One VT-16 pilot had the good fortune to see a Japanese bomber parked by a small hangar. He dropped several 500-pound bombs on it, most likely destroying it, one of the three planes claimed as destroyed by the group.

Low overcast that hung over the airfield prevented the American fighter pilots from making their preferred high-angle dives, and the absence of scattered clouds made it harder to find occasional cover from antiaircraft fire while they did so. This was another reason pilots found Japanese opposition more intense.

The *Monterey's* Avengers concentrated on aircraft revetments and buildings and their bombs inflicted serious harm to several hangars. In the revetment area they hit several aircraft and crews saw several fires break out after their dives. Six VF-34 Hellcat pilots saw a series of revetments covered by foliage that held eight Japanese fighters after they dropped their bombs. They promptly attacked, making several strafing runs on the planes, described as "vicious .50 cal. strafing." The planes had no fuel and none burned, but the assessment of the Hellcat pilots was that "the Jap planes took an awful beating and could definitely be classified as non-operational after the attack." Two VF-34 pilots, Ensigns William Pumphrey and Alfred Bianchetti, found four Betty bombers. They strafed them, setting one on fire and blowing pieces off the other three so that they became, at the least, "non-operational"; both were claimed as destroyed. The Hellcats of VF-47 bombed antiaircraft positions, like their comrades from VBF-16, and then made two strafing runs that damaged a few planes. Avengers from VT- 47 bombed aircraft dispersal areas, claiming one of the two planes destroyed by the group during the raid.[431]

The raids on the airfields, particularly those around Misawa, dealt a blow to an operation the Japanese Navy had planned, with the Japanese Army, called "Ken-Go." They planned to attack B-29 airfields in the Marianas on a much larger scale than the one mounted by the Japanese Army on May 24. On that raid, nine Sally bombers had attempted to land troops on Yontan Airfield, on Okinawa, but only one of the bombers succeeded in reaching the American airfield and crash landing on it. The dozen special raiding troops on board, however, managed to destroy seven American planes and more than 2,000 drums of gasoline, effectively making the field non-operational for several days.

The Japanese Army lost interest in promoting such missions after this initial raid, but by mid-July the Navy began to plan another using two-engine Betty or Nell bombers to carry 300 soldiers from the Army's 1st Airborne Raiding Group on a suicide mission to destroy airfields on Saipan and Tinian. The attacks of August 9 destroyed the bombers, forcing cancellation of the mission. Although the end of the war was only days away, the mission could have been mounted as one of the last-ditch efforts by the military as peace drew near.[432]

The loss of Lieutenant Rogers at Misawa was balanced by VF-27's shootdown of a Zeke, the only aerial victory over Japan on the 9th. It occurred during the second strike on the airfield at Koriyama by the same groups that flew the morning strike described earlier. This strike comprised twenty-one Corsairs, twenty Hellcats, forty-five Avengers, and ten Helldivers from Air Groups 27, 50, 85, 86, and 88. The target coordinator was the experienced Commander Sherrill of Air Group 85, an important figure in this account.

After a two-hour flight, the strike force arrived over the enemy airfield and Sherrill assigned aircraft revetments holding up to one hundred planes to Air Groups 27 and 50. Excepting four *Independence* Hellcats, the photo plane to record the raid's damage and its escort, a dozen Hellcats and fourteen Avengers from both groups attacked aircraft revetments. As the *Cowpens* Hellcats carried only rockets, they did not make glide-bomb attacks, but came in on the enemy field only one hundred feet off the ground, firing their rockets at enemy planes up close as the remaining planes bombed the aircraft and buildings on the field. After their bomb run, the *Independence* Hellcats strafed the railroad yard and rail station near the airfield while VF-50 returned to the airfield for a second, low-level strafing run, firing their remaining rockets at a chemical factory located near the airfield.

Smoke and explosions during and after the attack, however, made it difficult for pilots to observe the results of their efforts. Air Group 85 Corsairs made a high-angle dive-bomb attack that destroyed four enemy aircraft, but the TBM crews couldn't see any Japanese planes on their portion of the field, and bombed "installations" on the airfield as consolation.

Wasp's Corsairs and Hellcats also didn't carry bombs, only rockets. Not finding any enemy planes during their first attack, both squadrons rocketed hangars and repair shops, as well as some revetments near them, then returned for several strafing runs at low level. Two Hellcats finally found some enemy planes and, using both rockets and machine guns, exploded one fighter and set another on fire, destroying both. Before leaving the area, pilots fired rockets into a railway station at Ononii, then moved on to another rail station, at Nogami, where they found four trains they strafed and rocketed, causing a large explosion. The flight of Hellcats then turned to Iwaki Airfield, where they not only strafed the field but fired rockets into hangars, starting several fires.

Although initially assigned to target hangars at Koriyama, most of the Avengers from *USS Wasp* hit barracks and repair shops on the airfield, as the hangars were already destroyed or extensively damaged. One pilot, who had to make a second run as his bomb wouldn't release, found an undamaged hangar and hit it squarely.

The *Yorktown* sent Corsairs, Avengers, and Helldivers on the strike. The Corsairs dove first, followed by the Helldivers and Avengers, bombing buildings, including hangars, repair shops, and barracks. Two Corsair pilots destroyed an antiaircraft position with direct hits as other pilots destroyed two Willows, potential *kamikazes*.

After finishing at the airfield, the Helldivers and Avengers flew to the rendezvous point for the flight home while the Corsairs went in search of more targets. They found one, the Japan Refining Company, and fired more than twenty rockets into the facility, setting storage tanks on fire. Then, on the way to the rendezvous, they stopped off at Iwaki Airfield, too, firing rockets at hangars and destroying two more Willows.

Reports of Japanese antiaircraft opposition at Koriyama varied from meager to moderate. All the planes on the mission returned, but flak damaged a VT-88 Avenger, hitting it in a fuel tank. The tank was full, however, without fumes that could explode, so the plane remained in the air and returned safely. Two VF-27 Hellcats took on the task of escorting it to the Task Force.

During the flight home, the two Hellcat pilots, Ensigns William Condon and William Sellers, saw a Japanese Zero flying on a reverse course to theirs a few thousand feet below. The enemy plane did not notice the Americans above, "apparently fat, dumb, and happy." The two Americans quickly turned around, dove to gain speed, gave chase, and came up on the Zero's tail. They both opened fire, Condon hitting the engine, which began to smoke, followed by Sellers, who fired a burst that sent the enemy plane down, where it crashed. The two pilots shared the credit for their victory.[433]

Eight more enemy planes went down to American guns during that afternoon and evening. Late in the afternoon, eight *Randolph* Hellcats from VF-16 were covering the radar picket destroyers, about fifty miles from the Task Force, when fighter controllers vectored them to a bogie approaching from Japan. Three pilots intercepted the enemy plane, identified as a Myrt, and bracketed it, two approaching from the left and one from the right. The Japanese pilot evidently saw the pilot on his right and turned left, right into the sights of Lieutenant James McPherson, who opened fire. His rounds set the Myrt on fire, but the Japanese rear gunner on the enemy bomber returned fire, damaging the Hellcat so McPherson had to return to a lower altitude to continue the patrol. One Japanese crewman was able to parachute from the stricken plane before it crashed into the sea.[434]

Another air patrol over the radar picket destroyers intercepted another enemy plane headed for the Task Force. Two Hellcats of VF-6 found the enemy plane, a Kate, flying near the water, probably in an unsuccessful attempt to avoid American radar. As they sped to open fire, the enemy plane began to execute a split-S turn that it never completed, as it crashed into the sea before the American flyers could open fire. Credit for the victory went to the division leader, Lieutenant Herschel Pahl.[435]

Two hours later, two Hellcat pilots of VF-88 each shot down a Grace bomber also trying to reach the Task Force. As eight F6Fs from the patrol were climbing to intercept the enemy, at 14,000 feet they saw the enemy bombers about 5,000 feet above them, headed in the opposite direction. The Navy flyers turned and began to close on the enemy planes, which immediately began to make turns to evade them. Suddenly one inexplicably went into a spin. Four Hellcats pursued, firing at it before it crashed into the sea. The pursuers later surmised that the pilot was inexperienced, not at all uncommon in the Japanese air forces in 1945, stalled the plane during a turn, went into an uncontrollable spin, and crashed. Ensign Leonard Komisarek got credit for this Japanese loss.

As the first Grace spun to its doom, the other tried to escape by diving. The remaining four F6Fs followed it, gaining slowly until they came within firing distance only 500 feet from the ocean. With two fighters on either side, the gunner in the Grace began to fire at the American planes, hitting the engine and wing of Lieutenant (jg) Robert Brown's Hellcat before it made a left turn. It was now lined up for shot by Lieutenant (jg) Robert Appling, who fired a burst from 900 feet that struck the enemy's left wing. The Grace continued its turn and Appling closed to only 150 feet and fired three more bursts. Lieutenant (jg) Brown and the section leader, Lieutenant John Adams, also fired bursts at the Grace. The enemy plane was only 200 feet above the water, with both wings on fire, when it suddenly plummeted into the sea. Appling received credit for the victory and described the shootdown: "I gave him a short burst and whambo—in he went."[436]

About an hour after VF-88 put down these two Japanese planes, VF-86 got one more. Four Hellcats, with four Corsairs from VBF-86, were on patrol when two Hellcat pilots saw a Grace, flying at about 8,000 feet, passing over the radar pickets on the way to crash into a ship of the Task Force. Lieutenant Armind Holderman, who had shot down a Japanese plane on July 28, and Ensign Clifford Gunn, Jr., whom we first met in chapter nine while he was strafing, climbed to intercept and closed with the enemy plane as it reached the Task Force and the ships below began to fire their antiaircraft guns. The Grace began to dive on *USS Wasp*, their carrier, and the pair began shooting at it when it was only 4,500 feet above the *Wasp*. Holderman got in a burst from the side and hit the engine and wing root. Gunn fired next; then both pilots fired together until the enemy plane began to burn. During the action, practically every antiaircraft gun in immediate vicinity of the *Wasp*, as well as from the carrier itself, fired at the Grace and the American pilots attacking it, who braved American flak to shoot down the *kamikaze*. Holderman and Gunn broke off the attack when flames engulfed the enemy plane and they could be sure it could not crash into the *Wasp*. The plane missed the carrier and Holderman received the credit for the shootdown.[437]

At 5:00 PM, four Corsairs from VBF-1 were patrolling over a lifeguard submarine off the coast of central Honshu when a Japanese plane suddenly appeared and dove on the submarine. The Corsairs set out in pursuit, but couldn't get within firing range before the enemy plane, a Judy, dropped a bomb that landed only a few hundred feet from the sub. The report of the action then reads: "The enemy pilot pulled out of his dive and had started a left turn towards the sub when the Corsairs nailed him. Lieutenant [Richard] Wright fired one long and one short burst into the wing roots and Lieutenant (jg) [Eric] Schloer fired a long burst into the fuselage just forward of the cockpit. The Judy flamed, turned over on its back and dived into the sea from 1,200 feet." Both pilots received half a victory credit.[438]

The last American aerial victories of the day went to Ensign J. C. Stires of VF(N)-91 during a dusk combat air patrol over the battleships and cruisers that had bombarded Kaimaishi early in the afternoon and now were returning to the Task Force. *USS Massachusetts*, *Indiana*, and *South Dakota*, with two British light cruisers, *HMS Gambia* and *Newfoundland*, had shelled the Japan Iron Works, the marshalling yards, and barracks in the town for almost two hours early that afternoon, without any Japanese opposition. During the operation, the destroyers *USS Strembel* and *USS Erben* sank small cargo ships and two luggers that had the great misfortune to blunder into the bombardment force.

As dusk gathered, two *Bon Homme Richard* Hellcats, flying over the warships at 10,000 feet, were vectored to a bogie at 3,000 feet to the west of them. The pair dove to 3,000 as the Fighter Direction Officer updated them on their distance from the enemy plane. The last report had it three miles from them, so they began to circle so they wouldn't overshoot their target. When two-thirds of the way through the circle, Stires, who had seriously damaged a Willow on July 25, saw the enemy plane off his left wing and moved toward it. Coming up on its tail, from below, he raised the nose of his Hellcat and opened fire when 200 feet away. The burst hit the underside of the enemy plane, under the cockpit. The Judy pulled up, fell off on its right wing, and went into a spin. Stires followed it down until it crashed into the water below.

Now only 300 feet above the sea, Stires spotted another Judy skimming the water below him, less than a mile off his nose. Pouring on the coal, he overtook the enemy and opened fire from 1,000 feet. The Judy began violent evasive action, never flying more than one hundred feet above the water in an attempt to lose its antagonist. Stires kept up the pursuit, firing multiple bursts into the Judy. The enemy plane began to smoke and when Stires fired a final burst from only 400 feet, the enemy's wing caught fire. By this time, the Hellcat had exhausted its ammunition, so Stires pulled away. The Judy disappeared into the darkness and haze, but as it was one hundred miles from Japan and on fire, Stires received credit for its destruction, as he did for the first plane shot down.[439]

To counterbalance the aerial victories during the combat air patrols, the Task Force also lost four planes that ditched during combat air patrols that afternoon. Fortunately, all the pilots were rescued. An unidentified VBF-88 Corsair pilot had to ditch during a late morning patrol. Lieutenant Marshall Lloyd of VBF-6 ditched early in the afternoon and a destroyer picked him up. Two VBF-94 Corsairs ditched late in the afternoon, but destroyers rescued both pilots, Ensign Earl Neff and Lieutenant (jg) George Lantz.

The VF-16 combat air patrol on which Lieutenant McPherson shot down the Myrt intercepted another Japanese plane about two hours later, after the action just described, but did not shoot it down with unfortunate consequences. Two other members of the patrol, not involved with the Myrt, were flying over the radar pickets at only 5,000 feet. At 2:45 PM, fighter controllers sent them to intercept another bogie approaching the destroyer screen at 26,000 feet. They climbed to intercept and at 14,000 feet spotted a Grace in a high-speed dive toward the destroyers below. The Hellcats turned and followed the Grace down, attempting to overtake it. They could not gain on it, but fired several bursts at long range with no apparent effect. Soon antiaircraft fire from the destroyers forced them to break off the pursuit as the Grace, obviously a *kamikaze*, continued down to crash on the destroyer *USS Borie*, the last ship struck by a *kamikaze* during World War II.[440]

The *Borie* was on station, with three other destroyers, as a radar picket about fifty miles from the Task Force. Japanese planes had been evident for several hours when, shortly before 3:00 PM, a Val approached the American ships from the northwest. It circled around the destroyers and then came in to attack the *Borie* from the stern. As the Val drew near, the destroyer turned to port to fire all guns at the attacker. The enemy plane continued on, however, and crashed into the destroyer's port side, near the mainmast and bridge. A 500-pound bomb it carried passed through the ship and exploded. The plane and bomb destroyed the bridge; damaged the forward guns, radar, and radio communications; and started a number of fires. Damage to the bridge made it impossible to steer the ship from there, so steering passed to the secondary "conn," or steering compartment, in the stern as speed slowed to fifteen knots and damage-control parties sprang into action. Within twenty minutes, the fires were under control and crews of the undamaged guns were back in action as a second Val began an attack, also from the stern. *Borie*'s guns shot this plane down several thousand yards from the ship and shared in the destruction of several more enemy planes that attempted to attack the radar pickets during the next few hours. This *kamikaze* attack left forty-eight men dead, including thirteen who disappeared in the explosion, listed as missing in action. Another sixty-six crewmen were wounded.[441]

Chapter Twelve

ON AUGUST 10, THE JAPANESE ANNOUNCED OVER THE RADIO THAT THEY would finally accept the terms of the Potsdam Declaration, if the Emperor was exempted from the terms of surrender. More than 400 Army Air Force long-range fighters based on Okinawa and Iwo Jima attacked airfields on Kyushu and B-29s bombed the arsenal in Tokyo. The Soviet Air Force was active over the Sea of Japan, attacking shipping and sinking two Japanese destroyers. Navy flyers continued air strikes on airfields ranging from northern Honshu to those near Tokyo. The weather had deteriorated from the previous day, forcing flyers to hit some alternate targets, but American planes still flew 1,215 strikes. The British hit targets near Sendai with 224 attack sorties, while the Americans spread their attacks from Yokosuka to Ominato. Enemy fighters did not make an appearance and the Allied aircraft lost went down to antiaircraft fire. The British sank three freighters and two small cargo ships while U.S. flyers sank three small enemy warships and a few merchant vessels.[442] American flyers also destroyed 150 aircraft on enemy airfields, with some air groups making up to a dozen attack passes on airfields.[443]

~~

The usual sweeps began the day; twenty-one took to the air by 6:00 AM. Twenty-four Corsairs from the *Shangri-La* and *Yorktown* with a dozen *Wasp* Hellcats attacked Kisarazu Airfield. With the exception of one Hellcat carrying several fragmentation bombs, each plane carried only rockets because of the extreme distance they had to fly to reach the field from the Task Force's position off northern Honshu, roughly 300 miles. As the flight crossed the coast, the weather was uncharacteristically clear and they could see Mount Fuji, almost one hundred miles away.

Arriving over Tokyo Bay, the *Wasp*'s Hellcats attacked first and one plane dropped the fragmentation bombs while the rest fired rockets at planes located along the seawall on the west part of the field, bordering Tokyo Bay. After the first pass, they returned to strafe. One pilot blew the tail off a Tabby as others hit some of the fourteen well-camouflaged enemy planes seen in the area. The *Shangri-La*'s Corsairs came next, firing rockets on the first run, then returning for strafing runs that destroyed five enemy planes on the northern part of the field. *Yorktown* Corsairs also struck aircraft along the seawall, destroying five aircraft with rockets, twin-engine Nicks and Franceses, most on the second pass after they reassembled over Tokyo Bay. VBF-88 also hit antiaircraft positions that were putting up intense opposition to their visit.

Air crews expected heavy antiaircraft fire, as the field was considered one of the most heavily defended on the Home Islands. Fire came not only from the field, but also from Yokosuka Naval Base across Tokyo Bay, and from a small island between Yokosuka and the Futtsu Peninsula that also bristled with antiaircraft guns.

After the attack ended, *Yorktown* planes had some rockets and ammunition left and got permission to make a pass a Mobara Airfield, twenty miles northeast of Kisarazu, shortly after 8:00 AM. The ten Corsairs dove on the field, then pulled out hugging the ground to avoid anticipated intense antiaircraft fire that failed to greet them. They sped away. Lieutenant (jg) Verlyn Branham Jr.'s engine began to malfunction, but he reached the sea, fortunately only a few miles away, and ditched about a half mile offshore. He got out of the plane but could not immediately inflate his life raft. As a section of *Yorktown* Corsairs circled above Branham, Lieutenant Harold Greene pulled his own life raft from under his seat and opened the canopy of his Corsair. With his flaps down to slow the plane, he shoved the raft over the side. It landed close to Branham and he inflated it, as well as his own. He threw the escape gear from one raft into the other, and climbed in. Greene then wrote a message telling him that a rescue submarine was on the way to him, placed it in a flight glove inside a pitot-tube cover, and dropped it directly onto the raft! By 10:00 AM, the submarine came into view of the pilots circling Branham, about fifteen miles away. The section leader, Lieutenant David Steele, flew over the sub, dipped his wing to signal he was friendly, and pointed the way to the raft. Within half an hour, Branham was safe and his squadron mates flew home to the *Yorktown*.[444]

Another pilot was less fortunate than Branham when Air Group 87 struck Aomori, almost 400 miles north of Kisarazu, on the north coast of Honshu. VBF-87 attacked the harbor and airfield in the town after a 4:00 AM takeoff from the *Ticonderoga*. There was no antiaircraft fire as some of the fourteen Hellcats bombed and rocketed hangars and buildings on the airfield and others struck the railroad yard in the town. Afterward, the flight reassembled over the bay north of the town and attacked ships. Antiaircraft gunners on the airfield had manned their guns by this time, and fired a moderate but accurate barrage at their recent antagonists. As the planes attacked a small cargo ship, flak hit Lieutenant William Petersen's Corsair. It began to smoke, bailed out at 3,000 feet, and hit the water. He was not seen again by his comrades circling above, nor by a Kingfisher floatplane sent to search for him. Petersen, who had consigned a Jill to the same fate on July 28, was later listed as killed in action.[445]

Fifteen Hellcats and eleven Helldivers from Air Group 87 followed up an hour later, striking dock and rail facilities in the town of Aomori, only a few miles from the Aomori Airfield. On the way to the target, the Task Force ordered four of the F6Fs to provide cover for a rescue submarine, while the remaining planes bombed warehouses and the rail yard in Aomori, adding to the damage done by 20th Air Force B-29s a few weeks earlier. The Hellcats bombed antiaircraft positions, a ferry slip, warehouses, as well as two Sugar Dogs, sinking one. The dive-bombers took out another ferry slip and warehouses, bombed a bridge, and scored a near miss on a cargo ship. An attack on a transport did not damage the vessel, but a Hellcat pilot, Lieutenant Robert Carman, was more successful. Antiaircraft fire was minimal, but one Hellcat received minor damage.

Carman decided to make a lone-wolf attack on the transport missed by the dive-bombers. He scored a direct hit with his 250-pound bomb, fired rockets at a small cargo vessel that instantly blew up before him, then finished this solo performance by strafing a small tanker.

After this main raid, the four Hellcats detached to the sub rejoined and all fifteen fighters visited Misawa Airfield, rocketing and strafing the field, and a few bridges nearby, before returning to the *Ticonderoga*.[446]

Another SubCAP, an early morning flight from VF-27, lost a plane during their search for targets of opportunity. As usual, after several hours circling above the submarine, their relief arrived and they set off in search of targets to attack. They found a small coastal vessel and promptly attacked. The ship fired back and hit one of the planes, flown by Ensign George Van Hagen. He had to ditch through a fog bank that extended down to the surface of the water. He got out of his plane, but the fog prevented his comrades from spotting him. They radioed his position and more *Independence* aircraft went in search of him, locating him that afternoon. A lifeguard submarine picked him up.[447]

∿

The second wave of morning strikes took off around 7:00 AM, fifteen missions targeting airfields, naval bases, and harbors in northern Honshu. Sixteen F6Fs and fourteen TBMs from the *Monterey* and *Bataan* teamed up to hit Aomori for a third time.

Air Group 34 Avengers bombed oil tanks at Nonai, close to the port, with the Hellcats from both ships following them down. Bombs ruptured most of the tanks and they caught fire, spreading burning oil to piers nearby that also caught fire. More attacks followed that destroyed all of them by the end of the day.

The Avengers attacked the transport hit a few hours earlier by Lieutenant Carman and scored two hits on the vessel, leaving it burning and listing. VF-34 Hellcats found seven floatplanes near Futago Hana, but the VT-34 Avengers attacked first, setting two on fire, then the Hellcats followed up, destroying two more. The fighter pilots had a large cargo ship all to themselves, however. They fired rockets and strafed, leaving the vessel enveloped in smoke that rose several thousand feet in the air.

The planes reformed over the bay and attacked more shipping. VF-47 led off the attack on the transport now on fire, scoring two more hits with rockets. VT-34 TBMs followed up with bombing and strafing runs on the vessel. Several bombs landed close aboard the ship and Ensign Donald Vanderzee scored a direct hit on the stern that caused a large explosion. VF-34 then strafed and rocketed the unfortunate transport, firing twenty-four rockets of which more than a third struck the superstructure and amidships. As the flight turned away, the ship was low in the water.

The next stop was a small tanker anchored near a small island, well-covered with camouflage netting. A five-inch gun on the bow fired at the attackers once the raid began, alerting the Americans to the ship's presence. Two VF-34 Hellcats fired six rockets that hit the vessel, creating explosions and fires that also knocked out the gun.

As the Hellcats dealt with the transport, the *Monterey* TBMs pulled away and quickly found some camouflaged floatplanes tethered along the shore of the bay. The Avengers quickly attacked, dropping 250-pound bombs and strafing the enemy aircraft, setting three on fire. Following an announcement of these new pickings over the radio, VF-47 Hellcats turned up and, in the words of *Monterey* crews, "simply cut [the floatplanes] to ribbons." Then VF-34 Hellcats arrived, fresh from their mauling of the transport, to add to the destruction. The result was seven totally destroyed floatplanes left derelict on the beach.

Two *Bataan* Hellcats that had turned back with engine trouble added to the score by bombing and rocketing a factory near Miyako, on the east coast of the main island, but the plant was so well dispersed that actual damage was minimal. Several planes received flak damage from Japanese antiaircraft fire described as moderate throughout the mission, but all returned safely to their carriers.[448]

While pilots from VF-34 and VF-47 had a good day at Aomori, Air Group 87 was attacking the naval base at Ominato, thirty-five miles across Mutsu Bay, losing a plane after the strike. Eleven Corsairs escorted thirteen Avengers to attack the biggest vessel at anchor in the harbor, a large troop transport. The Japanese naval gunners reacted sharply, putting up a barrage described in the mission report as "the most intense antiaircraft fire yet encountered by VT-87." As the planes dove on the harbor, every ship opened fire on them: the old minelayer attacked the previous day by Air Group 16, troop transports, a tanker, and six destroyer escorts, the latter particularly bristling with antiaircraft guns. Guns protecting the airfield and on the shore of the naval base also joined in.

The Avengers scored at least one direct hit on the large troop transport, with a number of near misses that damaged the vessel's hull. VF-87 Hellcats also attacked two more transports but failed to score any direct hits, so on the fight home, they fired their remaining rockets on revetments and hangars on the airfield at Misawa. Over the harbor, flak hit Lieutenant Granville Cowan's Hellcat. Escorted by some squadron mates, he reached open water off the coast and ditched his plane. Other pilots saw him get out of the plane, but he didn't inflate his life raft and soon disappeared in the swells of choppy water, later listed as killed in action.[449]

Farther south, ten Corsairs and ten Avengers from Air Group 6 attacked two airfields in central Honshu. The weather was bad on the east coast of Honshu and the planes had trouble locating a clear target. Visits to four airfields, starting at Yamada, found overcast at all of them, so the strike leader directed the Avengers to head for Matsushima Airfield, north of Sendai, while the Corsairs searched for another target.

The TBMs found about thirty-five enemy planes in revetments on the airfield and bombed them, but practically all were derelicts and they only destroyed one operational plane during their attack. Although there was only light antiaircraft fire, flak hit the Avenger flown by Lieutenant (jg) Joseph Newton during its dive during the second pass on the field. He managed to pull out but the plane was emitting heavy smoke and suddenly nosed down and crashed into Matsushima Bay, killing Newton and his two crewmen, ARM3c Raymond Lee and AOM3c Thomas Shawski.

The Corsairs had better luck than the Avengers. They located a previously unknown field near the town of Morioka, ninety miles north of Matsushima. They went in to attack and no one fired back, so they quickly destroyed ten enemy planes in the open and hidden in trees near the field. Not satisfied with this score and having more rockets to use, they turned to the rail yard in the town of Morioka. Dropping bombs, firing rockets, and strafing, the F4Us destroyed three locomotives and fifteen rail cars, and also damaged the roundhouse and other buildings in the yard. On the way home, they found two trains near Ichinosaki and Yamada and destroyed them both.[450]

Air Groups 1 and 94 shared a mission to strike airfields in the central Honshu area. Unfortunately, the persistent overcast that covers much of Japan during August stymied the twenty Avengers, eight Hellcats, and eight Corsairs. Overcast covered the three airfields investigated, so the groups eventually settled on striking Sakata Harbor, but not before enterprising pilots of VT-94 found an opening over the airfield at Tsuruoka, where they dropped five bombs on the runway and administration building.

The rest of the flight arrived over the harbor at Sakata to find a small tanker, two armed troop transports, and six Sugar Dogs at anchor. Air Group 94 attacked first, followed by Air Group 1. Shore batteries kept up a steady barrage during the raid, described as "meager" to "moderate" by crews. Two of the four *Lexington* Hellcats on the mission bombed and rocketed the troop transports, but without obvious severe damage, while the other two bombed a bridge, damaging it heavily on one end. The Avengers hit dock facilities and warehouses, setting the latter on fire, and bombed the rail yard in the town.

One VT-94 Avenger, flown by Lieutenant (jg) Robert Mullen, had mechanical problems on the return flight and had to ditch near the carrier. Fortunately, plane-guard destroyer *USS John Rodgers* was at hand and rescued the crew quickly.

The Corsairs of VBF-1 made three attack runs on the harbor, getting a direct hit on one of the troop transports near the stern that made a twenty-foot hole in the deck. The Helldivers scored three hits on the tanker—one on the stern, another on the bow, and the third amidships— as some bombed warehouses and harbor installations.

After the Corsairs had strafed the two troop transports, forcing their antiaircraft crews under cover, two flights of Avengers bombed them and scored a hit on the stern of one, on their first pass. On the second pass, they sank a Sugar Dog and went after the transports again, inflicting more damage. The third flight, which had not attacked the first time, bombed a Sugar Dog during the second pass and hit it. One pilot, Ensign John Leslie, bombed the small tanker, hitting it squarely, and it sank in less than three minutes.[451]

Aomori got more attention later in the morning from a sixteen-plane strike by VF-16, one of the twenty late morning sweeps and strikes dispatched by the Task Force before noon. After taking off from *USS Randolph*, the Hellcats flew to Aomori Airfield, which had escaped the direct attention of the early morning attacks. The F6Fs dived on the field, targeting antiaircraft positions, hangars, and the few planes visible in revetments. Bombs planted on revetments probably destroyed several aircraft, but pilots couldn't be sure. With hangars also set on fire, some Hellcats aimed for antiaircraft guns on the south part of the field. Their 250-pound bombs hit some positions, silencing them, but this was not enough to prevent Japanese antiaircraft gunners from hitting Ensign Marilyn Voss's Hellcat, destroying the hydraulics and setting the plane on fire. Voss kept the plane in the air until he reached the coast, and made a good water landing about five miles off the coast, south of port of Hachinhoe. Within two hours of his hitting the water, a Kingfisher from *USS Pasadena* rescued him.

The Hellcats were not done harassing the Japanese, so they dropped bombs and fired rockets at a small highway bridge near Misawa. Their aim was good, as they destroyed a span of the bridge. With rockets still left over, the flight found and attacked a railway bridge and strafed fishing boats in the town of Yamada farther down the coast as a finale.[452]

Another flight of Hellcats had taken off from *USS Ticonderoga* at the same time as VF-16. On reaching their target, Misawa Airfield, they dived on hangars and aircraft dispersal areas, with pilots assigned specific targets based on current reconnaissance photos. On the first attack run, VF-87 dropped 1,000-pound bombs, bombing hangars and dispersals. One hangar blew up and bombs nicely covered the dispersals. Following the initial pass, the Hellcats made two more passes, strafing more dispersals and setting two, possibly three, aircraft on fire, as well as thoroughly riddling a Zeke, a Betty, and a Topsy. The latter did not burn and could not be claimed as destroyed, but VF-16 certainly did not leave them in flying condition. Most of the other planes seen on the field were the usual wrecks or dummies.

Japanese antiaircraft batteries were in action during the raid, firing scattered bursts that caught one Hellcat during its dive. Lieutenant (jg)

Andrew Sawyer never pulled out and crashed on the enemy airfield, killed instantly. The squadron reported: "This was a particularly bitter loss to the squadron, coming in the course of a well-planned and executed attack during the final stages of the war."[453]

Another fighter was lost when the *Yorktown*, *Shangri-La*, and *Wasp* teamed up again to attack the airfield at Niigata, on the west coast of central Honshu. Carrying a mix of 500-pound bombs and 260-pound fragmentation bombs, sixteen VF-88 Hellcats (with four more from VF-86 for the photo flight) and twenty-three Corsairs from VBF-85 and VBF-86 arrived to find the airfield covered by overcast. The strike leader ordered *Yorktown* and *Wasp* pilots to hit the harbor at Niigata, while the Corsairs from VF-85 stayed overhead as high cover.

The Hellcats from VF-88, armed only with rockets, dove on ships offshore, facing medium and light flak described as "very heavy" by returning pilots, even heavier than the flak they had found at Yokosuka Naval Base. Their target of choice was a sizeable cargo ship underway, headed toward the docks. The planes fired more than eighty rockets at the ship, scoring sixteen hits that heavily damaged it, but as the planes headed home, it was still above the waves. The intense flak damaged six planes and shot down a seventh when Lieutenant (jg) William Tuchima's Hellcat went down in flames.

The flight leader told the damaged Hellcats to return to the *Yorktown*, with an escort of two more, and then the remaining six Hellcats dove on more ships and damaged two armed merchant ships. One ship caught fire and another exploded. A small tanker also got a good riddling from machine-gun fire. Heading for home, two pilots strafed some luggers, sinking two of them.[454]

VBF-86 dove after the *Yorktown* planes. One flight spotted a small cargo ship in the Shinano River, which flowed through the city, and hit the ship with two bombs and some rockets; the ship immediately began to sink by the bow. After this dive, the Corsairs fired rockets into some oil storage tanks, then strafed luggers and small vessels in the Sea of Japan, just offshore of the city.

The second section of VBF-86 Corsairs decided to try to attack the original target, Niigata Airfield, now in the clear. They found few aircraft on the field so bombed, rocketed, and strafed buildings on their first pass, then returned to strafe and claimed two planes as probably destroyed. These pilots reported that the antiaircraft fire from the city of Niigata was the most accurate they had yet seen, but fortunately the gunners did not shoot down any Air Group 86 planes.

Reforming after these attacks, VBF-86 headed east toward their carrier, but stopped at Shiogama Airfield, north of Sendai. Making low-level passes, they bombed and rocketed the field and parts of the town near it. Matsushima Airfield, also north of Sendai, got some attention from two pilots after they rocketed a factory in Shiogama. Although the fifty planes visible on the field were mostly wrecks, they did spot a Betty and a fighter that they pummeled with their machine guns.[455]

After covering the initial stages of the attack at Niigata, the VF-85 flight leader decided to head east, to find a suitable target to attack. The flight found the airfield at Sendai and the aircraft factory next to it, on the east coast, clear. There were no airplanes in sight on the airfield, but despite moderate antiaircraft fire, they dove and dropped 500-pound bombs on the aircraft factory and hangars on the airfield. Then, strafing the area, they riddled a number of aircraft fuselages of new, uncompleted aircraft. Moving on to Matsushima Airfield, they strafed this field as well, although few planes were in sight.[456]

The action continued as before noon, the *Randolph* dispatching eight Corsairs and ten Helldivers to attack Aomori once again, aiming for the ferry slips. When they arrived over the harbor, thick, black smoke was billowing from the burning oil storage tanks at Nonai, destroyed by Air Group 34 early that morning. There were no ships in the harbor, so the planes attacked docks and piers. Antiaircraft fire was evident, with one battery plugging away at one Helldiver as it plummeted down to bomb a ferry pier, fortunately without getting hit itself. The SB2Cs bombed all three ferry piers in the harbor, scoring hits on all of them.

VBF-16 Corsairs fired rockets into antiaircraft positions, including the persistent antiaircraft battery, warehouses, and piers during the attack. Although this diminished flak, it was not enough to prevent AA fire from damaging one Helldiver. The pilot, Ensign Keith Moore of VB-16, found that his engine was not giving him full power and reported he would have to ditch. He flew north to the Tsugaru Strait, and then found he could probably reach a lifeguard submarine off the east coast of Honshu. He nursed the plane to the vicinity of the sub and made a good water landing, and the sub soon rescued him and his radioman, ARM3c Charles Lux. This was the third water adventure for the pair since early July. They had already gotten wet after a takeoff crash during training before the Task Force reached Japan, and flak shot them down during the July 14 strike on Hakodate, as recounted in chapter four. After the attack at Aomori, Corsairs escorted the damaged Helldiver toward home while the remainder looked for trouble elsewhere. These pilots rocketed a railway bridge near Misawa before they returned to the *Randolph*.[457]

The last morning strike on Kisarazu Airfield also left another plane in the drink. Two squadrons completed the mission: eleven Corsairs from VBF-88 and eleven Hellcats from VF-86, but mechanical problems left only five of the *Shangri-La* Corsairs to fly the mission. This reduction in force led the Task Force to change VBF-85's mission to a SubCAP. After flying over the lifeguard submarine for a few hours, the arrival of their relief permitted them to do some rocketing and strafing at barracks in the town of Iioka before they headed home.

At Kisarazu, *Wasp* Hellcats attacked aircraft revetments, while the *Yorktown*'s planes bombed hangars and any enemy planes they could see parked on the runways and taxiways. VF-86 dropped bombs and strafed the field's northern revetments on their first pass, then returned to fire rockets and machine guns at hangars and repair shops. VBF-88 fired rockets into hangars from 500 feet, setting two on fire, also locating Nicks and Dinahs in the open to rough up. The enemy planes didn't burn when hit, so they could only be claimed as damaged. As was expected, the flak encountered was intense, but all planes began the flight back to their carriers.

On the flight home, VF-86 Hellcats rocketed and strafed a train and a factory in the town of Ohara. The train exploded and the factory caught fire. Two VBF-88 Corsairs, leading the flight home, made a stop at the airfield at Mobara. While they were strafing the airfield, antiaircraft fire hit both planes. One of the Hellcats, flown by Lieutenant Lee Horacek, suffered severe engine damage and ditched about ten miles offshore of

Mobara. As several squadron mates circled above him, he got into his raft to await rescue. It came in the shape of a lifeguard submarine that picked him up within three hours of his water landing.[458]

~⚬~

Shortly after the two late morning strikes recounted above had taken off, the saga of Lieutenant Coumbe that began in the last chapter came to a happy ending. Following a short nap during the night, he found himself a mile off the fishing village of Nakanosawa, about seven miles east of his location the night before. Spying a beach fronting a wooded area near the town, he paddled to shore at about 3:30 AM. He pulled his raft into the woods, covered it with foliage, and then dozed until 6:00 AM, when *Essex* Corsairs flying to Hachinhoe Airfield for an early morning sweep passed overhead in an effort to locate him. The pilots spotted a flare he fired, and then saw him waving on the beach. They dropped a raft to him, radioed the Task Force that a rescue should be mounted, then continued on their way to Hachinhoe, where they found strafed the ten derelict aircraft on the field.

Coumbe launched his raft, climbed in, and paddled into the bay against the current, eventually reaching a point about 300 yards from the beach. He stayed there for about three hours, until the effort to maintain his position against the current became too much, then returned to the beach. Shortly before noon, rescue planes arrived in the form of two Kingfishers launched from *USS North Carolina* that morning. Their rear armament was removed and both pilots flew with an empty rear seat to carry Coumbe when, with luck, they picked him up. Eight *Essex* fighters escorted the floatplanes and the flight arrived at Coumbe's last reported location at about 11:45 AM.

As the rescue planes began to circle overhead, one flown by Lieutenant (jg) Clinton Wear came in low to drop a life raft to Coumbe, but turned too sharply and crashed into the bay offshore before he could do so, killing him. His squadron mates speculated that the raft became tangled in his controls, causing the crash.

Coumbe left his own raft on the beach and began to swim out into the bay just as the Kingfisher flown by Lieutenant (jg) Raphael Jacobs landed and taxied to within fifty yards of the beach. Jacobs threw a line from the cockpit for Coumbe to grab. As Coumbe swam closer, Jacobs stood on his seat, placing one foot outside the cockpit, on the wing. The water was very choppy and the Kingfisher was rocking up and down. Suddenly Jacobs lost his footing and fell into the sea. The throttle of the Kingfisher moved forward as this was going on and the plane began to move forward, away from both men in the water. As it did so, guns from Ominato Naval Base, across the bay, began to fire at the floatplane and two shells landed within fifty yards of the two pilots in the water. The wayward Kingfisher still served a useful purpose, as it drew the enemy shells away from the men in the water as it moved away. Several planes from the fighters circling above flew over to Ominato to strafe these guns. One pilot, Lieutenant William Farnsworth, who described a dogfight in chapter eight, later reminisced that he thought the Japanese antiaircraft gunners were aiming directly between his eyes as he strafed a ship in the harbor.

The second Kingfisher now landed and the pilot, Lieutenant Almen Oliver, taxied over and picked up Coumbe and Jacobs. After it took off, the remaining Corsairs, still orbiting overhead, came in and strafed the Kingfisher, which eventually sank. Oliver and his two passengers arrived at the *North Carolina* at 6:15 that evening, both survivors in good shape. The Corsairs in the escort flight returned to the *Essex* after seven and a half hours in the air.[459]

The fifteen early afternoon strikes targeted airfields, with 117 aircraft from Air Groups 27, 50, 85, 86, and 88 working together again to strike Koriyama and Yabuki Airfields. Occasional bursts of Japanese antiaircraft fire encountered during the mission managed to knock down one American plane.

Air Groups 27 and 50 went in to attack first. Hellcats from VF-50 fired rockets into antiaircraft positions to suppress enemy fire so the *Independence* planes could bomb and strafe. They made direct hits on gun positions and some buildings. Torpedo 50 bombed aircraft seen under trees in earlier photographs, but none of them caught fire. Air Group 27's

Hellcats and Avengers bombed and strafed repair shop buildings, and then VF-50 Hellcats came back for second run, strafing parked aircraft, destroying three planes.

Yorktown's planes attacked next. The Corsairs strafed aircraft on field on their first pass, then returned for four more passes. They destroyed three planes, fired rockets into barracks and the chemical factory near the airfield, and also destroyed a locomotive in the marshalling yard. Bombing Eighty-Eight Helldivers hit hangars and barracks on the airfield, along with the chemical factory, and their radiomen strafed the barracks during the run. The torpedo bombers looked the field over for viable targets since so much was already destroyed from earlier raids and attacked any targets they could find. As the mission report stated, "the scramble [for targets] began." They found and bombed almost a dozen barracks, damaging five, and also hit hangars. One of the latter, possibly a fuel dump, exploded. The chemical factory and rail yards near the field also got their attention, and on the return flight *Yorktown*'s Corsairs made a strafing pass on Harano Airfield, but found only dummy aircraft.

Wasp's planes attacked Koriyama last. They first dive-bombed hangars, aircraft dispersals, and barracks, but couldn't see many results because of smoke although they did claim one aircraft destroyed. Japanese gunners evened the score, however, when they shot down the Hellcat flown by Lieutenant (jg) Warren Anderson as he dove on the field. With a wing on fire, he was able to bail out, but his parachute streamed and didn't open. On the second pass, the Hellcats looked for hidden aircraft. One pilot found a heavily camouflaged plane and blew it apart with rockets while others hit antiaircraft positions and the marshalling yard near the field. A few pilots made another pass to strafe the field for a third time.

Air Group 85's aircraft bombed, strafed, and rocketed Yabuki Airfield, about fifteen miles south of Koriyama. The Corsairs destroyed only three planes, as few were on the field, concentrating mostly on buildings, warehouses, and the rail yard in the town itself. The Helldivers bombed buildings and repair shops on what crews reported was "a routine strike." Torpedo 85 bombed aircraft revetments, saturating them with 500 pounds although very few planes were visible. An interesting footnote occurred on the flight home. As they neared the radar picket destroyers, crews had a grandstand view of a *kamikaze* attack on the destroyers and saw one ship shoot down a diving Japanese plane. Fortunately, the attack did not damage any American ships.[460]

———

Another large strike went to airfields around Sendai: fifteen Corsairs, twenty-nine Hellcats, and forty-seven Avengers from Air Groups 1, 6, 31, 49, and 94. The American attackers, for the most part, encountered very little antiaircraft fire while attacking these fields. In fact, the only VT-49 Avenger damaged was hit by .50 caliber rounds from another American plane.

At the beginning of the strike, VF-49's aircraft, detailed to cover the attacking aircraft, discovered a previously unknown airfield between the two target airfields. By flying at low altitude they discovered about seventy enemy fighters cleverly hidden under camouflage nets and foliage up to a mile from the main landing strip. The Hellcats pounced and made more than fifteen runs on this unexpected cornucopia of enemy aircraft. Planes made a wing-over at the end of one attack run to begin another, all at very low level. Bombs hit enemy fighters and biplane trainers on the first pass; then the strafing began.

Two VF-49 fighters that didn't get word of the target bonanza continued on to Obanazawa, but finding no enemy planes there, flew on to Jimmachi Airfield just as Air Group 94 finished their attack, as we shall see. The pair took up the attack, burning eight twin-engine planes, eight biplanes, and a Zeke destroyed. The total bag for VF-49 was twenty-nine enemy planes destroyed and another fifteen probably destroyed.

At Mamurogawa, some of the Avengers of VT-49 joined in attacking this field, but the traffic over the field was so dense that the strike coordinator told some of the torpedo bombers to join VF-49 at the "gold mine" a few miles farther south. The planes that stayed at Mamurogawa had difficulty in spotting camouflaged planes on the ground at the altitude at which it was safe to drop their 500-pound bombs, but they did manage to flush a two-engine bomber, another twin-engine plane, and two fighters, all destroyed.

Air Group 94 started at Mamurogawa, sending four Hellcats low to spot targets. Then the Avengers and all the Hellcats bombed the field before heading to their next stop, Obanazawa. Not finding any aircraft here, they continued on to Jimmachi, where they found aircraft, including many training biplanes, parked on runways and by hangars. After the first bombing run, all planes returned for strafing and rocket attacks. An F6F pilot strafed a Baka suicide bomb hidden two miles from the main airfield. After hitting these airfields, where the TBMs racked up eight enemy planes destroyed and the Hellcats ten, most planes headed home—but three Avengers made a side trip and bombed the rail yard in Yamagata while a division of the fighters struck the training airfield near the town, destroying four more training biplanes.

Air Group 1 also bombed Mamurogawa as the Corsairs of VBF-1 hit hangars and the village of Aramachi near the airfield. Following the first pass, the F4Us formed a traffic circle over the field, to facilitate individual pilots locating heavily camouflaged enemy planes. On the first strafing pass, machine-gun fire poured into brush near the field and set four planes on fire. More was to follow as the Corsairs made repeated strafing runs for the next hour, nailing enemy planes hidden with a variety of guises from tree-top level, without any flak to disturb them. The camouflage techniques included hiding planes under brush, camouflage nets, and trees, while some had roofs built over them to resemble houses. These techniques, while certainly clever, were ultimately to no avail, as when viewed from the air, it was apparent to American pilots that something wasn't quite right. A low-level inspection and a burst of machine-gun fire into the suspicious area often resulted in a fire, revealing the fraud. The Avengers made only one pass on the airfield, bombing a wooded area that probably contained enemy planes, but crews could not be certain they had destroyed any, although up to dozen were later reported burning. The strike ended with seventeen enemy planes completely destroyed.

Air Group 31 struck both Matsushima and Matsuda Airfields. At Matsushima, the *Belleau Wood*'s Avengers destroyed the power plant and a barracks as the Hellcats turned to railway cars near the field when they couldn't find any planes on the airfield to attack. The dozen aircraft then moved on to Masuda Airfield, where they bombed barracks, repair shops, and hangars, setting the last on fire and demolishing a barracks. Following these two strikes, most planes headed back to the *Belleau Wood*, but two Avengers with bombs that had hung up at Masuda looked for another target and were rewarded by the discovery of yet another previously unknown airfield about five miles northwest of Masuda. The pair bombed a hangar and destroyed a fighter parked next to it.

Air Group 6 heard the report of the new airfield while near Mamurogawa and flew over to investigate, following up on VF-49's introduction. They made four separate attacks, the first with bombs and subsequent runs with rockets and machine guns, aiming at any aircraft they could find camouflaged in revetments or hidden in groves of trees. Their attacks ended with twenty-eight of the Japanese planes on the new field destroyed.

Flak hit Ensign John Petersen's Corsair during the raid and he made a forced landing close to the new airfield. Petersen got out of the plane and waved to the planes above to signal he was OK. A VT-6 Avenger tried to land to pick him up, but there was not enough open ground for it to do so and Japanese civilians soon captured him. They tied him up, stripped him bare, then gestured they would burn him alive. A stoning, followed by a beating, left him unconsciousness. Later, Japanese soldiers arrived, tied him to a motorcycle, and forced him to run alongside it until he reached a Japanese military base. Fortunately, the war ended a few days later and he survived, to be repatriated to the United States a few weeks later.[461]

Chapter Thirteen

The fleet retired to refuel following the August 10 strikes, with much of the British Pacific Fleet moving south for maintenance and upkeep. The only British warships remaining off Japan were the battleship *HMS King George V* and the carrier *HMS Indefatigable*, with cruisers and destroyers as escorts.[462] The appearance of yet another typhoon forced the Task Force to maneuver to the southeast to avoid it, preventing more air strikes until August 13, when the typhoon moved away.

Bad weather had forced the cancellation of B-29 raids planned for the 11th, but the press misinterpreted the pause as a cease-fire order in preparation for an armistice. Rather than risk the impression that peace negotiations had failed, President Truman ordered a temporary halt to B-29 operations on the 11th, not to resume until August 14.[463]

Also on August 11, senior Japanese commands outside Japan received word of the Emperor's intention to surrender.[464] Intercepted radio messages, however, made it apparent that many senior Japanese commanders had no intention of following a surrender order. This resulted in the resumption of B-29 raids on August 14, preceded by Task Force 37 and 38's strikes on the 13th. In the meantime, Soviet forces had invaded Korea and the Japanese-held portion of Sakhalin Island, north of Japan, on August 12.

On the 13th, the Task Force had received news that a Japanese surrender was imminent.[465] Long-range fighters of the Army Air Force attacked airfields in Korea, shooting down sixteen Japanese planes. Navy strikes continued and airmen set out on missions as they had in the past, to hit airfields in the Tokyo area and as far north as Sendai, as poor weather prevented attacks on many intended industrial targets. Flying almost 1,000 attack sorties, American and British flyers destroyed 254 enemy planes on the ground, as no Japanese fighters rose to meet them. Attacking planes made up to a dozen passes on airfields, an unusual circumstance given the usual heavy response from Japanese antiaircraft guns in the past. Japanese aircraft did, however, mobilize to attack the fleet throughout the day. Fighters flying combat air patrol over the fleet shot down eighteen of the attackers, and a fighter returning from a strike accounted for another. Intense antiaircraft fire drove off the few planes that reached the Task Force.[466] During the day some units of the fleet began to assemble to act as an occupation force to meet the hoped-for surrender of the Japanese.[467]

The early morning saw the first shootdown of the day, a Myrt attempting to sneak into the Task Force. Only a few minutes after taking up position over the radar picket destroyers, fighter controllers ordered four Hellcats of VBF-16 to intercept an enemy plane approaching the Task Force at 5,000 feet. Climbing to 6,000 feet, they found thick clouds, including "mattress" overcast, between 1,000 feet and 4,800 feet. Informed that the enemy plane was descending to 1,500 feet, the flight split into two pairs. One remained at 6,000 feet as the other flew below the cloud cover. Lieutenant (jg) Eldin Murray and his wingman flew under the clouds. Once under the clouds, Murray saw the enemy plane off his left wing a few miles away, flying away from him. Using the speed built up as the pair descended from 6,000 feet, they closed with the enemy plane, identified as a Myrt carrying a torpedo, the pilot apparently unaware of their presence. Murray flew to one side of the enemy plane, looked it over, then got on its tail and opened fire. His rounds hit the left wing near the fuselage and started a fire. He fired again into the fuselage and the Myrt suddenly exploded. Murray had to pull up sharply to avoid hitting the debris and the enemy plane did a half roll and plunged into the sea. Murray reported: "One Myrt splashed."[468]

Following this initial shootdown, an early morning strike became the highlight of the day: the targeting of two electric plants in Tokyo. It was the first mission since July 28 that used almost all of Task Force 38 air groups. Fourteen groups took part, the exception being Air Group 27, as *USS Independence* had sailed for Iwo Jima the day before. The carrier returned to the Task Force on the 14th, just in time for its aircraft to take part in the last strike of the war, early on August 15.[469]

The strike was composed of 101 Hellcats, sixty-eight Corsairs, 147 Avengers, and 105 Helldivers, all briefed to attack Electric Factory No. 1 and Electric Factory No. 2 in Kawasaki, southwest of central Tokyo. Factory No. 1 was a primary strategic target, a manufacturer of radio tubes. The plan was for planes from Task Groups 38.1 and 38.3 to attack Factory No. 1 and those of 38.4, Factory No. 2. Typical Japanese summer weather, however, conspired to prevent all but a handful of planes from bombing either plant. Groups spent between a half hour and an hour circling the total overcast in the Tokyo area, waiting for a break in the clouds that really never came. There was very little antiaircraft fire as the groups circled Tokyo until the target coordinator ordered them to hit targets of opportunity, as most did.

Air Group 1 circled for an hour before receiving the order to hit another target. As they turned to fly to the Japanese International Aircraft Factory in Hiratsuka, a few miles north of the Shibaura factories, a hole in the overcast suddenly appeared and the group leader ordered his planes to attack the factories. The Helldivers of VB-1 didn't hit the two factories, but were able to bomb the waterfront of Kawasaki, a few miles away from them, where they hit three oil storage tanks that caught fire, a warehouse, and a factory. VT-1's Avengers had better luck, eight planes bombing through one of the holes that appeared in the overcast over the Shibaura plants. Six Corsairs of VBF-1 dove on the primary target, Factory No. 1, using the Tama River nearby as a reference point. Two pilots actually saw the factory and hit it with their bombs. Impressions of the flak that met the attackers over Kawasaki varied from moderate to intense. Rounds hit one Avenger that had to ditch inside Tokyo Bay. The pilot, Lieutenant (jg) Lee Pasley and his gunner, ARM3c John McCarthy, exited the sinking aircraft as the squadron commander of VT-1, Lieutenant Robert Ramage, dropped a life raft to them before leaving the scene. No fighter could circle the flyers because of the flak positions that ringed Tokyo Bay, and they both became prisoners of war for a short time until repatriated the next month.

The only other plane lost by Air Group 1 went down during takeoff, when the Helldiver piloted by Ensign William Rebman lost power after takeoff and ditched near the destroyer screen. Rebman and his radioman, ARM3c J. Fox, both got out of the plane before it sank. *USS Maddox* picked them up.[470]

Twenty-two planes from Air Group 6 also managed to bomb the primary target, despite the weather, attacking the two factories after Air Group 1. After circling Tokyo, the Avengers spotted the target and reported this to the strike commander. He ordered them to return to the rendezvous point and lead the group's Corsairs and Helldivers, and planes from other groups, back to the target. On arriving at the rendezvous point, no other planes were evident, so the Avengers returned to the Shibaura plants and attacked them, with their fighter escorts, braving intense antiaircraft fire to do so. Four Hellcats and six Avengers bombed Factory No. 1 while eight Corsairs and four TBMs bombed Factory No. 2. All carried 1,000-pound bombs for this raid.

The Helldivers of Bombing Six, low on fuel, received the order to hit the secondary target, the International Aircraft Factory in Hiratsuka, where they scored eight hits with 1,000 pounds on the factory and the arsenal next to it. Two others who lost the aircraft factory in clouds bombed Yokosuka Naval Base and Hiratsuka town.[471]

Lexington's Air Group 94 was the third group that actually bombed the Shibaura factories. Ten Corsairs continued the search for the primary targets and found another hole in the overcast through which they could bomb. With no time to coordinate their attacks before clouds again covered the two factories, these Corsairs bombed from all directions, with nine crews actually seeing their bombs hit Factory No. 1.

VT-94 attempted to find the Air Group 6 planes, ordered to lead them to the factories from the rendezvous, after circling Tokyo, but missed them and used radar to find the primary target. A break in the overcast rewarded them as they arrived over the two factories. The Avengers followed the Corsairs in high-speed dives that reached about 300 miles per hour. The pilots' aim was good; ten 1,000-pound bombs hit Factory No. 1 and five hit Factory No. 2. Japanese antiaircraft gunners around the factories met them, as they did the other two air groups attacking the Shibaura factories, with moderate to intense flak that was well-aimed, although it did not shoot down any of the *Lexington*'s planes.

Like Air Group 6, Bombing Ninety-Four's Helldivers ran low on fuel during the extended circling before they found an open target. Told to bomb the International Aircraft Factory at Hiratsuka with four of the Corsair escorts, they scored a few hits on the plant but also bombed another factory in the vicinity.[472]

Two more air groups found and bombed the International Aircraft Factory. Most of the Hellcats of Air Group 49 bombed and rocketed buildings in the factory complex. Despite haze, crews saw three bombs hit installations, causing explosions and starting fires. Lieutenant Robert Foltz, however, could not line up properly at the factory and attempted a second run, but found the factory completely covered by overcast. He flew to Yokosuka Naval Base and while over the base spotted a submarine underway in Tokyo Bay near the base. He attacked it, always a difficult task on a vessel underway. His bomb landed about seventy-five feet from the vessel. Some of the VT-49 Avengers, with a Hellcat, attacked the Air Technical Arsenal north of Yokosuka, dropping bombs and firing rockets that hit several buildings. A few other Avengers decided to cross Tokyo Bay and bomb Kisarazu Airfield, as visibility there was somewhat better. They bombed and strafed the field, damaging at least one plane. A VF-49 Hellcat had mechanical problems on the flight home and had to ditch near the radar picket destroyers. A destroyer, *USS Brush*, rescued the pilot, Ensign William Henwood, who had shot down an enemy plane on July 24.[473]

Planes from *USS Belleau Wood* also bombed the Hiratsuka aircraft factory, encountering little antiaircraft fire, too. Ten Hellcats and five Avengers dropped their bombs from about 3,000 feet, but couldn't see results because of thick haze. The remaining fighters and bombers hit the arsenal in the town, and a factory in Yoshida, a few miles to the east.[474]

The thirty-eight planes dispatched from *USS Ticonderoga* came close to the primary targets, bombing docks and a factory in Kawasaki. After circling over Tokyo for half an hour, the Hellcats, Helldivers, and Avengers bombed docks in the vicinity of Yokohama and what they believed was an electronics factory in Kawasaki, but heavy cloud cover, made it impossible for crews to explicitly say where their bombs landed.

Although Japanese antiaircraft guns did not open up on them until they attacked, Air Group 87 did lose one plane in a collision while circling over the Tokyo area. Ensign Giovanni Brega's Avenger pulled up underneath another plane and the propeller of the latter cut off the tail of his aircraft. Brega and his two crewmen bailed out and landed in Tokyo Bay, close to the Kawasaki shore. Each man deployed his life raft and dye markers. The trio floated in the bay with the current slowing pushing them toward the eastern shore. After more than six hours floating in the heart of the Empire, an Army Air Force Catalina appeared overhead, beginning one of the most spectacular air crew rescues of the Pacific War.

The Catalina, from Rescue Squadron 4 based on Iwo Jima, had just arrived on station over the radar pickets when a lifeguard submarine radioed that three Navy air crew were in a raft inside Tokyo Bay. The plane, with the radio call sign "Playmate 97"and piloted by 1st Lieutenant Charles Oates and 2nd Lieutenant John Ree, set out for Tokyo with two *San Jacinto* Hellcats, flown by Lieutenant (jg) Anthony Royster and Ensign Harold Azbell, from a SubCAP patrol as escort. Approaching Tokyo Bay from the south, the plane flew east of Tsurugi Point, then over the eastern shore of lower Tokyo Bay to avoid the large number of antiaircraft guns around Yokosuka Naval Base on the western side of the bay.

Locating the raft in the middle of the bay, midway between Kisarazu Airfield and Yokohama, the plane landed as a Japanese destroyer, underway from the naval base, began to fire at it. The two *San Jacinto* Hellcats flew over and began to strafe the enemy vessel. Painted white to facilitate identification by American forces, the Catalina was not hard for Japanese gunners to spot. Shore batteries and a motor-torpedo boat also joined in firing at the seaplane, on the bay for a very long thirteen minutes, as it picked up Brega and his crew. The torpedo boat approached the plane at high speed, shooting the whole time with intense machine-gun fire that fortunately did not hit the Catalina.

Once the Navy flyers were aboard, Oates began to dump fuel to lighten the plane for takeoff as the destroyer and torpedo boat continued to head toward him. The two Hellcats above continued to strafe the destroyer as the latter fired a round that landed underneath the Catalina's wing. Oates immediately stopped dumping fuel and took off, northwards toward Tokyo. At this point the destroyer was about an uncomfortable 2,500 yards away.

After reaching 7,000 feet, circling over the bay to gain altitude, the plane turned south, flying over the eastern shore of the bay again while antiaircraft guns on the warships and the shore continued to fire at it. The Catalina flew south to Iwo Jima, landing safely with the three passengers who returned to the *Ticonderoga* a few days later. Admiral Halsey radioed his personal thanks to the crew of Playmate 97 for their "magnificent performance."[475]

Of the other eight air groups flying this strike, three hit airfields as secondary of alternate targets. Air Group 16, assigned an airfield as their secondary target, eventually found Miyakawa open. During the first pass, Corsairs, Helldivers, and Avengers dropped 500-pound bombs on hangars and aircraft revetments. Crews could not see the results, but photos show at least one hangar hit. There was no antiaircraft fire and all planes returned home safely.[476]

The airfield at Tateyama got the attention of two air groups: 50 and 86. *Wasp's* Corsairs didn't find any aircraft, but hit a large seaplane hangar, although several of the new "Tiny Tim" rockets they fired failed to explode. A light cruiser anchored on the north side of Tokyo Bay, along with several other ships in the bay, fired a fairly heavy barrage at the planes, but did not hit them. TBMs also bombed the field, using enormous 2,000-pound bombs that inflicted serious damage to workshops and possibly damaged the only two planes seen on the field. The Helldivers bombed warehouses, as well as a lighthouse and radar station near the field, when clouds suddenly appeared over the airfield and spoiled their approach. The warehouses, at least, suffered considerable damage.

Bombs from Air Group 50 Hellcats destroyed a hangar and seriously damaged a barracks on their first pass at Tateyama. The Avengers also destroyed a hangar and several repair shops, and left a barracks burning as the fighters returned for a second strafing pass on the barracks. The most notable aspect of the mission occurred on the flight home. Radar on one Avenger picked up a large return signal on his scope that became stronger as the flight approached it. When the planes broke through overcast into the area of the strongest return, they found not a flight of Japanese fighters, but a flock of seagulls diving on a school of fish.[477]

Air Groups 34, 47, and 83 bombed factories as the targets of opportunity. Air Group 83 hit a factory, and a dam, in what may have been the town of Tomi Hama, southwest of Tokyo, meeting very little antiaircraft fire. Their attack, however, left a column of smoke 1,000 feet high. The Hellcats and Avengers of Air Group 47 bombed another factory near Atsugi, when it became visible through the overcast. The attack, made through moderate antiaircraft fire, started fires inside the factory area, but the poor visibility made positive identification of the target impossible. *Monterey's* aircraft chose another factory and rail lines, also possibly near Tomi Hama, encountering little flak. Because of heavy cloud cover, the best crews could say was that their bombs landed in the area of the target.[478]

Air Group 85's aircraft flew over to Sagami Wan, to see if the submarines seen by one of their pilots on July 30 in a bay near Shimoda Ko, mentioned in chapter ten, were still there. They eventually found two subs still anchored and, without any opposition, the Corsairs, with some Helldivers and Avengers, bombed the subs, sinking one and damaging the other. The remaining bombers targeted docks and warehouses in the town of Shimoda and luggers in a cove, inflicting general damage. VT-85 suffered an operational loss when the engine of Lieutenant Richard Paland's TBM stopped on the flight back to the carrier, forcing him to ditch the aircraft. (Paland had sunk a freighter on July 15, as described in chapter five.) The crew succeeded in escaping the plane before it sank. Paland and AMM3c Harry Mandville were rescued by a destroyer, but unfortunately ARM3c James Shirley drowned before he could be picked up.[479]

Air Group 88 also attacked targets along the west coast of Sagami Wan. Corsairs struck small cargo ships and luggers in Inatori Harbor, then flew on to Shimoda, hitting some more small vessels. Bombing Eighty-Eight hit warehouses and a factory in the town and strafed small ships in the harbor, while the TBMs also hit buildings and a bridge. Both groups reported very little antiaircraft fire on the mission.[480]

Besides the major raid on the Shibaura factories, twenty other strikes and sweeps took off from their carriers before 8:00 AM. Eight Corsairs from VBF-1 flew a sweep to airfields on the Chiba Peninsula, after they found their assigned fields near Mito Airfield completely overcast. They started at Katori Airfield, near Kashima, making four passes on hangars, barracks, repair shops, and what appeared to be five operational fighter planes among the twenty on the field that were mostly wrecks. With bombs and rockets, the F4Us set a hangar and two repair shops or barracks on fire and damaged the five fighters. Moderate antiaircraft fire hit the plane flown by Lieutenant (jg) Charles Moxley, who was involved in the aerial melee on July 24, as he pulled out from one pass. The plane crashed near the field, killing him.

Undeterred by this loss, the flight flew on to Miyakawa Airfield. The only planes on the airfield were wrecks, or "duds," so the Corsairs fired rockets into a hangar before their last stop, Naruto Airfield, where they made one strafing pass on the field, finding the aircraft there to be wrecks as well.

Another Corsair went down as the flight reached the *Bennington*. Ensign John Lundgren ran out of gas and ditched for the second time in a month, near the carrier before he could land. The plane-guard destroyer *USS DeHaven* rescued him.[481]

Air Group 16's Hellcats visited Tateyama, their briefed target, a few hours after Air Groups 50 and 86 hit the field. Before this, however, they attacked the airfield at Mobara, the only field they could find open in the heavy overcast that covered the Tokyo area. They bombed hangars, barracks, and aircraft dispersals through thick haze that made it impossible to see the results before their second stop at Tateyama. Here visibility was no better, with haze covering this field, so the Hellcats fired rockets into the hangars and were rewarded with fires.

Antiaircraft fire at Tateyama was intense, as it was earlier in the morning, and Japanese gunners downed a Hellcat. During their last dive on the field, two pilots saw a plane crash into Tokyo Bay near the airfield. After pulling out, they flew over to investigate and saw an oil slick in the water at the scene of the crash. The pilot of the lost Hellcat was Lieutenant James McPherson, who had shot down a Myrt only four days earlier, as described in chapter eleven. Unfortunately, he was killed in action.[482]

Japanese aircraft continued to try to reach the Task Force throughout the morning. Before 11:00 AM, fighter controllers vectored a defensive combat air patrol flying at 25,000 feet, two *Shangri-La* Corsairs and two *Wasp* Corsairs, to intercept a bogie, identified by fighter controllers as a Nick bomber cruising at 28,000 feet. The four climbed to meet the enemy plane and the two VBF-86 pilots, Lieutenants (jg) Elbert Swinden and Lewis Farmer, sighted the Nick when they reached 27,000 feet, off their right, about three miles distant. The Nick saw them and started to climb, and the four American planes gave chase. Three of them could not climb above 29,000 feet, but Swinden's Corsair could and overtook the Nick as it leveled off at 32,000 feet. He then climbed 1,000 feet higher to make a pass on the Nick from above and the side. Swinden found his guns would not work, as the ammunition had frozen in its boxes at the high altitude. Swinden maneuvered to force the Nick to dive and succeeded. He followed the enemy plane down as the rear gunner took potshots at him and directed the other three pilots to the enemy plane. Farmer reached it first and fired a burst that hit the port engine of the bomber and shot pieces off the starboard wing. According to the action report, "The Nick went down to the deck and finally splashed," and Farmer got credit for the kill.[483]

Around the same time, the fighter director ordered four Corsairs of VBF-85, flying at 25,000 feet over the radar pickets, to investigate an enemy plane flying from the west toward the Task Force. Spotting the enemy plane at about 29,000 feet four miles away from them, the flight climbed to 32,000 feet. One pilot, Ensign Wallace Moessmer, then made a pass at the enemy, another Nick, from the rear and hit its left wing. The enemy plane turned right and started to dive as Lieutenant Douglas Dok fired a burst with the only gun working on his plane. Both pilots followed the Nick downward, almost to the deck. As they reached lower altitude, a second gun on Dok's Corsair began to function and both pilots made runs at the sides of the enemy, to avoid the rear gunner, firing bursts into the fuselage and cockpit. Their fire eventually took its toll as the Nick rolled onto one wing and crashed into the sea. Each pilot received a half victory credit for the shootdown.

Almost an hour later, the other two members of the VBF-85 patrol also shared a victory. Vectored to a bogie flying at 16,000 feet east of the destroyer line, they soon "tallyhoed" a Grace about 2,000 feet below them, heading east toward the Task Force. The pair attacked from nine o'clock high, with Lieutenant (jg) Peter Hopkins firing a burst. The enemy plane turned into them and Hopkins and his wingman, Ensign Howard Wilbern, both fired at it. The Grace began to slowly spiral down toward the sea as Wilbern followed the plane down, close enough that flames burned the wingtips of this Corsair. The pair shared the credit for the shootdown.[484]

———

Two dozen more strikes and sweeps took to the air between 9:45 AM and noon. Less than half an hour after VF-16 hit Tateyama, another squadron attacked the field, the latter having the dubious honor of being one of the few airfields not covered by heavy overcast that morning. Eight Hellcats from VF-88 hit the field after finding their assigned airfields totally covered by mattress. Pushing over from 11,000 feet, the planes made a rocket attack on hangars and any aircraft they could see on the field, although the latter were most likely wrecks. During the pullout, antiaircraft gunners' aim was as accurate as it was during the VF-16 attack a few hours earlier and hit Lieutenant Wilson Dozier's F6F, blowing a wing off the plane. It immediately crashed into Tokyo Bay, killing him instantly. Antiaircraft fire also damaged two other planes that returned to the *Yorktown*. The five undamaged planes proceeded to the town of Katsuura, where they rocketed and strafed a factory, before returning to the carrier.[485]

VBF-85 swept airfields in the Kasumigaura area, hitting Yatabe Airfield first. During their first pass, pilots dropped 500-pound bombs and fired rockets at Japanese planes they were lucky enough to find on the airfield, destroying seven. Coming back for a second pass, despite moderate antiaircraft fire, they then strafed the field. Enemy fire, however, hit one Hellcat's engine and the pilot, Ensign John Chapman, had to make a water landing in Kasumigaura Lake. He got into his life raft, unharmed, and was taken prisoner. Turning to the seaplane base at Kashima, the flight dropped a single bomb, then strafed and rocketed the base before heading home.

After passing over the radar picket destroyers on the return flight, Lieutenant Richard DeMott and his wingman, Lieutenant (jg) Roy Bean, came upon a Jill bomber flying toward the Task Force. It suddenly flew out of clouds only 1,000 feet away from DeMott, so he immediately closed and fired a burst, setting the enemy plane's wing on fire before it flew back into a cloud. When it reappeared, Bean then got on its tail and fired, setting the port wing on fire just as DeMott came in from starboard and fired another burst. The Jill went down to the sea and crashed. Both men shared the credit for the aerial victory.[486]

Air Group 31's Hellcats took off just before noon to fly a sweep of airfields early but ran into intense, medium flak that caused two planes to ditch. Sixteen F6Fs arrived at Tsukuba West Airfield, near Yatabe, around 1:00 PM and found operational aircraft to destroy. Pilots dropped bombs on hangars and strafed aircraft during the first pass on the field, which destroyed two twin-engine planes that burned and damaged more. Some of the intense flak reported damaged the wing of a Hellcat that turned for home with a squadron mate as escort. It eventually ditched near the *Belleau Wood* and the plane guard *USS Brush* picked up the pilot, Lieutenant George Shimeck, unhurt. The remaining fighters made six more strafing runs on the field, despite the antiaircraft fire, and set six more planes on fire with rockets and machine-gun fire. The fourteen Hellcats then turned their attention to Kasumigaura Airfield, making a single pass on the airfield, firing rockets and strafing a row of aircraft lined up on the field, both single and twin-engine types. Only two burned, as the remainder were likely "duds." Flak greeted the attackers here, as well, and damaged one plane, so the flight turned for home with the engine of the damaged Hellcat smoking. The pilot, Ensign Arthur Tarabusi, made a water landing near the radar picket destroyers, one of which rescued him.[487]

A portion of the strike, VF-49 took off at the same time as VF-31, hitting Tsukuba West shortly after VF-31. The strike had attacked Koga Airfield before this, where they found camouflaged planes to burn, hidden in wooded areas surrounding the airfield. *San Jacinto*'s pilots didn't fall for dummy planes laid out on the field as a diversion. Half the Hellcats made a low-level strafing attack on the field while the others remained overhead as top cover. There was very little antiaircraft fire on the first pass, so the fighters high above were soon released to attack Tsukuba West. Those remaining at Koga made fifteen more low-level strafing runs on the airfield, most on planes parked in the woods. When the attackers left, their fragmentation bombs, rockets, and machine guns left fourteen planes burning, both single-engine and twin-engine.

The Hellcats that attacked Tsukuba West strafed camouflaged planes hidden in trees, where pilots claimed twenty single-engine and twin-engine enemy planes destroyed. One of the pilots found a locomotive after his last pass and strafed it, causing it to explode. The higher score here than that compiled by VF-31 is difficult to explain. They could have found more enemy planes to strafe by flying lower, enabling pilots to spot well-camouflaged planes hidden in less obvious places.[488]

The early afternoon's action began with the interception of more enemy planes by fighters flying combat air patrols over the radar picket destroyer line. Beginning at 1:00 PM, seven air combats took place within the next four hours.

The first occurred when fighter controllers told four VF-86 Hellcats to intercept a bogie approaching the Task Force. Two of the Hellcats couldn't maintain the climb during the interception, but Lieutenant (jg) Jesse Hopkins and Ensign John Trycinski did, continuing to climb and eventually reaching 32,000 feet. Here they leveled off, then began to descend slowly until Trycinski spotted two enemy planes, Graces, flying in tandem below, toward the fleet. At 18,000 feet, Trycinski took on one Grace and fired from 1,000 feet. He scored hits and the Grace caught fire, rolled over, and dove straight down, exploding into pieces when still 5,000 feet above the water. At the same time, Hopkins had attacked the second Grace. Coming in on its tail, he fired two bursts as he closed, killing the pilot. The enemy aircraft began to smoke and started a slow spiral. A wing caught fire before the plane hit the water and exploded.[489]

At 1:30 PM, eight VF-16 Hellcats patrolling over the radar picket destroyers received orders to intercept a bogie approaching from the

Empire. Three of the planes responded and spotted the enemy plane, immediately identified as a Grace, flying at 15,500 feet. One pilot, Ensign John Ritter, got on its tail first and made two firing passes, followed by the other members of the flight: Lieutenant Eugene R. Hanks and Ensign John F. Spaulding, who also shot at the enemy plane. Parts of the tail flew off from the machine-gun burst they fired. Ritter then closed with the enemy and fired a burst from very close range and the Grace exploded, forcing Ritter to pull up sharply to avoid debris. The enemy plane then spiraled down. At about 5,000 feet, the pilot jumped but his parachute did not open, as the plane continued on to the sea below.[490]

The next enemy plane shot down fell to the guns of a VF-1 radar picket combat air patrol that intercepted a Judy intent on wreaking havoc on American warships. While cruising at 12,000 feet at 1:45 PM, fighter controllers directed the planes to climb to intercept an enemy plane twelve miles away. At 19,000 feet, the pilots saw a Judy dead ahead and above, diving on the radar picket destroyers below. When the Japanese pilot saw the Hellcats approaching, he pulled out of his dive and turned northeast, then climbed to evade them. Dropping their auxiliary fuel tanks, the Hellcats gave chase. After twenty miles, the Judy began to dive and, at 7,000 feet, flew into some nearby clouds as the Hellcats drew near. Lieutenant (jg) Winston Gunnels got the plane in his sights about 1,500 feet ahead of him and opened fire. Ten short bursts hit the wing and engine; smoke began to billow from the Judy and small bits flew off as it disappeared into the clouds. The four Hellcats followed, some flying above the clouds, another below them. After thirty seconds, the enemy plane came out of the clouds, no longer smoking. The pilot flying below the clouds, Lieutenant (jg) Charles LePage, opened fire, setting the plane on fire again. As he repositioned his plane for another attack, two unidentified Corsairs cut in front of him, but LePage kept after the Judy as it entered more clouds. After flying through the cloud, LePage emerged to see the Judy enveloped in flames. LePage got in another burst, as did the two Corsairs, just before the Judy hit the drink. LePage received credit for the victory.[491]

As these shootdowns were taking place, the early afternoon strikes took off, despite the fact that it was becoming increasingly likely that the war would end very soon. Planes from only ten air groups were involved, seventy-three Hellcats and fifty-three Corsairs without any bombers. The fleet had obviously decided to reduce operations in anticipation of the end of hostilities.

Air Group 6 sent three Hellcats and seven Corsairs to Nagano Airfield. There was no antiaircraft fire as planes attacked the airfield and the aircraft factory next to it. Corsair pilots destroyed seven planes with rockets after bombing a nearby aircraft factory, and one Hellcat pilot strafed six enemy planes in revetments, setting two biplanes on fire. Another F6F pilot also bombed the aircraft factory, while the third bombed the roundhouse in the railroad yard in the vicinity. Then two of the Hellcats fired rockets at two different locomotives, setting one afire and blowing up the other.

The Corsair flight leader, Lieutenant Marshall O. Lloyd, described the mission:

We rendezvoused seven Corsairs and three Hellcats and proceeded to Mito on the East Coast of Honshu. . . . We arrived over the target one hour and forty-five minutes after takeoff. No AA or enemy opposition was encountered during the 125-mile approach over land to the target. I decided that our bombs would do more damage to an aircraft assembly plant near the field than on the airfield as the field had already been hit earlier in the day. [In two attacks by Hancock fighters earlier in the day, pilots claimed a total of thirty-two planes destroyed at the field.] A bombing run was made from 18,000 feet during which the Corsairs used diving brakes. The assembly plant was under one roof and the first eight bombs dropped were direct hits on the roof. Large explosions and much debris flew into the air, but no fires were observed after the attack.

We rendezvoused north of the of the field at 8,000 feet and proceeded to look the airfield and revetments over. I split the flight into two divisions of five each and made a strafing run on the revetments. My division took the revetments on one side of the field and Lieutenant [George] Pyne's took the other. There were fifty or sixty revetments around the field and many had two or three training planes in them.

Strafing runs were carried to a low altitude as there was no AA [anti-aircraft fire].

I again rendezvoused the flight and made a rocket attack on the railroad yards in the town of Nagano. Each pilot picked his own target and fired four rockets on this run. After the attack, two large, raging fires were burning; the roundhouse had collapsed, a locomotive was steaming, and fifteen to twenty railway cars were burning. A large storage tank was also strafed, with no observable results. We made the attack toward the field so we could make a strafing run on the planes on our pullout.

We rendezvoused and were preparing for another attack on the field when Ensign [Curtis] Weaver spotted four trucks stopped on the highway south of town. I ordered a right-hand pattern and we made several strafing runs on the trucks. No fires were observed.

By now, the pilots had all spotted targets and were calling me for permission to attack. Permission was given and during the next ten minutes pilots strafed targets of opportunity. I called for a rendezvous south of the field and we made another split strafing attack on the revetments.

We had been over the target for about forty minutes by then, so I rendezvoused the flight and returned the same way we had approached.

All planes returned safely to the *Hancock*.[492]

⬥⬥

Fighters from four air groups flew a joint sweep of airfields that afternoon: Air Groups 50, 85, 86, and 88, whom we have met flying together several times already. Lieutenant Commander Cleo Dobson of VF-86 was the target coordinator. After takeoff and assembly, the squadrons split up to attack different airfields upon arriving over Cape Oarai, about seventy-five miles northeast of Tokyo.

Dobson took VF-86 to Katori Airfield. Medium-caliber antiaircraft fire was moderate as half the sixteen Hellcats on the mission fired rockets and dropped their 250-pound bombs on hangars and workshops on their first pass. The other Hellcats did the same on aircraft revetments. On the second pass, all planes rocketed and machine-gunned twenty-five planes parked on the field, many of which were apparently dummies, although pilots claimed two as probably destroyed.[493]

Dobson ordered VBF-85 to strike Kasumigaura Airfield, which they did in an initial dive-bombing and strafing attack, followed by more strafing runs, while encountering little antiaircraft fire. Besides damaging hangars, *Shangri-La* pilots claimed six aircraft destroyed. After finishing here, they stopped at the seaplane base in Kasumigaura, where they fired rockets and their machine guns at buildings on the station, as no aircraft were on the field.[494]

The eight Hellcats contributed by Air Group 50 started at the airfield at Miyakawa. Armed only with rockets, they fired at hangars since no planes were visible on the field. Turning to Naruto Airfield, when they arrived planes from Air Group 87 were already working the field over. Neither field offered much resistance.

Hellcats from VBF-16 had reached Naruto first, the first stop on their afternoon mission. They bombed hangars and revetments on their first run, then fired rockets and machine guns at revetments on the second, but could not see any readily apparent results. *Ticonderoga* pilots of VBF-87 then arrived at Naruto at about the same time as VF-50, it being the second airfield they attacked on the mission. They only strafed the field with rockets and machine-gun fire, as they had expended their bombs on the airfield at Mobara, not reporting any observable results at either.

The Hellcats of VF-50 were glad to join the action at Naruto after leaving Miyakawa. On their first attack they fired rockets into aircraft revetments and were gratified to see two aircraft burn, classified as destroyed. On the second run, they strafed eight aircraft on runways, with VBF-87 Hellcats, but concrete results were elusive.[495]

Yorktown's fighters, carrying only rockets, hit Yatabe Airfield, strafing camouflaged aircraft on their first strafing run, but none burned as Japanese gunners fired a moderate barrage at the attackers. On this pass, Lieutenant David Steele's Corsair lost much of the fabric covering one wing. As it tore off, Steele thought flak had hit the aircraft. After he readily determined the cause, pilots slowed the speed of subsequent dives to prevent a recurrence. Climbing to 10,000 feet, they made another dive on the field, again strafing planes on another part of the field, but again none caught fire.

Getting little satisfaction from these strafing runs at Yatabe, the flight flew off to investigate a few other airfields in the area. Overcast covered most of them, but they finally found Hyakurigahara Airfield, near Utsunomiya, ripe for an attack with a number of planes in revetments on the south side of the field. Diving out of the sun to affect the aim of anti-aircraft gunners who were fairly accurate, the sixteen Corsairs and three Hellcats fired rockets and their machine guns throughout their dives. Lieutenant Steele dove, despite the damage to the wing of his plane, and fired a rocket at one enemy plane at low altitude, destroying it completely. The other planes also strafed at very low level and strafed some cleverly camouflaged planes, but none burned, so claims of aircraft destroyed were limited to Steele's victim.

Besides flak, pilots also encountered barrage balloons tethered at one end of the airfield, an unusual hazard at Japanese airfields in the Home Islands that summer. *Yorktown* pilots simply flew through them, assessing that the small size of the balloons, similar to small weather balloons, would not permit them to carry cable strong enough to damage the aircraft.

All planes returned to the *Yorktown*, but had to circle over the radar pickets for about forty minutes while *Yorktown* combat air patrol dealt with a *kamikaze* attack at 5:20 PM.[496]

—◆—

The last aircraft loss of the day was a Corsair that went over the side of the *Wasp* while landing in the early evening. The pilot, Lieutenant Edward Ruane, returning from a combat air patrol, was quickly rescued by a destroyer. The Japanese, however, continued to lose more planes attempting to reach the fleet.

The downing of enemy planes continued throughout the afternoon and into the early evening, as Japanese pilots continued to try to sink an American ship. Late in the afternoon, VBF-87 destroyed two more enemy planes over the Task Force. A flight of eight *Ticonderoga* Hellcats, flying at 20,000 feet, received the order to intercept a bogie approaching, very fast and low, from the east, not from Japan as expected. Diving to 5,000 feet to pick up speed, the enemy plane would be difficult to see among the thick clouds and rain showers that reduced visibility to only a mile. The Hellcats eventually saw the enemy plane, a Jill, carrying a bomb underneath, when it was about forty miles from the Task Force. The Japanese pilot dropped his bomb when he saw them and poured on the coal to escape. The Hellcats did likewise. Lieutenant William Hemphill got within firing range first, behind the plane, and fired. His rounds hit home and the Jill caught fire at the wing roots. It dove for the water and the other Hellcats got in a few shots before it hit the water, but the victory credit went to Hemphill.

After this action, the flight climbed back to 10,000 feet to continue their patrol when fighter controllers informed them of another bogie heading for the fleet from the same area as the first. Turning toward it, the Hellcats found the enemy, a Judy this time, flying at 2,500 through the heavy clouds. Ensign Robert Butcher, on his first day as a combat flyer, got on the Judy's tail and fired at the cockpit. It turned slowly to the right and crashed into the ocean as other members of the flight also fired at it. Butcher got the credit for the kill.[497]

Shortly after 4:00 PM, American pilots stopped another potential *kamikaze* from reaching the Task Force. Within minutes of being catapulted from the deck of *USS San Jacinto*, Lieutenant (jg) Jack Gibson, who had shot down a Frank on July 24, downed a Judy ready to dive on the British Task Force. Gibson later described the event:

As soon as the three planes of our scramble CAP were airborne, we received orders to leave the Task Force screen and intercept bogies closing from the northwest. I had just picked up my flaps and started to climb when I saw an enemy plane go behind a cloud about a mile ahead, . . . at an altitude of about 2,000 feet. I immediately tally hoed and started in pursuit. Before I could get close to machine-gun range, two VF [fighters] from another air group made passes on the same plane, but both overshot and were in no position to immediately resume their attack. I closed rapidly and began to fire into the plane from dead astern. In the meantime, he went right down to the water. The only evasive maneuver the enemy pilot tried was skids. He would

Some of the types of Japanese aircraft encountered by the Task Force in the summer of 1945, labeled with their American code names, on an airfield in the South Pacific in 1944.

The view of the *USS Essex* as seen by a radioman in a Helldiver, July 1945.

The Japanese naval base at Kure under attack by American naval aircraft in the spring of 1945. A similar scene, with flak bursts covering the harbor, greeted flyers of the Task Force who attacked the base over several days in July.

A Helldiver of VB-88 lands on the carrier *Yorktown* after one of the raids on Kure on July 24.

An American aircraft, hit by Japanese antiaircraft fire, on fire as it goes down near Kure during the raid of July 28.

The plane in the previous photo explodes as it hits the ground. The plane and its crew are not identified.

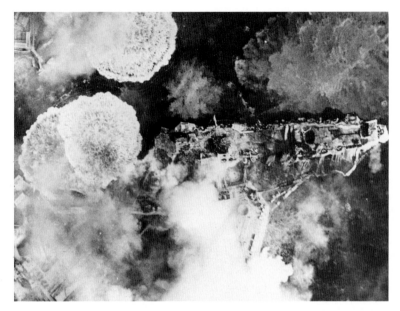

One of the Japanese aircraft carriers moored at Kure under attack during one of the raids of July 24.

Lieutenant Commander Arthur Maltby (R) and his radioman, of VB-85, examine damage to their Helldiver after the July 30 raid on Kure.

The Japanese carrier *Aso* under attack at Kure.

The Japanese heavy cruiser *Tone* under attack at Kure on July 24. American naval planes sank the cruiser that day.

American planes bomb a light Japanese cruiser, either the *Oyodo* or *Aoba*, at Kure on July 28.

The Japanese carrier *Amagi* sunk at Kure during the raids of July 24.

American bombs straddle the Japanese battleship *Haruna* at Kure on July 28. The vessel sank the same day.

A Helldiver of VB-83 flies past Mount Fujiyama following one of the strikes flown on July 30.

A Chinese War Correspondent interviews Ralph Koontz (R) of VF-88, who ditched on July 14, several weeks after the ordeal.

An American submarine on lifeguard patrol off the coast of Japan, about to pick up an American flyer, inside the circle, during July 1945.

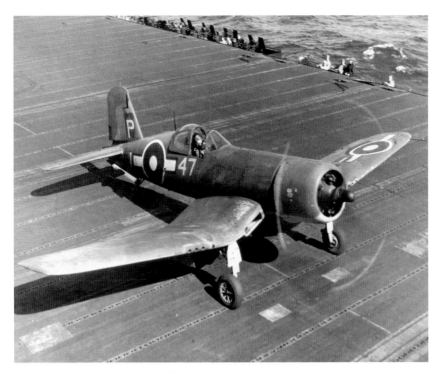

A British Corsair lands on the flight deck of an American carrier, August 1945. Mechanical problems, damage from enemy fire, and low fuel reserves led many aircraft to land on the nearest carrier during combat operations.

The gun layer of a 40mm antiair-craft gun on the *USS Yorktown*, August 1945.

USS Cowpens, the light aircraft carrier, that was home to pilots and air crew of Air Group 50.

Flight deck personnel cover a Helldiver with foam after it crash landed into a five-inch gun turret on the *USS Lexington* following a strike on August 13.

Carriers and destroyers of Task Group 38.4 maneuver off the coast of Japan, August 1945.

A Corsair of VBF-1 takes off from *USS Bennington* for one of the strikes flown just before the Japanese surrender in August 1945.

A *kamikaze* aircraft heads for the sea near *USS Wasp* after Lieutenant Armind Holderman of VF-86 shot it down over the Task Force during the air attacks of August 9.

The plane in the previous photo hits the sea just near the bow of the carrier.

A Japanese suicide plane, a Zero, shot down attacking the Task Force, August 1945. In this photo, a vertical stabilizer on the tail has been shot away.

The Zero shown in the previous photo just before it plunged into the sea.

Japanese aircraft hidden in camouflaged revetments on the airfield at Hachinhoe in northern Honshu in the summer of 1945. More aircraft may have been hidden in the tree line in the distance.

Hellcats from VF-85, carrying drop tanks to extend their range, in flight just after the surrender, August 1945.

The characteristic mushroom cloud from an atomic blast towers over the Japanese city of Nagasaki after the second atomic bomb attack on that city on August 9, 1945.

Lieutenant Thomas Reidy describes his victory over the last Japanese plane shot down by an American flyer, on the afternoon of 15 August.

Admiral John Tower with four repatriated prisoners of war from Air Group 85. Left to right: Ensign John Chapman of VBF-85 and Ensign Edward Dixon, VF-85, both shot down before the summer strikes, with Lieutenant John Dunn, also of VF-85, the last man taken prisoner of war on August 15, 1945, and ARM3c Robert Hanna of VB-85, shot down over Kure on July 24.

Pilots of Air group 31 celebrate VJ Day in the ready room of *USS Belleau Wood*, 15 August 1945.

skid violently . . . [causing] his plane to raise thirty or forty feet . . .
then I would overshoot. Finally, after expending about 300 rounds of
ammunition into the Japanese plane, it began to blaze. I closed, firing
all the way and then he dove straight into the water. As . . . [the plane]
crashed, a violent explosion . . . [took place], apparently caused by the
bomb he was carrying under the starboard wing. My plane was [then]
covered in oil, water, and debris as I flew over the Jap.

Fortunately, the explosion caused little damage to the Hellcat and
Gibson returned to the *San Jacinto* to claim his victory.[498]

A half hour later, four VF-34 Hellcats were patrolling over the Task
Force as the low-altitude patrol when fighter controllers informed them
of an enemy plane that had eluded patrols over the radar pickets, nearing
the carriers. Climbing to intercept, they spotted the bandit off to their
right, five miles away and a few thousand feet lower, heading directly
for the carriers. The enemy pilot saw them at the same time and jinked
around to keep the Hellcats in the dark about where he would attack.

The Japanese pilot made a turn to port just as Lieutenant Oscar
Rupert got on his tail after gaining on the enemy in his dive. Rupert
fired a burst from 900 feet that hit the enemy fighter, a Frank, in the
wing roots, starting a fire. After firing two more bursts, the speed from
Rupert's dive caused him to overshoot the Frank. As he did so, the Japanese pilot turned and went into a dive. One of the other pilots, Lieutenant
(jg) Lowell Wessels, turned inside the Frank and followed him down. At
about 1,500 feet, the Frank, still burning, leveled off and Wessels, on its
tail, "gave it a 300-round dose of .50 cal," scoring hits in the fuselage and
cockpit. The Frank dropped its right wing and crashed into the ocean,
leaving only an oil slick. Rupert received credit for the kill.[499]

The last Japanese victim of the day to fighters of the fleet went down
over the radar pickets, shortly after 6:00 PM. Two Hellcats and two Corsairs from Air Group 88 were preparing to land on the *Yorktown* at the end
of their patrol. Still at 23,000 feet when the fighter controller told them
to intercept a bogie approaching the Task Force at 34,000 feet, the flight
set out in pursuit and climbed. The two Hellcats, flown by Lieutenant
Malcolm Cagle and Lieutenant (jg) Raymond Gonzalez, whom we have

met before several times, dropped their auxiliary fuel tanks after Gonzalez reported he made visual contact with the enemy plane, an Irving. Gonzalez took the lead and caught up with the enemy plane at 34,000 feet. Pulling up the nose of the F6F, he fired a burst from the extreme distance of 1,000 feet. His aim was dead on as his round set the Irving's left wing on fire. He fired a second burst and the enemy plane exploded. Two other planes fired some bursts at the enemy plane as it fell toward the sea, but Gonzalez got credit for the victory.[500]

Victories over Japanese planes continued into the early evening, after sunset, as VF(N)-91 made the final contributions to the tally of planes destroyed that day. Lieutenant Robert Kieling and Ensign Philip McDonald took off from the *Bon Homme Richard* at 5:45 to fly a dusk combat air patrol that continued after sunset at 6:30 PM.

Shortly after the pair arrived over the radar picket destroyers, fighter controllers ordered them to investigate unidentified planes about twenty-five miles away, approaching the picket line. Kieling soon spotted two Nicks flying below the Hellcats. The latter overtook the two enemy planes and took up position to attack, with Kieling lined up on the side of the left-hand enemy and McDonald the right.

From a distance of 750 feet, Kieling fired a burst that blew off the Nick's canopy and set an engine fire. The Japanese plane dived, with Kieling in pursuit, and crashed into the water. Four of the Hellcat's guns jammed during the encounter, but Kieling fired with those still functioning.

While Kieling dispatched one Nick, McDonald was at work on the other. He fired from 800 feet, setting the enemy plane's right engine on fire. His second burst hit the fuselage, and the enemy plane turned over and spiraled into the sea below.

The pair began to climb to regain altitude and continue their patrol when McDonald saw a Frances three miles dead ahead and only a few hundred feet below them. He attacked from behind, again setting an engine on fire. As the Frances started to descend, Kieling fired a burst. The enemy continued downward; a crewman jumped and opened his parachute a scant one hundred feet above the water, and then the plane crashed, leaving only a fire on the surface of the water.

Immediately, fighter controllers informed both pilots of another intruder. They soon found another Frances a few hundred feet above them, flying in the opposite direction. McDonald, in a better position to attack first, got on its tail and fired a long burst of machine-gun rounds. Kieling then fired a short burst from his two functional guns and McDonald followed up with a second. The Japanese pilot immediately bailed out and the plane crashed into the ocean.

Japanese flyers were not done trying to reach American ships that evening. Fighter controllers soon reported a fourth vector that led them back to the scene of their first victories, where a fire was still burning on the water. Here they saw yet a third Frances, also flying above them, on McDonald's side. He made a head-on attack that set the port engine of the enemy plane on fire, then turned sharply and got on its tail, just as Kieling did so. They both fired again before the Frances disappeared into the clouds, on fire. They could not locate it again, but during the search, McDonald spotted a third Nick flying across his patch, a few miles ahead. He took up pursuit, got into position behind the enemy aircraft, and fired a burst that set the left engine on fire. A second burst left the right engine alight. The Nick turned and flew into a cloud, only a hundred feet above the water, and disappeared.

McDonald then saw two more blips on his radar and, excited by his victories, began to close for more until he realized he was over the coast of Honshu and Lieutenant Kieling ordered him back to the radar picket line. These air combats lasted about forty minutes, all after sunset. McDonald was credited with four enemy planes destroyed, Kieling with one.[501]

Chapter Fourteen

REFUELING TOOK PLACE ON THE 14TH AS PREPARATIONS WENT AHEAD for continued strikes against Tokyo-area airfields on August 15. After intercepts of Japanese messages on the 11th gave Washington the impression that the Japanese military was not yet ready to surrender, despite the Emperor's stated wish to do so, President Truman ordered a resumption of strategic bombing attacks on Japan on August 13. B-29s resumed attacks the next day with 410 bombers that hit two arsenals and a marshalling yard.[502] By the 14th, senior Japanese commanders knew that surrender was imminent, including the commander of Japanese air forces.[503] During the night of the 14th, Army officers in Tokyo made an unsuccessful attempt to stop the Emperor's recorded announcement of the surrender, scheduled to be broadcast on the morning of the 15th. The news of the imminent surrender filtered down the chain of command and Japanese Army and Navy squadrons protecting the Home Islands were aware of it. On the 14th at an airfield south of Tokyo, the commanding officer announced the imminent surrender, ordering them to accept the Emperor's decision. The flights of Japanese fighters on the morning of the 15th that met the final missions of American and British naval aircraft, and the air battles that ensued, were a reaction to this news, a final opportunity for Japanese pilots to engage the enemy.[504]

Slightly more than one hundred planes from American carriers took off at 4:15 AM, just after the British also launched a strike. A second American strike soon followed as the attempted revolt by Japanese Army officers was collapsing in Tokyo. The first strikes ran into more than fifty Japanese fighters that rose to oppose them in air battles that Task Force 38 later described as "the most determined air opposition since the Okinawa operation."[505] VF-88 lost the four Hellcats described in chapter one and *USS Shangri-La* lost a Corsair, as we shall see. The British lost an Avenger and a Corsair.[506]

The first strike had already attacked their targets and the second was in the air when CINCPAC's order to "Suspend air attacks" came at 6:15 AM. The Task Force radioed the recall order and cancelled all offensive air operations. Although the Task Force steamed away from Japan after the last aircraft landed on their carriers, Japanese aircraft attempted to attack the fleet throughout the day, but all were repulsed without damage to any Allied ships. After receiving the message from CINCPAC to "Cease offensive operations against Japan" midmorning, *USS Missouri*, flagship of Task Force 38, sounded her whistle and siren for one minute to signal the end of the war.

Ultra intercepts of Japanese Navy communications on the 15th revealed that planning of military operations continued. The air battles that morning likely ensued from this, along with the reluctance of many Japanese military men to accept the surrender, resulting in air battles to get some "last licks" against the enemy.[507]

Eleven of the thirteen sweeps and strikes that took off by 4:55 that morning either attacked a target or tangled with enemy aircraft before receiving word of the cease fire. Two missions in the first wave, and all the missions that took off after 5:20 that morning, were recalled before they reached their targets.

VBF-1 arrived at Hyakurigahara Airfield at 5:50 AM, with time for a full course of bombing and strafing before receiving the recall order, spending about an hour over the target. They became the targets of intense flak as they did so, but all twelve Corsairs returned safely.

Before reaching the airfield, one division of Corsairs took a few minutes to attack a long train chugging along between the cities of Asahi and Saruta. The train ran into a tunnel before the planes got within range, but they fired rockets into one end of the tunnel that blocked it. Continuing on to Hyakurigahara, the dozen F4Us initially bombed and strafed a portion of the field, revetments in one corner shown in earlier photos to hide more than twenty enemy fighters. This attack left five planes destroyed and ten more damaged. The three strafing passes that followed burned four more fighters previously identified in photos as hidden under trees.

After this attack they flew over to Ishioka Airfield, but low fog covered the field and pilots couldn't spot any enemy planes before receiving the recall order.[508]

Air Groups 85, 86, and 88 flew a joint mission to sweep airfields in the Tokyo area. Nine Corsairs from VBF-86 also attacked Hyakuriga-hara Airfield after VBF-1 left, also reporting intense medium- and light-caliber antiaircraft fire. Using bombs, rockets, and machine guns, they struck hangars and other buildings on the field on their first pass. But before they could make a second pass, word of the cease fire reached them and they returned to base.[509]

A division of VBF-85 also made a pass at Hyakurigahara, minutes before *Wasp*'s Corsairs reached the field, but reported little flak before they also received the recall order. Before arriving at Hyakurigahara, their nine Corsairs had found Kashima to be the only other field in the area not covered by overcast. The flight dropped bombs on the hangars, following up with rocket and machine-gun strafing attacks. Japanese gunners responded with little antiaircraft fire, but some of their rounds hit the engine of Lieutenant (jg) John Dunn's Corsair, forcing him to ditch in Kasumigaura Lake. After he got out of the aircraft and into his raft, he was taken prisoner, apparently the last American to become a prisoner of war during World War II. His captivity at a Japanese prisoner of war camp in Tokyo was fortunately brief. He was freed and repatriated the next month.

Six of *Lexington*'s Hellcats also attacked Hyakurigahara Airfield after they also found their assigned target covered by overcast. Attacking a few minutes after VBF-86, they found antiaircraft fire to be "moderate" as four of the planes dropped bombs on hangars and workshops in the airfield, destroying one hangar with a direct hit, as well as a repair shop. Then, while they looked the field over for planes to strafe, they received the recall order and returned to the *Lexington*.[510]

VF-88 Hellcats received the recall before they reached their target, but fought the air battle recounted in the first chapter at about the same time Japanese radio broadcasts told the Japanese people that a rescript from the Emperor would be broadcast at noon. This final dogfight ended with nine Japanese fighters and four American Hellcats shot down as two

VF-88 planes orbited over the coast, ordered to relay radio messages sent by the sweep leader to the *Yorktown*. As their mission ended, they fired their rockets at a barracks on Chosi Point, a parting shot at the Empire before turning for home.[511]

The *Yorktown*'s Hellcats were not the only squadron to fight Japanese planes that morning. Fifteen minutes earlier, in the penultimate air battle of World War II, VBF-6 shot down three Franks, but without loss to themselves. Eight Corsairs and four Hellcats from VF-6 had taken off from the *Hancock* to sweep Nagano Airfield in western Honshu. Bad weather on the flight separated four Corsairs from the other planes, and only eight planes continued on to Nagano. With the field in sight, the flight received the order to return to base. Obviously the cease fire was in effect and pilots drowned out the entire message with yells and whistles over their radios. Confirmation followed, so the flight turned east, passing very near Mount Fuji, prominent as it stood above the overcast.

The Hellcats were now flying behind, and below, the Corsairs when Japanese fighters appeared. The flight commander, Lieutenant Commander Lavell Bigelow, radioed the commander of Air Group 6, Commander Henry Miller, whom we have met before, also in the air on another cancelled strike. He told him that the Japanese fighters appeared to be preparing to attack and asked how to respond. Miller told him to "shoot them down gently" if they began to attack. A similar remark is generally attributed to Admiral Halsey later that morning.[512]

The F6Fs mixed it up with the Japanese while the Corsairs remained above them, to cover the Hellcats from any potential attacks from above. Lieutenant Herschel Pahl of VF6, who had shot down a Kate and enjoyed himself strafing Jimmachi Airfield on August 9, described what happened:

As we approached Sagami Wan at 13,000 feet, at 0705, we observed two enemy Franks below and in front of us, but we were ordered by CTG 38.1 [Commander of Task Group 38.1, Admiral Theodore Sprague] by radio not to attack except in self defense. We just watched them. A few minutes later we know them to be decoys for a group of at least five enemy fighters closing very rapidly from astern and below, directly behind Lieutenant Wickham and Ensign Killian, who were at least a thousand feet below and behind the F4Us . . . abeam of us. Our flight leader, Lieutenant Commander Bigelow, then became aware of the developing attack and ordered us to attack and shoot them down. I saw the first three Zekes very close to Lieutenant Wickham's section and saw one of them open fire at long range. I swung over sharply and fired on the Zeke closest to them with my wingman, Ensign Daryl Grant, alongside of me. Then the fight was on. I got a good, full-deflection shot and saw glass and bits of metal torn from . . . [a Zeke which] made a tight turn and went into a very deep diving spiral to the left. I followed him, still firing. More pieces came off . . . and he started smoking and . . . to burn on the port side of his engine. I broke off [at] about 8,000 feet and zoomed back into the fight as the Zeke went into the water.

I very quickly picked up another Frank which was starting a run on an F6F chasing a smoking Jack. (At this point I missed a collision with an F4U by inches.) I got in good shots at this Frank in a tight turn and followed him into a split "S" [turn] and [then] a screaming dive. He didn't burn but was smoking badly when I broke off a little above a cloud. As I zoomed for altitude again, I got a quick, snap shot at a Frank going straight down with terrific speed. I didn't follow him because of other planes above us which later turned out to be F4Us keeping high cover for us. Below I saw a burning plane just as it went through the cloud below us.

Lieutenant Charles Wickham, who shot down a Jack, picked up the tail-end plane in the group of five which were spiraling up from behind [us]. He hit the Jack from behind, in the engine, with his six 50's [machine guns]. . . . The plane immediately started smoking, the propeller stopped, and as he passed close aboard he [Wickham] could see the pilot slumped over. The plane did a flip and crashed into the water.

Ensign Ray Killian, Wickham's wingman, shot down the third enemy fighter and later described his victory: "Our Hellcats splashed two of them in a hurry while I made a pass at a Jack, one of the latest and fastest Jap fighters. After I gave him a long burst, he attempted a slow roll. He was only half way over when another burst from my guns drew smoke and fire from his engine. The pilot apparently had been killed as the plane was now out of control. It spun down, flaming, and crashed into the water."

Pahl, Wickham, and Killian each received credit for one enemy aircraft destroyed. Following the fracas, all planes returned to the *Hancock*.[513] Having begun the war over Pearl Harbor, as we saw in chapter one, it is fitting that the same air group should take part in one of the final air battles of the war in the Pacific.

Another Air Group, AG-87, didn't run into Japanese fighters that morning, but did succeed in making one pass on Chosi Airfield before receiving the recall order. Fifteen F6Fs from VBF-87, including a photo plane and its escort, dropped 500-pound bombs and fired rockets into hangars and a factory near them, as well as the buildings of the gunnery school located on the base. There was very little antiaircraft fire and following this initial pass, the flight returned to the carrier.[514]

Hellcats from the first sweep launched from *USS Randolph* also had time to complete several attacks before the recall order. Assigned to attack Kisarazu Airfield, they dove through the cloud layer that covered most of the field, encountering moderate flak, to drop fragmentation bombs and fire rockets at hangars and aircraft revetments. After this first run at Kisarazu, the flight flew over to Katsuura, where they bombed a warehouse and docks and fired rockets into a small cargo ship and a dredge. An explosion followed, along the docks, and the dredge caught fire. After the flight reformed, pilots heard the recall order and made an uneventful return to the *Randolph*.[515]

Though the recall order denied Hellcats and Corsairs of Air Group 83 the opportunity to attack an airfield, they did have time to shoot down one enemy plane before their war ended.

While still off the coast of Honshu, the flight encountered a Myrt flying 1,000 feet above them, headed toward the Task Force. One section of Corsairs jettisoned their bombs and took up pursuit, followed by the four Hellcats on the mission. The Corsair flight leader, Lieutenant Thomas Reidy, who had already shot down a George on July 25, closed on the Myrt from astern and opened fire. His rounds set the left wing root on fire, but this soon went out. Two of the F6Fs then cut in and opened fire as well, without any apparent effect. Reidy got in a second burst that started a fire in both wings that increased in size. The Myrt sought refuge in a cloud as one of the Hellcat pilots continued to fire at it. The enemy plane soon emerged from the cloud, on fire and smoking. It exploded in the air with the debris crashing into the sea, and Reidy got the credit for the shootdown.[516]

Air Groups 31 and 49 both shot down more enemy planes shortly after crossing the coast. At about 6:00 AM, the eight VF-31 Hellcats saw fifteen Japanese fighters at three o'clock, flying above them. The Japanese planes appeared to be positioning themselves to attack British planes, Seafires and Avengers, bombing a factory in the Tokyo area.

The four *Belleau Wood* Hellcats climbed to gain an altitude advantage on the enemy fighters, climbing to 8,000 feet, as did the VF-49 F6Fs. On their first dive into the air battle developing between the Japanese and British, VF-31 pilots didn't open fire, as it was very difficult to distinguish British from Japanese fighters. Then the Japanese planes, Zekes, began to dive individually on the British Avengers and could be readily identified and attacked. The Zekes would dive on an Avenger, then zoom back into clouds above. VF-31 pilots took on the Zeros as they did so, shooting down five of them, as well as an Oscar that joined the fray, by getting on their tails and letting loose with the six .50 caliber machine guns. Lieutenant James Parker, Jr., and Lieutenant (jg) Edward Toaspern each shot down two Zeros. Ensign Francis Clifford got another Zero and Ensign Robert Karp accounted for the Oscar.[517]

The four Hellcats from VF-49 jettisoned their bombs when they saw the enemy planes attacking the British flight and also joined the air battle. Japanese pilots began to attack the Hellcats in what became a chaotic aerial battle.

Lieutenant Allen Lindsay got on the tail of a Zero as another Zero began to follow him. Lieutenant Jack Gibson, who had already shot down two Japanese fighters in the past three weeks, got behind the Zero following Lindsay and fired a long burst that hit the fuselage and wing root of the Zero, which immediately caught fire and fell toward the ground in flames. After Gibson shot at two more enemy planes from a poor position, another Zero pulled up directly in front of him. He fired several bursts and the enemy burst into flames.

At the same time, Lindsay got astern of a Zero and fired a long burst as it made a climbing turn, and it fell toward the ground, smoking. He then found another target and fired a burst from long range. As he drew closer, he fired again, setting the enemy ablaze. It dove toward the ground, in flames.

Lieutenant George Williams, whom we met shooting down a Frank on July 24, then strafing on August 9, spun out trying to nail the first Zero he pursued. When he recovered, he found another right in front of him and opened fire as the Zero started a wide turn, blowing pieces off the enemy fighter until it burst into flames and headed for the ground. After he regained some altitude, Williams encountered yet another Zero. He got on its tail as the enemy pilot jinked back and forth in an attempt to throw off his aim. Williams fired a burst that hit the plane, which instantly caught fire and then exploded.

At the beginning of the fracas, a Zero dived on the last man in the Hellcat flight, Lieutenant (jg) Elwood McDonald. He turned toward his attacker, firing several bursts of machine-gun rounds as the enemy plane flew toward him and scoring hits as it flew past him, trailing smoke with pieces flying off the aircraft. The Zero then went into a dive toward the ground. McDonald got a shot at a second Zeke that was making a run on some Hellcats from behind and below, after the Japanese pilot made the mistake of pulling up in front of him. McDonald fired four bursts and the enemy plane began to trail smoke and rolled. McDonald fired two more bursts, causing the Zero to plummet toward the ground in flames. A fourth Zero then made a pass at McDonald from above him, off his right wing. The American turned toward the attacker and flew straight at him. The Zero pilot blinked, then passed him, giving McDonald a chance to fire one long burst, along the length of the enemy fuselage. The Zero looked like it had come apart when pieces flew off as it dived for clouds below. McDonald followed it down, fired one more burst, and the Zero blew up. Then, the fight was suddenly over, as quickly as it began. No more than five minutes later, pilots heard the order to return to their carriers.

The tally of enemy fighters for VF-49 pilots was one destroyed and one probable for Lindsay, two destroyed and one damaged for Gibson, two destroyed for Williams, and two destroyed, two probables, and one damaged for McDonald. At total of seven enemy fighters were shot down.[518]

British Seafires shot down four more of the Japanese fighters, but lost a Seafire as well as an Avenger that had to ditch on the return flight.[519]

The last enemy planes downed over the Home Islands of Japan were three Myrts, shot down by Corsair pilots from VBF-88. Before 8:00 that morning, a Dumbo took off to rescue Lieutenant Dunn, last seen in a raft on Kasumigaura Lake. Eleven Corsairs from VBF-88 escorted the rescue plane in case some Japanese either didn't hear, or ignored, the news that peace had broken out. When the fight arrived at the Japanese coast, eight planes remained with the Dumbo while three, flown by Lieutenant Raymond McGrath and Lieutenants (jg) George Lewis and Robert Wohlers, flew to the lake to see if they could locate Dunn.

Arriving over the lake, the trio could only see the oil slick where Dunn's aircraft had ditched. He was not in sight, since the Japanese had already taken him prisoner. While Japanese antiaircraft gunners fired at them, they turned east, flying at only 1,000 feet, to head home. As they passed over Hokoda Airfield, they saw two Myrts taking off. Perhaps annoyed because of the antiaircraft fire, the Corsairs intercepted the enemy planes.

McGrath climbed to gain altitude, and then dived on one Myrt from astern. When 600 feet away from the enemy plane, he fired a short burst and the Myrt exploded only one hundred feet in front him. He pulled up sharply, avoiding damage to his plane. At the same time, Lewis made a pass on the second Myrt, then got on the tail of the enemy aircraft and fired again. It exploded, crashing to the earth. The third member of the section, Wohlers, had spotted a third Myrt in the vicinity. He attacked and set the enemy's wing root on fire during his first pass, then, like Lewis, made his second pass from astern. After he fired, the plane went into a spin, never recovering before it crashed into the ground. The trio then rejoined their squadron mates flying with the Dumbo and returned to the *Yorktown*, where they landed at 12:30 PM.[520]

As the last strikes and sweeps returned to their carriers, jubilant air crews salvoed their bombs and some did loops on their return to the carriers. Offensive flight operations ceased, but combat air patrols still took to the skies to prevent dedicated Japanese pilots who wanted to die for the Emperor from reaching the Task Force. When asked by his staff how the Allies should deal with any Japanese planes that approached the Task Force after the cease fire was in effect, Admiral Halsey responded, "Shoot them down in a friendly fashion."[521]

Launched for a combat air patrol over the Task Force before 11:00 that morning, four Corsairs of VBF-6 received orders to intercept a bogie approaching the British Task Force as they were climbing to their assigned altitude.

When they reached 18,000, they spotted the "meatball," a Kate torpedo bomber carrying a torpedo, flying below them. Attacking immediately, the Kate turned into the Corsairs, but three of them overshot the enemy plane as it began to dive on the British carrier *HMS Indefatigable*. Lieutenant Robert Farnsworth, already discussed in chapters eight and twelve, was able to roll into a vertical dive and hold it until he had the Kate in his sights. The first two bursts he fired missed, but the third hit home as Farnsworth held down the trigger on his joystick until the enemy plane exploded. It crashed into the ocean only one hundred yards from the British carrier. Farnsworth got credit for the victory and his squadron a message of thanks from *HMS Indefatigable*.[522]

Less than an hour later, another Japanese plane headed for the fleet went down. Two planes of an eight-plane patrol from VBF-85 got a vector for two approaching Japanese aircraft just as their patrol over the radar picket destroyers was about to end. The two Corsairs intercepted a Judy, with a Frank in trail, several thousand feet below them. Ensign Falvey Sandridge went after the Judy, coming up on its tail, firing several bursts that hit the cockpit and engine. The enemy aircraft caught fire and began to fall to the ocean as pieces dropped off. Sandridge followed it down to about 4,000 feet, where he broke off, as it was obvious the enemy plane was doomed. He later received credit for the victory.

The other Corsair pilot, Lieutenant Bayard Webster, attacked the Frank, scoring several hits on the left wing root and engine. The enemy plane was smoking as he came around for another pass and it dived into some clouds below. Although the enemy plane's blip disappeared from Task Force radar screens, Webster only got credit for a damaged enemy aircraft.[523]

VF-86 made the penultimate kills while four pilots were on patrol over the radar pickets, flying in two sections at different altitudes. At about 1:00 PM, the two lower planes saw an enemy fighter a few thousand feet above them, coming out of some clouds and heading for the Task Force. The pair put on full power and closed with the enemy plane, a Zero. Lieutenant (jg) Ora Myers made the first pass on the Zero, scoring hits on its engine and fuselage. As the plane caught fire, he made a second pass, striking the engine again. His wingman, Lieutenant (jg) Carl Baker, joined him for this attack and both men poured more machine-gun rounds into the Zero. Myers then made a third attack, from behind, as the enemy plane dove toward the sea, firing until he pulled out at 4,000 feet. The Zero continued on and crashed into the sea.

About a half hour after the pursuit of the Zero began, the two planes flying at higher altitude got some trade, as well. Given a heading for another enemy plane, they intercepted a Judy, and one of the pilots, Lieutenant Mahlon Morrison, was in a better position to initiate an attack. He got on the Judy's tail, fired, and scored hits. The enemy began to trail smoke, turned, and headed for the water as the other member of the team, Lieutenant Commander Cleo Dobson, whom we met in chapter thirteen, also attacked, from astern as well. His bursts hit the fuselage and left wing and the Judy burst into flames, rolled, and then went into a spin. As it plummeted toward the sea, a wing tore off and the plane became engulfed in flames before it hit the water. Myers received credit for an aerial victory while Dobson and Morrison shared the credit for their accomplishment.[524]

Ensign Clarence Moore of VF-31 scored the last American aerial victory of World War II shortly thereafter. Moore returned from the morning strike, expecting to enjoy the end of the war, but got a combat air patrol assignment instead. At about 2:00 PM, while he was flying over the Task Force, fighter controllers ordered his flight of twelve Hellcats to intercept an enemy plane approaching at an altitude of 7,000 feet. When they spotted the plane, a Judy carrying a bomb, it immediately turned back toward Japan and jettisoned the bomb.

The Hellcats had the advantage of altitude and quickly gained on the enemy plane. The flight leader, at the front of the formation, prepared to attack the plane first, but the Japanese pilot pulled back his throttles and the Hellcat overshot. Then Moore, a section leader, got on the enemy's tail and fired a few bursts, hitting the wings. The Judy caught fire, exploded, and crashed into the ocean, making VF-31's total score for the last day of the war eight Japanese planes shot down.[525]

Besides the five planes shot down over Japan, two more planes became operational losses that day. A Helldiver of VB-6 flying in the second wave of strikes ditched in the ocean. *USS Collett* rescued the unidentified crewmen. The last operational loss before the war ended occurred an hour after news of the cease fire reached Task Force 38. A VF-94 Hellcat crashed while being launched for a combat air patrol. *USS Dashiell* rescued the pilot.

Conclusion

Some may view the final days of World War II as "end of the war" operations with little risk to the participants. As we have seen, this was decidedly not the case with Task Force attacks on the Japanese Home Islands. The Americans lost a total of 229 aircraft during the combat operations described in this book: sixty Corsairs, seventy-three Hellcats, fifty-four Helldivers, forty Avengers, and two Kingfishers. From these aircraft, seventy crewmen were killed, twenty-six became prisoners of war, and 174 crewmen were rescued. The numbers rescued, mainly from ditching off the coast of Japan but some accomplished under fire, reveal that the air-sea rescue, although still in its infancy, managed to save a number of air crewmen, although some were lost. In many cases, communications failures prevented rescue aircraft from appearing on the scene while squadron mates were still circling the man, or men, in the water. On occasion, there were simply too many men in the water with too few rescue planes to reach them all. The rescue squadrons, both Navy and Army Air Force, however, did perform many remarkable rescues along the coast of the Japanese Home Islands. The Japanese military should have recognized such rescues, occurring so often, as another sign that the American and British forces had the Japanese homeland in an unbreakable grip.[526]

Although the Task Force's air operations, even combat air patrols, were offensive, not defensive in nature, it was still difficult for Navy flyers to find Japanese aircraft in the air that summer.[527] The Japanese were conserving their aircraft, and experienced pilots, for the impending invasion of the Home Islands, making it very difficult for American flyers to rack up many aerial victories that summer.

American pilots from Task Force 38 shot down 123 Japanese planes over Japan or off the coast. Hellcats accounted for ninety-eight: thirty-five during combat air patrols off the coast and sixty-three during strikes and sweeps. Corsairs shot down another twenty-five: fifteen on combat air patrols and ten on strikes and sweeps. The difference in these numbers does not reflect on the skill of Corsair pilots or the performance of the airplane. Hellcat squadrons were simply in the right place, at the right time, to run up a higher score.

The Corsair was a superior aircraft in many respects, in performance, durability, and firepower, and the Navy was in the process of replacing the Hellcat with it, although the latter could still more than hold its own against Japanese fighters. The commander of Air Group 6, Commander Henry Miller, described the Corsair as "The finest airplane in the carrier Navy, the F4U-4 has performed beyond any pilot's expectations." He went on to describe the Avenger as "the old dependable." The Curtiss Helldiver, however, received poor marks. Besides its difficult handling characteristics, it had a longer takeoff distance that led to numerous ditchings at takeoff. Almost one quarter of the SB2Cs lost on combat operations described in this book went down during takeoff.[528] The aircraft also had a relatively limited range that led to even more ditchings following strikes on Japan. In addition, its relatively slower flying speed was a constraint on the planning and execution of missions. Miller described the aircraft as "a lame duck . . . a nightmare throughout [its service]."[529]

The main purpose of the strikes flown by these four aircraft types during July and August 1945 was to degrade Japanese air power in preparation for the impending invasion of Kyushu, as well as to halt all Japanese merchant traffic along the coasts of the Home Islands. The importance of hitting Japanese airfields to destroy aircraft stored in, and near, them is confirmed by the state of Japanese air power during the summer of 1945. The Japanese envisaged using 6,000 Army and Navy suicide planes, with the pilots to fly them, to thwart the invasion of Kyushu. They had 5,350 planes for this purpose in August 1945, and during the summer of 1945 Japanese aircraft plants could still produce 1,700 aircraft a month. The attacks against the invasion fleet would have been made hourly with 300–400 planes in each attack wave. Almost one half the American ships damaged in the Pacific were victims of *kamikaze* attacks, and projections of shipping losses, based on previous experience, were ninety ships sunk and 900 damaged. This number would have undoubtedly included a fair number of transports, so the loss of American lives, before they hit the invasion beaches, would have been considerable.[530]

Although there were 125 airfields in Kyushu, Shikoku, and western Honshu for launching these *kamikaze* attacks, the Japanese hid the planes earmarked for this purpose on and near airfields all over the Home Islands, including the aircraft returned to the Home Islands from Southeast Asia between April and June. They also intended to stage more aircraft from airfields in Korea, Manchuria, and China to the Home Islands for use in these attacks. Many of the aircraft intended for use as *kamikazes* were training planes, many biplanes, so their destruction by Task Force pilots was of more importance than might be apparent at first glance. The Japanese Navy had 2,500 training planes earmarked for suicide attacks in August 1945, with more than enough pilots to fly them.[531] The use of training planes for suicide missions fit perfectly into the circumstances Japan found itself in, in the summer of 1945, as they required lower octane fuel and used less of it than fighter aircraft. They also required much less skill to fly on one-way missions.[532]

The Japanese had 18,000 pilots ready for combat in August 1945, most with an average of only one hundred hours of flight training. Half had less than this amount, insufficient for combat operations but military leaders believed it was enough for one-way *kamikaze* attacks on the American invasion fleet.[533] By the time the Task Force began their strikes against the Home Islands in July, the Japanese air forces had stopped advanced flying training, concentrating on developing pilot skills for *kamikaze* pilots with primary training only. Army pilots had about seventy hours of flight training, while Navy pilots had less, thirty to fifty.[534]

The reduction in flying hours during training was a direct result of the effective loss of the Philippines in early 1945, which cut off the Home Islands from sources of oil in the East Indies and Southeast Asia. The effect on the Japanese Army and Navy air forces was considerable, both tactically and strategically. As mentioned earlier, pilots with so little flight time were not expected to perform well in combat, but did possess sufficient skill to reach and dive on an American ship. This bald fact effected Japanese strategy to oppose the invasion with *kamikaze* attacks as the primary means of defense. The Japanese also had enough fuel to carry out such attacks, as the overall consumption of oil products in the Home Islands fell dramatically from the summer of 1944 to the summer of 1945, enabling the stockpiling of fuel.

The reduction in oil consumption worked in tandem with poorly trained pilots and the need to conserve aircraft for the invasion to curtail Japanese air opposition to most Task Force strikes during July and August. There were few interceptions of American aerial missions, as we have seen. The order to conserve planes, issued in April 1945, was eventually rescinded in July as B-29s laid waste to secondary Japanese cities and Navy planes struck the remnants of the Japanese fleet and destroyed the planes hidden by the Japanese. Although enemy fighters met some Navy strikes in the closing days of the war, there was still no all-out defensive effort to stop these strikes as the Japanese hoarded aircraft for the invasion. Japanese commanders also believed that if they tried to oppose American air attacks that summer with the poorly trained pilots available, this would have depleted the manpower required to stop an invasion. Hence the defense of airfields was left to antiaircraft artillery, the primary agent that shot down Navy planes over the Home Islands in the summer of 1945.[535]

The effect of the Task Force strikes during July and August was considerable. The raids of July 14–15 aimed to reduce the shipment of coal to industries farther south, as ferries between the two islands carried more than three-fourths of coal production. The strikes on these two days reduced coal shipments by more than eighty percent and arguably had as great a strategic effect as the strategic bombing of Japanese industry and cities by the Army Air Force's 20th Air Force. The accuracy with which naval aviators dropped their bombs on Japan during the summer of 1945 is remarkable. More than half landed within 250 feet of the target, a truly impressive accomplishment for the time.[536]

As mentioned in chapter two, the goal of the Navy raids on the remains of the Imperial Fleet from July 18 through July 28 was to destroy the major naval units that could still pose a threat to American convoys expected to cross the northern Pacific in the fall 1945 with supplies for the invasion of Japan. The likelihood of these ships escaping from Kure and disappearing into the northern Pacific, as the German battleship *Bismarck* had done in 1941, was very low and Navy planners were aware that these remnants were mainly useful only as antiaircraft gun platforms. But Navy commanders continued to follow one of their major aims throughout the war: to sink enemy ships. Although American planes would likely have found and sunk them at sea, it was more efficient to do so while they could be easily located in harbors, regardless of the cost, rather than search for them on the high seas. At any rate, the Task Force air attacks on Japanese warships during July and August left the Japanese with only a few destroyers, supported by small suicide craft, to oppose any invasion.[537]

There were few merchant ships available, as well, by this time to import the raw materials vital for both military and civilian production. Eighty-eight percent of Japanese merchant shipping was sunk by the Allies during World War II and forty percent destroyed by Allied aircraft, including American naval aviation.[538] Hence the sinking of even very small merchant craft by Navy flyers became significant, as these ships had become vital to the Japanese by 1945.

The destruction of these small cargo ships, down to the Sugar Dogs often sunk by Navy flyers that summer, was more important than might be thought at first glance, in the context of an impending Kyushu invasion. The supply of the Japanese defenders on Kyushu was made by sea and even the smallest vessels were part of the supply chain. The more small cargo vessels that could be destroyed around the Home Islands, the fewer that were left to carry supplies and troops to oppose the invasion. After the surrender, Japanese officers admitted that, although they had stockpiled sufficient ammunition, food, and equipment on Kyushu to oppose an invasion for the first three weeks of battle, the outcome of a longer struggle would have been very much in doubt because of the increasing difficulty of supplying the island.[539]

Although the invasion fortunately never took place, American preparations were similar to the Allied aerial campaign over France in the spring of 1944 that destroyed enemy aircraft and rail lines before the invasion of France. Although concerted attacks on Japanese railways only began just before the Japanese surrender, Navy flyers' destruction of Japanese planes on airfields and small shipping was a major part of the strategy to degrade Japanese aerial opposition and interdict their transport of supplies.[540] Until the two atomic bombs fell on Hiroshima and Nagasaki, every member of the Task Force expected to partake in the invasion of Japan. The dedication with which Navy flyers attacked naval targets and airfields would prevent Japanese ships and planes from killing the soldiers and Marines hitting the beaches of Kyushu, as well as the sailors offshore.

The goal of aerial strikes and raids, by the Army Air Force and Navy flyers, changed, of course, following the second atomic bomb attack. On August 10 the strategic goal of air attacks, including those of the Task Force, changed from preparation for the invasion to continuing military pressure to convince the Japanese military to accept peace,[541] as it became evident to the men of the Task Force that the Japanese would very likely soon quit the war. On August 9, the Japanese cabinet decided upon a plan for surrender, but Army and Navy commanders insisted on terms unacceptable to the Allies. A message intercepted by American intelligence on August 11 revealed that senior Japanese commanders had no intention of following a surrender order.[542] Hence Allied leaders saw the necessity for continuing both Army Air Force and Navy attacks on the Home Islands, even after the second atomic bomb fell on Nagasaki.[543]

The air battles and attempted suicide attacks on the Task Force on August 15, the incipient mutinies among overseas Japanese military commands, the attempted coup of August 14 in Tokyo, and the final *kamikaze* mission by Japanese Navy flyers based at Otta Airfield on the afternoon of August 15 (lost without a trace over the ocean) underline the reluctance of many Japanese military men to accept the shame of defeat. Fortunately, the surrender did come, but the loss of each airman in the final days of the war was particularly bitter for their comrades, with peace so near. The men who flew and died in the last few days of the Pacific War were as professional and dedicated as the pilots and air crew of Scouting 6 on the first day of the war at Pearl Harbor.

ENDNOTES

1 Report of Attack on Pearl Harbor, Report of Ensign P. L. Teaff.
2 Report of Attack on Pearl Harbor, Report of Lieutenant Commander H. L. Young, Commander Enterprise Air Group.
3 Report of Attack on Pearl Harbor, Report of Ensign W. E. Roberts.
4 Report of Attack on Pearl Harbor, Report of Ensign E. T. Deacon.
5 Report of Attack on Pearl Harbor, Report of Lieutenant Commander H. L. Hopping.
6 Report of Attack on Pearl Harbor, Resume of Events by Ensign F. T. Weber.
7 Report of Attack on Pearl Harbor, Report of Lieutenant (jg) Frank A. Patriarca.
8 Report of Attack on Pearl Harbor, Report of Lieutenant C. E. Dickinson.
9 Aircraft Action Report VF-88, No. 35, 15 August 1945; Action Report of Task Force 38.4, 2 July–15 August 1945, Carrier Division Six, Air Force Pacific Fleet, 34–35.
10 Headquarters, USAFFE and Eighth U.S. Army, *Homeland Air Defense Operations Record*, 80–81.
11 Aircraft Action Report VF-88, No. 35, 15 August 1945.
12 Aircraft Action Report VF-88, No. 35, 15 August 1945.
13 Aircraft Action Report VF-88, No. 35, 15 August 1945; Individual Deceased Personnel File of Eugene E. Mandeberg, National Personnel Records Center, NARA.
14 Richard Frank, *Downfall*, 30.
15 Frank, *Downfall*, 34, 36; United States Strategic Bombing Survey (USSBS), *Japan's Struggle to End the War*, 10.
16 Frank, *Downfall*, 333.
17 John Ray Skates, *The Invasion of Japan*, 44–45, 53, 55, 58.
18 Frank, *Downfall*, 334.
19 Frank, *Downfall*, 152; Edward Drea, *MacArthur's Ultra*, 206.
20 Drea, 202; Frank, "Ketsu Go," 77.
21 Drea, 204, 213.
22 Drea, 222.
23 Kenneth Werrel, *Blankets of Fire*, 193, 201, 227.
24 Werrel, 175, 231.
25 John S. Thach, *Reminiscences*, 463.
26 Eric Bergerud, *Fire in the Sky*, 255–257, 260–261, 296.
27 Bergerud, 336.
28 Stuart S. Murray, *Reminiscences*, 381–382.
29 Bergerud, 562–564.
30 Thach, 470.
31 Headquarters, USAFFE, *Homeland Air Defense Operations Record*, 118.
32 USSBS, *Japanese Air Power*, 49–50; Bergerud, 465.
33 Headquarters, USAFFE, *Homeland Air Defense Operations Record*, 58–60.

34 Bergerud, 204–205, 210–211.

35 Bergerud, 223–225.

36 Bergerud, 225–226.

37 Bergerud, 466, 479–480, 491.

38 Headquarters, USAFFE and Eighth U.S. Army, *Air Defense of the Homeland*, 17–18, 27, and *Homeland Air Defense Operations Record*, 162–63; Air Intelligence Group, *The Air War against Japan 1–15 June 1945*, 7–8.

39 Headquarters, USAFFE, *Homeland Air Defense Operations Record*, 119–20.

40 Headquarters, USAFFE, *Homeland Air Defense Operations Record*, 60–61.

41 Werrel, 191.

42 Third Fleet War Diary, July 1945, 18, and United States Pacific Fleet, Third Fleet Operational Summary, Task Force 38 both list the number of attack sorties on July 10 at 1,160. Commander Second Carrier Task Force, Action Report 2 July–15 August 1945, 30, lists 1,303 attack and photo sorties. The latter participated in these strikes although they did not attack the target, so they will be included in the total number of strike sorties, and Second Carrier Task Force daily strike sortie totals will be used throughout this work.

43 Aircraft Action Report VF-50–9, 10 July 1945.

44 Task Group 38.3 Action Report, 1 July–15 August 1945.

45 Aircraft Action Reports VBF-83, No. 114, and VF-83, No. 104, 10 July 1945.

46 Aircraft Action Reports VBF-6, No. 51, and VF-6, No. 40, 10 July 1945.

47 Aircraft Action Report VF-34, No. 8-45, 10 July 1945.

48 Aircraft Action Report CAG-16, No. 1-45, 10 July 1945.

49 Aircraft Action Report VF-31, No. 1, 10 July 1945.

50 Aircraft Action Report VF-32, No. 2, 10 July 1945.

51 Aircraft Action Report CAG-94, No. 3, 10 July 1945.

52 Aircraft Action Report CVG-83, No. 92, 10 July 1945.

53 Aircraft Action Report VT-34, No. 1-45, 10 July 1945.

54 Aircraft Action Report VB-1, No. 64, 10 July 1945.

55 Aircraft Action Report VB-1, No. 64, 10 July 1945.

56 Aircraft Action Reports VBF-1, No. 2-45, and VF-1, No. 2-45, 10 July 1945.

57 Aircraft Action Report VT-1, No. 1-45, 10 July 1945.

58 Aircraft Action Report CVLG-27, No. 1; Action Report Carrier Division Six, 2 July–15 August 1945.

59 Aircraft Action Reports CVLG-27 No. 1, AG-50 No. 8, CVLG-27 No. 1, VB-85 No. 32, VT-85 No. 27, VB-88 No. 1, VBF-88 No. 3, and VT-88 No. 1.

60 Aircraft Action Report VBF-1 No. 3, 10 July 1945.

61 Aircraft Action Report VF-88 No. 4, 10 July 1945.

62 Aircraft Action Report VF-31 No. 3, 10 July 1945.

63 Aircraft Action Report VF-49 No. 1-31, 10 July 1945.

64 Aircraft Action Reports VBF-85, No. 34, and VBF-88, No. 2, 10 July 1945.

65 *USS Lexington* War Diary, 10 July 1945.

66 Aircraft Action Reports VBF-88, AG-27 No. 2, VT-50 No. 10, VBF-85 No. 35, VB-85 No. 33, and VF-85 No. 28, 10 July 1945.

67 Aircraft Action Reports VBF-1 No. 4, VB-1 No. 65, and VT-1 No. 2, 10 July 1945.

68 Aircraft Action Report CVG-16, No. 7, 10 July 1945.

69 Aircraft Action Report CVG-16, No. 7, 10 July 1945.

70 Aircraft Action Report AG-47, No. 98, 10 July 1945.

71 Aircraft Action Report CVG-6, No. 32, 10 July 1945.

72 Action Report 2 July–15 August 1945, Commander Second Carrier Task Force, 30; Third Fleet Operational Summaries of Carrier Strikes, 10 July 1945.

73 Aircraft Action Report VBF-88, No. 4, 10 July 1945.

74 Aircraft Action Report VBF-88, No. 1, 10 July 1945.

75 Aircraft Action Report AG-6, CVG-6 No. 32, 10 July 1945, 23.

76 Third Fleet War Diary, July 1945, 18; Joint Army-Navy Assessment Committee, *Japanese Naval and Merchant Shipping Losses During World War II by All Causes*.

77 Thach, 461.

78 Aircraft Action Report VBF-1, No. 6, 14 July 1945.

79 Aircraft Action Report VF-85, No. 40, 14 July 1945.

80 Aircraft Action Report VF-88, No. 5, 14 July 1945.

81 *USS Lexington* War Diary, July 1945, 78.

82 Aircraft Action Report VF-34, No. 11, 14 July 1945.

83 Action Report, Task Force 38, 2 July–15 August 1945; Task Group 38.1 War Diary; *USS Hancock* War Diary; Aircraft Action Report CAG-6, No. 33, 14 July 1945.

84 Aircraft Action Reports CVG-16, No. 10-45, and AG-47, No. 101, 14 July 1945.

85 Aircraft Action Report AG-47, No. 101, 14 July 1945.

86 Aircraft Action Reports CVG-83, No. 94, and VT-34, No. 11, 14 July 1945.

87 Aircraft Action Reports VB-85 No. 84, VBF-85 No. 37, VT-85 No. 29, and All Hands, November 1945, 30.

88 Aircraft Action Report VF-50, No. 13, 14 July 1945.

89 Aircraft Action Report VT-50, No. 14, 14 July 1945.

90 Aircraft Action Report CVLG-27, No. 4, 14 July 1945.

91 Aircraft Action Report VBF-88, No. 5, 14 July 1945.

92 History of Fighting Squadron Eighty-Eight, 1 March 1945–3 September 1945, 10; Aircraft Action Report VF-88, No. 6, 14 July 1945.

93 Aircraft Action Report VB-88, No. 3, 14 July 1945.

94 Aircraft Action Report VT-88, No. 3, 14 July 1945.

95 Murray, 385–386.

96 Aircraft Action Reports VB-1, No. 66, and VBF-1, No. 9, 14 July 1945.

97 Aircraft Action Report CVG-16, No. 12-45, 14 July 1945.

98 Action Report, Task Force 38, 2 July–15 August 1945, 55.

99 Aircraft Action Reports VB-88 No. 4, VBF-88 No. 7, and VT-88 No. 4, 14 July 1945.

100 Aircraft Action Report VBF-85, No. 38, 14 July 1945.

101 Aircraft Action Report CVLG-27, No. 5, 14 July 1945.

102 Aircraft Action Report VT-50, No. 15, 14 July 1945.

103 Action Report, Task Force 38, 2 July–15 August 1945, 48, 52.

104 Aircraft Action Reports CAG-34, No. 7-45, and CVG-83, No. 95, 14 July 1945.

105 Aircraft Action Report VF-85, No. 39, 14 July 1945.

106 *USS Bataan* War Diary, July 1945, 13, 37.

107 Third Fleet War Diary, July 1945, 21.

108 Aircraft Action Report VB-1, No. 67, 15 July 1945.

109 Office of the Chief of Naval Operations, *Battle Experience*, 83–12.

110 Aircraft Action Report VBF-1, No. 15, 15 July 1945.

111 Third Fleet War Diary, July 1945, 22; Robert J. Cressman, *Official Chronology of the U.S. Navy in World War II*, 334; Joint Army-Navy Assessment Committee, *Japanese Naval and Merchant Shipping Losses.*

112 Aircraft Action Reports VBF-85, No. 39, and VF-88, No. 12, 15 July 1945.

113 Aircraft Action Report VBF-85, No. 39, 15 July 1945.

114 Aircraft Action Report VF-88, No. 10, 15 July 1945.

115 Aircraft Action Report VBF-88, No. 11, 15 July 1945.

116 Aircraft Action Report VF-85, No. 40, 15 July 1945.

117 Aircraft Action Reports VBF-85 No. 40, VB-85 No. 36, VT-85 No. 33, VBF-88 No. 11, VB-88 No. 5, VT-88 No. 5, CAG-50 No. 17, and CVLG-27 No. 6, 15 July 1945.

118 Aircraft Action Reports CVG-16, No. 12, 14 July 1945, and VF-88, No. 7, 15 July 1945.

119 Aircraft Action Report VF-85, No. 112, 15 July 1945.

120 Aircraft Action Report CAG-16, No. 13-45, 15 July 1945.

121 Aircraft Action Reports VBF-88, No. 10, and VF-85, No. 41, July 1945.

122 Aircraft Action Report CAG-16, No. 18-45, 15 July 1945.

123 Aircraft Action Report AG-47, No. 106, 15 July 1945.

124 Aircraft Action Report CAG-16, No. 18-45, 15 July 1945.

125 Aircraft Action Reports VT-1 No. 5-45, VBF-1 No. 14, and VB-1 No. 69, 15 July 1945.

126 Aircraft Action Report VF-50, No. 174, 15 July 1945.

127 Frank, *Downfall*, 157–158.

128 Action Report, Commander Task Group 30.6, 19 July 1945; report of Antisubmarine Action, *USS Lawrence C. Taylor* (DE-415), 16 July 1945.

129 Second Carrier Task Force Report, 2 July–15 August 1945, 1.

130 Aircraft Action Report VF-6, No. 59, 17 July 1945.

131 Aircraft Action Report CVG(N)-91, No. 3, 17 July 1945.

132 Murray, 388.

133 Third Fleet War Diary, July 1945, 33; Joint Army-Navy Assessment Committee, *Japanese Naval and Merchant Shipping Losses.*

134 Aircraft Action Report VF-49, No. 39, 18 July 1945.

135 Aircraft Action Report CVG-16, No. 23, 18 July 1945.

136 Aircraft Action Report VF-31, No. 9, 18 July 1945.

137 Aircraft Action Report VBF-1, No. 17, 18 July 1945.

138 Aircraft Action Reports VBF-85, No. 43, and VBF-88, No. 14, 18 July 1945.

139 Aircraft Action Report VBF-83, No. 126, 18 July 1945.

140 Aircraft Action Reports VB-85, No. 37, and VT-50, No. 19, 18 July 1945.

141 Aircraft Action Report CVG-83, No. 98, 18 July 1945.
142 Aircraft Action Report VBF-85, No. 44, 18 July 1945.
143 Aircraft Action Report CVLG-27, No. 8, 18 July 1945.
144 Aircraft Action Reports VB-1 No. 70 and CAG-94 No. 12, 18 July 1945.
145 Aircraft Action Report VB-1, No. 70, 18 July 1945.
146 Aircraft Action Report CVG-6, No. 37, 18 July 1945.
147 Aircraft Action Report VF-88, No. 12, 18 July 1945.
148 Aircraft Action Report VB-1, No. 70, 18 July 1945.
149 Aircraft Action Report VB-85, No. 37, 18 July 1945.
150 Aircraft Action Report CVG-16, No. 24, 18 July 1945.
151 Aircraft Action Report AG-83, No. 98, 18 July 1945.
152 Aircraft Action Report AG-47, No. 109, 18 July 1945.
153 Aircraft Action Report CVG-16, No. 24, 18 July 1945.
154 Aircraft Action Reports CVG-16, No. 24, and VT-34, No. 6, 18 July 1945.
155 Aircraft Action Report CVG-16, No. 24, 18 July 1945.
156 Aircraft Action Report CVG-16, No. 24, 18 July 1945.
157 Aircraft Action Report CVG-16, No. 24, 18 July 1945.
158 Aircraft Action Report CVG-16, No. 24, 18 July 1945.
159 Aircraft Action Report AG-83, No. 98, 18 July 1945.
160 Aircraft Action Report VT-88, No. 6, 18 July 1945.
161 Aircraft Action Report VT-85, No. 32, 18 July 1945.
162 Aircraft Action Report VB-85, No. 37, 18 July 1945.
163 Aircraft Action Report VT-50, No. 19, 18 July 1945.
164 Aircraft Action Report VT-88, No. 6, 18 July 1945.
165 Aircraft Action Report VB-88, No. 6, 18 July 1945.
166 Aircraft Action Report VBF-88, No. 126, 18 July 1945.
167 Aircraft Action Report CAG-27, No. 8, 18 July 1945.
168 Aircraft Action Report CAG-27, No. 8, 18 July 1945.
169 Aircraft Action Reports VB-1 No. 70, CAG-6 No. 37, and CAG-94 No. 12, 18 July 1945.
170 Aircraft Action Report VT-49, No. 20, 18 July 1945.
171 Aircraft Action Report VT-1, No. 6, 18 July 1945.
172 Aircraft Action Reports VB-1 No. 70, VT-1 No. 6, and CAG-94 No. 12, 18 July 1945.
173 Aircraft Action Report VT-1, No. 6, 18 July 1945.
174 Aircraft Action Report VT-1, No. 6, 18 July 1945.
175 Aircraft Action Report VT-31, No. 6, 18 July 1945.
176 Aircraft Action Report VT-49, No. 20, 18 July 1945.
177 Aircraft Action Report VBF-1, No. 18, 18 July 1945.
178 Aircraft Action Report VF-1, No. 23, 18 July 1945.
179 Aircraft Action Report VB-1, No. 70, 18 July 1945.
180 Aircraft Action Report CVG-6, No. 37, 18 July 1945.
181 Aircraft Action Report CAG-6, 1 No. 37, 18 July 1945.
182 Aircraft Action Reports VF-1, No. 23 and VB-1 No. 70, 18 July 1945.

183 Aircraft Action Report CAG-94, No. 12, 18 July 1945.

184 Aircraft Action Report VF-49, No. 40, 18 July 1945.

185 Aircraft Action Report VF-31, No. 11, 18 July 1945.

186 Aircraft Action Report VB-88, No. 6, 18 July 1945.

187 Aircraft Action Report VB-1, No. 70, 18 July 1945.

188 Aircraft Action Report VT-1, No. 6, 18 July 1945.

189 Individual Deceased Personnel File, Milton J. Adams, NPRC.

190 Aircraft Action Report CVG-16, No. 24, 18 July 1945.

191 Aircraft Action Report CVG-16, No. 24, 18 July 1945.

192 Aircraft Action Report VT-50, No. 19, 18 July 1945.

193 Aircraft Action Report CVG-16, No. 24, 18 July 1945.

194 Aircraft Action Report VB-85, No. 37, 18 July 1945.

195 Aircraft Action Report VBF-1, No. 18, 18 July 1945.

196 Aircraft Action Report CAG-6, No. 37, 18 July 1945.

197 Aircraft Action Report CAG-27, No. 8, 18 July 1945.

198 Aircraft Action Report AG-49, No. 109, 18 July 1945.

199 Aircraft Action Report VF-1, No. 23, 18 July 1945.

200 Aircraft Action Report VT-50, No. 19, 18 July 1945.

201 Encounter Report of 1st Lieutenant Robert Worton, 47th Fighter Squadron, 19 July 1945, Record Group 18, Entry 7, Box 2247, NARA.

202 Frank, *Downfall*, 157–158.

203 Second Carrier Task Force Report, 2 July–15 August 1945, 2; Joint Army-Navy Assessment Committee, *Japanese Naval and Merchant Shipping Losses*; John Winton, *The Forgotten Fleet*, 323. The Americans and British both claimed credit for sinking the carrier.

204 Aircraft Action Report CVG-6, No. 38, 24 July 1945.

205 Aircraft Action Report VBF-6, No. 72, 24 July 1945.

206 Aircraft Action Report CAG-6, No. 38, 24 July 1945.

207 Aircraft Action Report CAG-6, No. 38, 24 July 1945.

208 Aircraft Action Report CAG-6, No. 38, 24 July 1945.

209 Aircraft Action Report CAG-87, No. 22, 24 July 1945.

210 Aircraft Action Reports VF-31, No. 12, and VT-31, No. 7, 24 July 1945.

211 Aircraft Action Report VT-49, No. 21, 24 July 1945.

212 Aircraft Action Reports VBF-1, No. 20, and CAG-6, No. 38, 24 July 1945.

213 Aircraft Action Report CAG-6, No. 38, 24 July 1945.

214 Aircraft Action Report CAG-6, No. 38, 24 July 1945.

215 Aircraft Action Report CAG-6, No. 38, 24 July 1945.

216 Aircraft Action Report CAG-6, No. 38, 24 July 1945.

217 Aircraft Action Report CAG-6, No. 38, 24 July 1945.

218 Aircraft Action Report CAG-6, No. 38, 24 July 1945.

219 Aircraft Action Report CAG-6, No. 38, 24 July 1945.

220 Aircraft Action Report CAG-6, No. 38, 24 July 1945.

221 Aircraft Action Report CAG-94, No. 13, 24 July 1945.

222 Aircraft Action Report VF-1, No. 27, 24 July 1945.

223 Aircraft Action Report CAG-6, No. 38, 24 July 1945.

224 Aircraft Action Report, VBF-1, No. 20, 24 July 1945.

225 Aircraft Action Report CAG-6, No. 38, 24 July 1945.

226 Aircraft Action Report VT-1, No. 7-45, 24 July 1945.

227 Aircraft Action Report VF-49, No. 12, 24 July 1945.

228 Aircraft Action Reports AG-27 No. 9, CAG-50 No. 21, and VT-85 No. 37, 24 July 1945.

229 Aircraft Action Report VB-85, No. 38, 24 July 1945.

230 Aircraft Action Report VB-88, No. 7, 24 July 1945.

231 Aircraft Action Report VT-88, No. 7, 24 July 1945.

232 Aircraft Action Report VF-88, No. 15, 24 July 1945.

233 Aircraft Action Report AG-27, No. 9, 24 July 1945.

234 Aircraft Action Report AG-27, No. 9, 24 July 1945.

235 Aircraft Action Report CAG-50, No. 21, 24 July 1945.

236 Aircraft Action Report VG-50, No. 24, 24 July 1945.

237 Aircraft Action Report AG-47, No. 110, 24 July 1945.

238 Aircraft Action Report CVG-87, No. 24, 24 July 1945.

239 Aircraft Action Report CVG-87, No. 24, 24 July 1945.

240 Aircraft Action Report AG-34, No. 8-45, 24 July 1945.

241 Aircraft Action Report AG-34, No. 8-45, 24 July 1945.

242 Aircraft Action Report CVG-16, No. 28-45, 24 July 1945.

243 Aircraft Action Report CVG-16, No. 28-45, 24 July 1945.

244 Aircraft Action Report AG-83, No. 99, 24 July 1945.

245 Aircraft Action Reports CVG-16 No. 28-45, AG-34 No. 8-45, and CVG-83 No. 99, 24 July 1945.

246 Aircraft Action Reports CAG-94, No. 13, and VF-49, No. 12, 24 July 1945.

247 Aircraft Action Report CVG-87, No. 24, 24 July 1945.

248 Aircraft Action Report AG-27, No. 9, 24 July 1945.

249 Aircraft Action Report VF-49, No. 42, 24 July 1945.

250 Aircraft Action Report VF-49, No. 42, 24 July 1945.

251 Aircraft Action Report VF-1, No. 27, 24 July 1945.

252 Aircraft Action Report VBF-1, No. 20, 24 July 1945.

253 Aircraft Action Reports VBF-1, No. 20, and CVG-16, No. 28, 24 July 1945.

254 Aircraft Action Report VF-88, No. 15, 24 July 1945.

255 Aircraft Action Report VBF-94, No. 25, 24 July 1945.

256 Aircraft Action Report VBF-94, No. 26, 24 July 1945.

257 Aircraft Action Report CVLG-27, No. 11, 24 July 1945.

258 Aircraft Action Report VF-31, No. 33, 24 July 1945.

259 Aircraft Action Report VBF-88, No. 16, 24 July 1945. No report from VBF-85 has been located.

260 Aircraft Action Reports VBF-88, No. 19, and VBF-85, No. 45, 24 July 1945. The Olynyk list credits each pilot with the shootdown.

261 Aircraft Action Report VBF-88, No. 19, 24 July 1945.

262 Aircraft Action Report VBF-88, No. 17, 24 July 1945.

263 Aircraft Action Report VBF-1, No. 21, 24 July 1945.

264 Aircraft Action Report VB-1, No. 72, 24 July 1945.

265 Aircraft Action Report VT-1, No. 8-45, 24 July 1945.

266 Aircraft Action Report VF-1, No. 29-45, 24 July 1945.

267 Aircraft Action Report CVG-6, No. 39, 24 July 1945.

268 Aircraft Action Reports VF-31, No. 12, and VT-31, No. 7, 24 July 1945.

269 Aircraft Action Report CAG-94, No. 14, 24 July 1945.

270 History of Torpedo Squadron Forty Nine, 10 August 1944–27 November 1945.

271 Aircraft Action Reports VT-49, No. 22, and VF-49, No. 1-44, 24 July 1945.

272 Aircraft Action Reports VBF-88, No. 17, and VBF-85, No. 48, 24 July 1945.

273 Aircraft Action Report VT-88, No. 8, 24 July 1945.

274 Aircraft Action Report CVLG-50, No. 10, 24 July 1945.

275 Aircraft Action Reports VB-85, No. 48, and VBF-85, No. 39, 24 July 1945.

276 Aircraft Action Report VT-85, No. 38, 24 July 1945.

277 Aircraft Action Report VT-50, No. 33, 24 July 1945.

278 Aircraft Action Report CVG-16, No. 31-45, 24 July 1945.

279 Aircraft Action Report CVG-16, No. 31-45, 24 July 1945.

280 Aircraft Action Report CAG-87, No. 27, 24 July 1945.

281 Aircraft Action Report CVG-83, No. 100, 24 July 1945.

282 Aircraft Action Report AG-34, No. 9-45, 24 July 1945.

283 Aircraft Action Report AG-47, No. 111, 24 July 1945.

284 Aircraft Action Report CAG-87, No. 27, 24 July 1945.

285 Aircraft Action Report VT-88, No. 7, 24 July 1945.

286 Aircraft Action Report CVG-16, No. 27, 24 July 1945.

287 Aircraft Action Report VBF-83, No. 129, 24 July 1945.

288 Aircraft Action Report CVG-16, No. 32, 24 July 1945.

289 Aircraft Action Report VT(N)-91, No. 4, 24 July 1945.

290 Second Carrier Task Force Report, 2 July–15 August 1945, 2; Third Fleet War Diary, July 1945, 41.

291 Third Fleet War Diary, July 1945, 44; Cressman, 337; Joint Army-Navy Assessment Committee, *Japanese Naval and Merchant Shipping Losses.*

292 Drea, 212.

293 Aircraft Action Report VT(N)-91, No. 5, 25 July 1945.

294 Aircraft Action Report VBF-1, No. 22, 25 July 1945.

295 Aircraft Action Report VBF-6, No. 77, 25 July 1945.

296 Aircraft Action Report VF-83, No. 121, 25 July 1945.

297 Aircraft Action Report VBF-83, No. 132, 25 July 1945.

298 Aircraft Action Report VF-49, No. 1-45, 25 July 1945.

299 Aircraft Action Reports VF-88, No. 18, and VF-85, No. 46, 25 July 1945.

300 Aircraft Action Reports VF-88, No. 18, and VF-85, No. 46, 25 July 1945.

301 Aircraft Action Reports VF-88, No. 16, and VF-85, No. 48, 25 July 1945.

302 Aircraft Action Report VF-31, No. 14, 25 July 1945.

303 Aircraft Action Report CVG-16, No. 33, 25 July 1945.

304 Aircraft Action Report VBF-6, No. 81, 25 July 1945.

305 Aircraft Action Report CAG-6, No. 40, 25 July 1945.

306 Aircraft Action Reports VF-50, No. 24, and VT-50, No. 31-8, 25 July 1945.

307 Aircraft Action Reports CAG-6, No. 40, and VF-50, No. 46, 25 July 1945.

308 Aircraft Action Reports VT-49, No. 23, and VF-50, No. 46, 25 July 1945.

309 Aircraft Action Reports VF-31, No. 15, and VT-31, No. 8, 25 July 1945.

310 Aircraft Action Reports CAG-94, No. 15, and CVLG-28, No. 12, 25 July 1945.

311 Aircraft Action Report VF-1, No. 32, 25 July 1945.

312 Aircraft Action Reports VBF-1 No. 24, VT-1 No. 9, and VB-1 No. 9, 25 July 1945.

313 Aircraft Action Reports VBF-88, No. 21, and VT-88, No. 9, 25 July 1945. No report for VB-88 has been located for this mission.

314 Aircraft Action Reports VF-16, No. 35, and VF-16, No. 37, 25 July 1945.

315 Aircraft Action Report VF(N)-91, No. 5, 25 July 1945.

316 Aircraft Action Report VF(N)-91, No. 7, 25 July 1945.

317 Third Fleet War Diary, July 1945, 48; Joint Army-Navy Assessment Committee, *Japanese Naval and Merchant Shipping Losses.*

318 Third Fleet War Diary, July 1945, 45; Cressman, 338.

319 Frank, *Downfall*, 234.

320 Aircraft Action Reports VF-85 No. 52, VF-86 No. 13, and VF-88 No. 17, 28 July 1945.

321 Aircraft Action Report CVG-16, No. 38, 28 July 1945.

322 Aircraft Action Report VF-31, No. 16, 28 July 1945.

323 Aircraft Action Report CVG-87, No. 32, 28 July 1945.

324 Aircraft Action Report VBF-1, No. 26, 28 July 1945.

325 Aircraft Action Report VF-83, No. 123, 28 July 1945.

326 Aircraft Action Report CAG-6, No. 41, 28 July 1945.

327 Aircraft Action Report VT-88, No. 10, 28 July 1945.

328 Aircraft Action Reports CAG-86 No. 6, VBF-85 No. 51, and VT-85 No. 39, 28 July 1945.

329 Aircraft Action Report CAG-86, No. 6, 28 July 1945.

330 Aircraft Action Reports VT-34, No. 10, and VF-34, No. 15, 28 July 1945.

331 Aircraft Action Report AG-47, No. 112, 28 July 1945.

332 Aircraft Action Report AG-47, No. 112, 28 July 1945.

333 Aircraft Action Report CVG-87, No. 34, 28 July 1945.

334 Aircraft Action Report CVG-87, No. 34, 28 July 1945.

335 Aircraft Action Report CVG-87, No. 34, 28 July 1945.

336 Aircraft Action Report AG-83, No. 101, 28 July 1945.

337 Aircraft Action Report VBF-1, No. 27, 28 July 1945.

338 Aircraft Action Report CAG-6, No. 41, 28 July 1945.

339 Aircraft Action Report VBF-1, No. 27, 28 July 1945.

340 Aircraft Action Report VB-1, No. 74, 28 July 1945.

341 Aircraft Action Reports VF-31, No. 17, and VT-31, No. 9, 29 July 1945.

342 Aircraft Action Report CAG-94, No. 16, 28 July 1945.

343 Aircraft Action Report VF-49, No. 49, 28 July 1945.

344 Aircraft Action Report VT-85, No. 39, 28 July 1945.

345 Aircraft Action Report VBF-85, No. 51, 28 July 1945.

346 Aircraft Action Report VB-85, No. 40, 28 July 1945.

347 Aircraft Action Report VT-50, No. 32, 28 July 1945.

348 Aircraft Action Report CAG-86, No. 6, 28 July 1945.

349 Aircraft Action Reports VT-88 No. 10, VB-88 No. 9, and VF-88 No. 19, 28 July 1945.

350 Aircraft Action Report VT-27, No. 13, 28 July 1945.

351 Aircraft Action Report CAG-6, No. 41, 28 July 1945.

352 Aircraft Action Report VBF-94, No. 31, 28 July 1945.

353 Aircraft Action Reports VBF-1, No. 29, and VBF-6, No. 84, 28 July 1945.

354 Aircraft Action Report VT-27, No. 13, 28 July 1945.

355 Aircraft Action Report VBF-88, No. 27, 28 July 1945.

356 Aircraft Action Report CVG-16, No. 16, 28 July 1945.

357 Aircraft Action Report VF-1, No. 39, 28 July 1945.

358 Aircraft Action Report VBF-1, No. 30, 28 July 1945.

359 Aircraft Action Report VBF-1, No. 30, 28 July 1945.

360 Aircraft Action Report CAG-6, No. 42, 28 July 1945.

361 Aircraft Action Report CAG-6, No. 42, 28 July 1945.

362 Aircraft Action Report CAG-6, No. 45, 28 July 1945.

363 Aircraft Action Report CAG-6, No. 42, 28 July 1945.

364 Aircraft Action Report CAG-6, No. 42, 28 July 1945.

365 Aircraft Action Report CAG-94, No. 17, 28 July 1945.

366 Aircraft Action Report VF-49, No. 50, 28 July 1945.

367 Aircraft Action Report VF-49, No. 50, 28 July 1945.

368 Aircraft Action Report VBF-88, No. 27, 28 July 1945.

369 Aircraft Action Reports VBF-88 No. 27, VB-88 No. 10, and VT-88 No. 11, 28 July 1945.

370 Aircraft Action Report CVG-86, No. 7, 28 July 1945.

371 Aircraft Action Report AG-27, No. 14, 28 July 1945.

372 Aircraft Action Reports VBF-85 No. 53, VB-85 No. 40, and VT-85 No. 36, 28 July 1945.

373 Aircraft Action Report VT-50, No. 33, 28 July 1945.

374 Aircraft Action Report CVLG-27, No. 14, 28 July 1945.

375 Aircraft Action Report CAG-6, No. 42, 28 July 1945.

376 Aircraft Action Report CVG-16, No. 16, 28 July 1945.

377 Aircraft Action Reports CVG-83, No. 102, and AG-47, No. 113, 28 July 1945.

378 Aircraft Action Report CVG-16, No. 16, 28 July 1945.

379 Aircraft Action Report AG-34, No. 11, 28 July 1945.

380 Aircraft Action Report CVG-87, No. 37, 28 July 1945.

381 Aircraft Action Report AG-47, No. 113, 28 July 1945.

382 Aircraft Action Report CVG-83, No. 102, 28 July 1945.

383 Aircraft Action Report CVG-87, No. 38, 28 July 1945.

384 Aircraft Action Report VBF-83, No. 138, 28 July 1945.

385 Third Fleet War Diary, July 1945, 51–52.

386 Third Fleet War Diary, July 1945, 53–54; Cressman, 339.

387 Aircraft Action Reports VT(N)-91, No. 7, 30 July 1945.

388 Aircraft Action Report CVG-16, No. 44, 30 July 1945.

389 Aircraft Action Report VF-94, No. 18, 30 July 1945.

390 Aircraft Action Report CAG-6, No. 43, 30 July 1945.

391 Aircraft Action Report CAG-6, No. 45, 30 July 1945.

392 Aircraft Action Report VF-49, No. 51, 30 July 1945.

393 Aircraft Action Reports VBF-85 No. 54, VB-85 No. 42, VBF-86 No. 18, VB-86 No. 9, VBF-88 No. 25, and VB-88 No. 11, 30 July 1945.

394 Aircraft Action Report CAG-94, No. 18, 30 July 1945.

395 Aircraft Action Reports VF-1, No. 41, and VT-1, No. 12, 30 July 1945.

396 Aircraft Action Report CAG-6, No. 44, 30 July 1945.

397 Aircraft Action Reports AG-34, No. 12, and AG-83, No. 104, 30 July 1945.

398 Aircraft Action Reports VT-50 No. 34, VT-86 No. 7, VF-86 No. 20, and CVLG-27 No. 15, 30 July 1945.

399 Aircraft Action Report VF-50, No. 29, 30 July 1945.

400 Aircraft Action Reports VBF-85, No. 55, and VT-85, No. 42, 30 July 1945.

401 Aircraft Action Reports VF-88, No. 23, and VT-88, No. 12, 30 July 1945.

402 Aircraft Action Reports VBF-85, No. 56, and VB-85, No. 43, 30 July 1945.

403 Aircraft Action Report VB-88, No. 12, 30 July 1945.

404 Aircraft Action Reports VBF-88, No. 26, and VT-49, No. 26, 30 July 1945.

405 Aircraft Action Reports VBF-86, No. 19, and VB-86, No. 10, 30 July 1945.

406 Aircraft Action Reports VF-49, No. 52, and VT-49, No. 26, 30 July 1945.

407 Aircraft Action Report VF-85, No. 43, 30 July 1945.

408 Aircraft Action Report VF-86, No. 23, 30 July 1945.

409 Aircraft Action Reports VBF-85, No. 57, and VF-50, No. 31, 30 July 1945.

410 Aircraft Action Report VF-31, No. 22, 30 July 1945.

411 Aircraft Action Report VF-88, No. 26, 30 July 1945.

412 Aircraft Action Report VBF-86, No. 22, 9 August 1945.

413 Aircraft Action Report VBF-88, No. 42, 8 August 1945.

414 Frank, *Downfall*, 157–158.

415 Third Fleet War Diary, August 1945, 13; 2nd Carrier Task Force Report, 108; Task Force 37 (British) Report July–August 1945, 134–135; Cressman, 341.

416 Aircraft Action Report CAG-87, No. 46, 9 August 1945.

417 Aircraft Action Reports VBF-6, No. 91, and VF-6, No. 83, 9 August 1945.

418 Aircraft Action Report VF-94, No. 21, 9 August 1945.

419 Aircraft Action Report VF-1, No. 45, 9 August 1945.

420 Aircraft Action Reports VBF-1, No. 35, and VB-1, No. 78, 9 August 1945.

421 Aircraft Action Reports VBF-85 No. 59, VB-85 No. 44, VBF-86 No. 23, VB-86 No. 11, VBF-88 No. 30, and VB-88 No. 13, 9 August 1945.

422 Aircraft Action Report VF-34, No. 18, 9 August 1945.

423 Aircraft Action Report VT-86 No. 9, 9 August 1945.

424 Aircraft Action Reports CVLG-27 No. 17, VT-50 No. 36, VF-86 No. 25, VT-86 No. 9, VF-85 No. 57, VT-85 No. 38, VBF-88 No. 31, and VT-88 No. 13, 9 August 1945.

425 Aircraft Action Report VT-85, No. 38, 9 August 1945.

426 Aircraft Action Report AG-83, No. 108, 9 August 1945.

427 Aircraft Action Reports VBF-1 No. 36, VT-1 No. 13, VF-49 No. 56, VT-49 No. 27, and VF-31 No. 11, 9 August 1945; Winton, 337.

428 Aircraft Action Reports VF-49, No. 57, and VF-94, No. 23, 9 August 1945.

429 Aircraft Action Reports CVG-16, No. 54, and AG-83, No. 109, 9 August 1945.

430 Aircraft Action Report CAG-6, No. 47, 9 August 1945.

431 Aircraft Action Reports CVG-16 No. 55, AG-34 No. 14, and AG-47 No. 117, 9 August 1945.

432 Air Defense of Homeland, 28–30; USSBS, *Japanese Air Power*, 73.

433 Aircraft Action Reports CVLG-27 No. 18, VF-50 No. 37, VT-50 No. 38, VBF-85 No. 61, VT-85 No. 47, VBF-86 No. 26, VF-86 No. 27, VT-86 No. 12, VBF-88 No. 33, and VT-88, No. 14, 9 August 1945. The report of VB-88 was not available.

434 Aircraft Action Report CVG-16, No. 53, 9 August 1945.

435 Aircraft Action Report VF-6, No. 86, 9 August 1945; History of Fighting Squadron 88, 1 March 1945–3 September 1945, 12.

436 Aircraft Action Report VF-88, No. 27, 9 August 1945 and History of Fighting Squadron Eighty-Eight (1 March–3 September 1945), 12.

437 Aircraft Action Report VF-86, No. 28, 9 August 1945.

438 Aircraft Action Report VBF-1, No. 39, 9 August 1945.

439 Aircraft Action Report VF(N)-91, No. 10, 9 August 1945.

440 Aircraft Action Report CVG-16, No. 53, 9 August 1945.

441 Action Report, *USS Borie*, 2 July–15 August 1945, Part III.

442 Third Fleet War Diary, August 1945, 20; Task Force 37 (British) Report July–August 1945, 136–137; Cressman, 341; Air Intelligence Group, *The Air War against Japan, 1–15 August 1945*, 3.

443 Second Carrier Task Force Report, 2 July–15 August 1945, 14, 30.

444 Aircraft Action Reports VBF-85 No. 62, VF-86 No. 29, and VBF-88 No. 34, 10 August 1945.

445 Aircraft Action Report VBF-87, No. 51, 10 August 1945.

446 Aircraft Action Report CVG-87, No. 52, 10 August 1945.

447 *USS Independence* War Diary, August 1945, 12.

448 Aircraft Action Reports AG-34, No. 15, and AG-47, No. 118, 10 August 1945.

449 Aircraft Action Report CVG-87, No. 53, 10 August 1945.

450 Aircraft Action Report CAG-6, No. 49, 10 August 1945.

451 Aircraft Action Reports VBF-1 No. 41, VB-1 No. 30, VT-1 No. 15, VF-94 No. 26, and VT-94 No. 8, 10 August 1945.

452 Aircraft Action Report CVG-16, No. 59, 10 August 1945.

453 Aircraft Action Report CVG-87, No. 54, 10 August 1945.

454 Aircraft Action Report VF-88, No. 29, 10 August 1945.

455 Aircraft Action Report VBF-86, No. 29, 10 August 1945.

456 Aircraft Action Report VF-85, No. 63, 10 August 1945.

457 Aircraft Action Report CVG-16, No. 60, 10 August 1945.

458 Aircraft Action Reports VBF-85 No. 64, VF-86 No. 31, and VBF-88 No. 36, 10 August 1945.

459 Aircraft Action Report CAG-83, No. 109, 9 August 1945; *USS North Carolina* War Diary, August 1945, Report of 10 August 1945; William D. Farnsworth, *The First Seventy Years.*

460 Aircraft Action Reports CVLG-27 No. 20, VF-50 No. 46, VT-50 No. 45, VBF-85 No. 65, VB-85 No. 47, VT-85 No. 49, VF-86 No. 32, VBF-88 No. 37, VB-88 No. 16, and VT-88 No. 16, 10 August 1945.

461 Aircraft Action Reports VBF-1 No. 43, VT-1 No. 16, AG-6 No. 51, VF-31 No. 27, VT-31 No. 14, VF-49 No. 62, VT-49 No. 30, VF-94 No. 29, and VT-94 No. 9; "Kin Beg: 'Punish Jap Torturers,'" *Chicago Herald-American*, August 31, 1945, 3.

462 Third Fleet War Diary, August 1945, 24.

463 Frank, *Downfall*, 303.

464 Frank, *Downfall*, 308.

465 Murray, 395.

466 Third Fleet War Diary, August 1945, 26; 2nd Carrier Task Force Report, 113; Task Force 37 (British) Report, July–August 1945, 134–135.

467 Third Fleet War Diary, August 1945; Office of the Chief of Naval Operations, Air Intelligence Group, *The Air War against Japan, 1–15 August 1945*, 3.

468 Aircraft Action Report CVG-16, No. 62, 13 August 1945.

469 *USS Independence* War Diary, August 1945, 13.

470 Aircraft Action Reports VBF-1 No. 47, VB-1 No. 32, and VT-1 No. 17, 13 August 1945.

471 Aircraft Action Report AG-6, No. 58, 13 August 1945.

472 Aircraft Action Reports VBF-94 No. 39, VB-94 No. 22, and VT-94 No. 10, 13 August 1945.

473 Aircraft Action Reports VF-49 No. 64, VT-49 No. 31, VF-31 No. 30, and VT-31 No. 15, 13 August 1945.

474 Aircraft Action Reports VF-31, No. 30, and VF-31, No. 15, 13 August 1945.

475 Aircraft Action Report CVG-87, No. 58, 13 August 1945; Recommendation for Awards, Air Sea Rescue Group, August 14, 1945 in History, Rescue Squadron 4, August 1945, 45; Larry Davis, "Air Force Search & Rescue, Part 1"; History of Fighting Squadron Forty-Seven, 17 September 1945, 16.

476 Aircraft Action Report CVG-16, No. 64, 13 August 1945.

477 Aircraft Action Reports VF-50 No. 49, VT-50 No. 48, VBF-86 No. 32, VB-86 No. 15, and VT-86 No. 13, 13 August 1945.

478 Aircraft Action Reports AG-34 No. 17, AG-47 No. 120, and AG-83 No. 115, 13 August 1945.

479 Aircraft Action Reports VF-85 No. 65, VB-85 No. 48, and VT-85 No. 42, 13 August 1945.

480 Aircraft Action Reports VBF-88 No. 38, VB-88 No. 17, and VT-88 No. 17, 13 August 1945.

481 Aircraft Action Report VBF-1, No. 44, 13 August 1945.

482 Aircraft Action Report CVG-16, No. 65, 13 August 1945.

483 Aircraft Action Report VBF-85, No. 68, 13 August 1945.

484 Aircraft Action Report CVG-16, No. 65, 13 August 1945.

485 Aircraft Action Report VF-88, No. 32, 13 August 1945.

486 Aircraft Action Report VF-85, No. 69, 13 August 1945.

487 Aircraft Action Report VF-31, No. 32, 13 August 1945.

488 Aircraft Action Report VF-49, No. 66, 13 August 1945.

489 Aircraft Action Report VF-86, No. 35, 13 August 1945.

490 Aircraft Action Report CVG-16, No. 67, 13 August 1945.

491 Aircraft Action Report VF-1, No. 54, 13 August 1945.

492 Aircraft Action Reports VF-6, No. 96, and VBF-6, No. 102, 13 August 1945.

493 Aircraft Action Report VF-86, No. 36, 13 August 1945.

494 Aircraft Action Report VBF-85, No. 71, 13 August 1945.

495 Aircraft Action Reports VF-50 No. 51, CVG-16 No. 68, and CVG-87 No. 62, 13 August 1945.

496 Aircraft Action Report VBF-88, No. 41, 13 August 1945.

497 Aircraft Action Report VBG-87, No. 63, 13 August 1945.

498 Aircraft Action Report VF-49, No. 67, 13 August 1945.

499 Aircraft Action Report VF-34, No. 20, 13 August 1945.

500 Aircraft Action Report VF-88, No. 34, 13 August 1945.

501 Aircraft Action Report VF(N)-91, No. 11, 13 August 1945.

502 Frank, *Downfall*, 311–313; Werrel, 221.

503 Frank, *Downfall*, 317.

504 William Craig, *The Fall of Japan*, 177–178, 197.

505 Third Fleet War Diary, August 1945, 35.

506 Winton, 344.

507 Drea, 225.

508 Aircraft Action Report VBF-1, No. 48, 15 August 1945.

509 Aircraft Action Reports VBF-86 No. 37, VBF-85 No. 72, and VF-88 No. 35, 15 August 1945.

510 Aircraft Action Report VF-94, No. 33, 15 August 1945.

511 Pacific War Research Society, *Japan's Longest Day*, 213.

512 Recollections of Rear Admiral Henry Miller, Volume 1, 92.

513 Aircraft Action Reports VF-6, No. 97, and VBF-6, No. 103, 15 August 1945.

514 Aircraft Action Report CVG-87, No. 64, 15 August 1945.

515 Aircraft Action Report CVG-16, No. 70, 15 August 1945.

516 Aircraft Action Report AG-83, No. 117, 15 August 1945.

517 Aircraft Action Report VF-31, No. 33, 15 August 1945.

518 Aircraft Action Report VF-49, No. 68, 15 August 1945.

519 Aircraft Action Report VBF-1, No. 48, 15 August 1945; British Fleet Air Operations, July–August 1945, 31.

520 Aircraft Action Report VBF-88 No. 43, 15 August 1945.

521 Thach, 476.

522 Aircraft Action Report VBF-6, No. 105, 15 August 1945.

523 Aircraft Action Report VBF-85, No. 73, 15 August 1945.

524 Aircraft Action Report VF-86, No. 37, 15 August 1945.

525 Aircraft Action Report VF-31, No. 34, 15 August 1945; Clarence A. Moore, *Autobiography*, unpaginated.

526 Figures calculated from author's database.

527 Thach, 465.

528 Derived from a database of missions and losses the author compiled as a reference for this book.

529 Air Operations of Carrier Air Group 6, Memorandum No. 4CM-45, August 24, 1945.

530 USSBS, *Japanese Air Power*, 24–25, 70–71; Air Intelligence Group, *The Air War against Japan, 16–31 July 1945*, 3; USSBS, *Summary Report (Pacific War)*, 17.

531 USSBS, *Japanese Air Power*, 71.

532 USSBS, *Japanese Air Power*, 71.

533 USSBS, *Japanese Air Power*, 36, 40.

534 USSBS, *Japanese Air Power*, 71.

535 USSBS, *Japanese Air Power*, 48, 70–71.

536 Frank, *Downfall*, 157–158; USSBS, *Summary Report (Pacific War)*, 17.

537 Thach, 467; Skates, 139.

538 USSBS, *Japan's Struggle to End the War*, 11.

539 Frank, *Downfall*, 17.

540 USSBS, *Summary War Report (Pacific War)*, 16–17.

541 The debate about the use of the two atomic bombs seems endless, with many books written about the subject, which is outside the immediate theme of this book. But given the intensity of the war in the Pacific, particularly the long and bloody Okinawa campaign, the casualty potential of an invasion *perceived* by American leaders at the time, and the imprecise information about Japanese attitudes concerning surrender, based on intelligence analyses of Japanese communications, it is not surprising that atomic weapons were first used in combat over Japan in August 1945. It is worth noting that a U.S. Strategic Bombing Survey of survivors of Hiroshima and Nagasaki (see USSBS, *Summary War Report [Pacific War]*, 25) found that only one-third of them believed that victory was no longer possible after the two attacks.

542 Frank, *Downfall*, 312. In response to this intercept, General Marshall ordered the examination of using the remaining atomic weapons tactically during the impending invasion of the Home Islands.

543 Frank, *Downfall*, 344.

GLOSSARY

AA: antiaircraft fire

AMM: Aviation Machinist's Mate

AOC: Aviation Ordnanceman

ARM: Aviation Radioman

Avenger: American Navy single-engine torpedo bomber, the Grumman TBM

B-24: American, Army Air Force Consolidated four-engine bomber

B-29: American, Army Air Force Boeing four-engine bomber that could carry a large bomb load and had a pressurized cabin; used for the strategic bombing of Japan

Baka bomb: piloted, jet-powered aerial suicide bomb launched from an aircraft

Betty: American code name for the Japanese Navy Mitsubishi G4M two-engine bomber

Bogie: code name for an unidentified aircraft

CAP: combat air patrol, a patrol by fighters based on a carrier to protect it and the Task Force to which it belonged

Catalina: American, two-engine Consolidated PBY seaplane used for air-sea rescue and maritime patrol

CINCPAC: Commander in Chief, Pacific Fleet

Corsair: American Navy single-engine fighter, the Voight F4U

Dauntless: American Navy SBD single-engine dive-bomber in use at the beginning of World War II

DE: destroyer escort

Dinah: American code name for the Japanese Army twin-engine Mitsubishi Ki-46 long-range reconnaissance aircraft

Ditch: water landing by an aircraft

Dumbo: American code name for an air-sea rescue aircraft, a Catalina or Mariner

Emily: American code name for the Japanese Navy four-engine Kawanishi H8K flying boat

Fast Carrier Task Force: assembly of attack carriers used by the American Pacific Fleet

Fighter controller: officers who directed fighters in defense of a Navy Task Force using radar

Firefly: British single-engine bomber

Flak: antiaircraft artillery

Fragmentation bomb: ordnance designed to explode over a target and widely spread deadly shrapnel

Frances: American code name for the Japanese Navy twin-engine Yokosuka P1Y bomber

Frank: American code name for the Japanese Army single-engine Nakajima Ki-84 fighter

F4U: Navy designation for the Corsair fighter

F6F: Navy designation for the Hellcat fighter

George: American code name for the Japanese Navy single-engine Kawanishi N1K2 fighter

Grace: American code name for the Japanese Navy single-engine Aichi B7A bomber

Heckler mission: nighttime mission to interdict enemy airfields

Helen: American code name for the Japanese Army two-engine Nakajima Ki-49 bomber

Hellcat: American Navy single-engine fighter, the Grumman F6F

Helldiver: American Navy single-engine dive-bomber, the Curtiss SB2C

Irving: American code name for the Japanese Navy two-engine Nakajima J1N fighter and night fighter

Jack: American code name for the Japanese Navy single-engine Mitsubishi J2M fighter

Jake: American code name for the Japanese Navy single-engine Aichi E13A reconnaissance floatplane

Jill: American code name for the Japanese Navy single-engine Nakajima B6N torpedo bomber

Joint Chiefs of Staff: supreme American military headquarters during World War II

Joint Intelligence Staff: the intelligence branch of the Joint Chiefs of Staff

Judy: American code name for the Japanese Navy single-engine Yokosuka D4Y bomber

Kate: American code name for the Japanese Navy single-engine Nakajima B5N torpedo bomber

Kingfisher: American Navy single-engine floatplane, the Vought S2U

Lugger: a small, wooden ship with sails

Magic: decrypted intercepts of Japanese diplomatic messages

Mariner: American Navy two-engine seaplane, the Martin PBM, used for air-sea rescues and maritime patrols

Mattress: World War II American naval aviation slang for heavy cloud overcast

Mavis: American code name for the Japanese Navy four-engine Kawanishi H6K flying boat

Myrt: American code name for the Japanese Navy single-engine Nakajima C6N reconnaissance aircraft and night fighter

Nell: American code name for the Japanese Navy two-engine Mitsubishi G3M bomber

Nick: American code name for the Japanese Army twin-engine Kawasaki Ki-45 fighter and night fighter

Oscar: American code name for the Japanese Army single-engine Nakajima Ki-43 fighter

PBM: the Martin Mariner seaplane

P-47: American, Army Air Force single-engine long-range fighter

P-51: American, Army Air Force single-engine long-range fighter

Pete: American code name for the Mitsubishi F 1M, a single-engine, biplane Japanese float reconnaissance aircraft

Radar pickets: destroyers stationed approximately fifty miles from the main Task Force, acting as early warning of incoming Japanese planes

Revetment: aircraft storage position on an airfield with berms for protection against bombs

RM: Radioman

Rope: a longer version of the metallic strips used to confuse certain Japanese radar frequencies

Rufe: American code name for the Nakajima A6MZ, the float-plane model of the Japanese Zero fighter

Sally: American code name for the Japanese twin-engine Mitsubishi Ki-21 bomber

SBD: American Navy's Douglas Dauntless single-engine dive-bomber

Seafire: British single-engine, carrier-born version of the Spitfire fighter

Sonia: American code name for the Japanese Army single-engine Mitsubishi Ki-51 attack bomber

Sonobuoy: a small float containing a sonar device dropped from aircraft, used to detect submarines

Sugar Dog: Navy code name for very small, wooden cargo boats of less than one hundred tons displacement

SubCAP: a fighter combat air patrol protecting surfaced submarines on lifeguard duty

Superfortress: B-29

Tabby: American code name for the Japanese Navy twin-engine Nakajima L2D transport, the Japanese version of the American DC-3

Target of opportunity: any worthwhile target that presented itself when the assigned primary target could not be attacked during a mission

Task Force: the combined force of American and British carriers and warships operating off the coast of Japan during the summer of 1945

Tony: American code name for the Japanese Army single-engine Kawasaki Ki-61 fighter

Topsy: American code name for the Japanese twin-engine Mitsubishi Ki-57 transport

Torpecker: American Navy slang for the Avenger torpedo bomber

Ultra: decrypted intercepts of Japanese military messages

Val: American code name for the Japanese Navy single-engine Aichi D3A dive-bomber

Willow: American code name for the Japanese Navy single-engine Yokosuka K5Y biplane training aircraft

Window: short aluminum strips used to confuse Japanese radar

Zeke: American code name for the Japanese Navy Zero fighter

Zero: Japanese Navy single-engine Mitsubishi A6M fighter

BIBLIOGRAPHY

Action Report: VC-13 Antisubmarine Action Report No. 19. 29 July 1945. Archives, Navy History and Heritage Command.

Air Group 1 Squadron Histories, Archives, Navy History and Heritage Command.

Air Group 6 Squadron Histories, Archives, Navy History and Heritage Command.

Air Group 16 Squadron Histories, Archives, Navy History and Heritage Command.

Air Group 27 Squadron Histories, Archives, Navy History and Heritage Command.

Air Group 34 Squadron Histories, Archives, Navy History and Heritage Command.

Air Group 47 Squadron Histories, Archives, Navy History and Heritage Command. History of Fighting Squadron Forty-Seven, 17 September 1945.

Air Group 49 Squadron Histories, Archives, Navy History and Heritage Command. History of Torpedo Squadron Forty Nine, 10 August 1944–27 November 1945, Navy History and Heritage Command.

Air Group 50 Squadron Histories, Archives, Navy History and Heritage Command.

Air Group 83 Squadron Histories, Archives, Navy History and Heritage Command.

Air Group 85 Squadron Histories, Archives, Navy History and Heritage Command.

Air Group 86 Squadron Histories, Archives, Navy History and Heritage Command.

Air Group 87 Squadron Histories, Archives, Navy History and Heritage Command.

Air Group 88 Squadron Histories, Archives, Navy History and Heritage Command. History of Fighting Squadron Eighty-Eight, 1 March 1945–3 September 1945, Navy History and Heritage Command.

Air Group (N) 91 Squadron Histories, Archives, Navy History and Heritage Command.

Air Group 94 Squadron Histories, Archives, Navy History and Heritage Command.

Air Intelligence Group, Navy Department, Office of the Chief of Naval Operations. *The Air War against Japan*: 1–15 June 1945, 16–30 June 1945, 1–15 July 1945, 16–31 July 1945, 1–15 August 1945. Washington: Navy Department, 1945.

Bergerud, Eric M. *Fire in the Sky*. New York: Basic Books, 2009.

Chappell, John D. *Before the Bomb: How America Approached the End of the Pacific War*. Lexington, KY: University Press of Kentucky, 1997.

Chicago Herald-American. "Kin Beg: 'Punish Jap Torturers,'" August 31, 1945.

Craig, William. *The Fall of Japan*. New York: The Dial Press, 1967.

Craven, Wesley F., and James L. Cate. *The Pacific: Matterhorn to Nagasaki, June 1944 to August 1945*. Volume 5, *The Army Air Forces in World War II*. Washington, DC: Office of Air Force History, 1983.

Cressman, Robert J. *Official Chronology of the U.S. Navy in World War II*. Annapolis, MD: Naval Institute Press, 2000.

Davis, Larry. Air Force Search and Rescue, Part I. *Wings of Fame*, Volume 13. London: Aerospace Pub. Ltd. 1998.

Dickinson, Clarence E. "I Fought Back at Pearl Harbor." *Saturday Evening Post*, October 10, 1942.

Division of Naval Intelligence. *Standard Classes of Japanese Merchant Ships*, ONI-208J (Revised), Supplement 3, January 1945.

Drea, Edward. *MacArthur's Ultra: Codebreaking and the War Against Japan, 1942–1945*. Lawrence, KS: University of Kansas Press, 1992.

Farnsworth, William Dewey. *The First Seventy Years; an Autobiography*. Privately printed. William Dewey Farnsworth Collection, AFC/2001/001/11538, Veterans History Project, Library of Congress.

Frank, Richard B. *Downfall: The End of the Japanese Empire*. New York: Random House, 1999.

Frank, Richard B. "Ketsu Go" in *The End of the Pacific War*, edited by Tsuyoshi Hasegawa. Stanford, CA: Stanford University Press, 2007.

Giangreco, D. M. *Hell to Pay*. Annapolis, MD: Naval Institute Press, 2009.

Hayashi, Saburo, in collaboration with Alvin D. Cox. *Kogun: The Japanese Army in the Pacific War*. Quantico, VA: The Marine Corps Association, 1959.

Headquarters, USAFFE and Eighth U.S. Army. *Air Defense of the Homeland*. Japanese Monograph No. 23. Office of the Chief of Military History, Department of the Army.

Headquarters, USAFFE and Eighth U.S. Army. *Homeland Air Defense Operations Record*. Japanese Monograph No. 157. *War in Asia and the Pacific, Volume 12*. New York and London: Garland Publishing, 1980.

History, Rescue Squadron 4, August 1945. Reel A0923, Air Force Historical Research Agency Microfilm Collection.

Intelligence Office, 47th Fighter Squadron AAF. "Encounter Report of 1st Lt. Robert A. Worton, 19 July 1945." National Archives and Records Administration, Record Group 18, Army Air Forces, Entry 7, Box 2247.

Joint Army-Navy Assessment Committee. *Japanese Naval and Merchant Shipping Losses During World War II by All Causes*. NAVEXOS P 468, February 1947.

Lambert, John W. *The Long Campaign: The History of the 15th Fighter Group in World War II*. Algen, PA: Schiffer Military History, 2006.

Miller, Henry. *Recollections of Rear Admiral Henry Miller*, Volume 1. Oral History Department, United States Naval Institute, 1973.

Moore, Clarence A. *Autobiography*. Privately printed. The Clarence A. Moore Collection, AFC/2001/01/81205, Veterans History Project, Library of Congress.

Morison, Samuel Eliot. *Victory in the Pacific*. Edison, NJ: Castle Books, 2001.

Murray, Stuart S. *Reminiscences of Admiral Stuart S. Murray*. Oral History Department of the United States Naval Institute, 1971.

Norton, Donald J. *Chippewa Chief in World War II*. Jefferson, NC, and London: McFarland & Co., 2001.

Office of the Chief of Naval Operations, Navy Department. *Battle Experience: Final Operations of the Units of the Pacific Fleet off the Shores of Japan July–August 1945*.

Olynyk, Frank J. *USN Credits for the Destruction of Enemy Aircraft in Air-to-Air Combat World War 2*. Published by the Author, October 1982.

Pacific War Research Society. *Japan's Longest Day*. New York: Ballantine Books, 1983.

Report of the Attack on Pearl Harbor and Attack on Japanese Submarine on 10 December 1941. 2 January 1942. Commander Aircraft, Battle Force, National Archives and Records Administration, Record Group 38, Entry 351, Box 5.

Skates, John Ray. *The Invasion of Japan: Alternative to the Bomb*. Columbia, SC: University of South Carolina Press, 1994.

Thach, John S. *Reminiscences of Admiral John S. Thach*. Oral History Department of the United States Naval Institute, 1977.

United States Strategic Bombing Survey. *Japanese Air Power*. Military Analysis Division, July 1945.

United States Strategic Bombing Survey. *Japan's Struggle to End the War*. Chairman's Office, July 1946.

United States Strategic Bombing Survey. *Summary Report (Pacific War)*. Washington, DC: United States Government Printing Office, 1946.

Weintraub, Stanley. *The Last Great Victory*. New York: Truman Talley Books/Dutton, 1995.

Werrel, Kenneth P. *Blankets of Fire*. Washington and London: Smithsonian Press, 1999.

Winton, John. *The Forgotten Fleet*. New York: Coward, McCann, 1969.

Naval Reports available in the Navy War Diaries on the website www.Fold3.com

Action Report, Commander Task Group 30.6, 19 July 1945, and report of Antisubmarine Action, *USS Lawrence C. Taylor* (DE-415), 16 July 1945. Navy War Diaries

Action Report, 2 July–15 August 1945, Commander Second Carrier Task Force

Action Report, 2 July–15 August 1945, *USS Borie* (DD-704)

Action Report, Sinking of Japanese Submarine, *USS Robert D. Keller*, 17 July 1945

Air Group 1 Aircraft Action Reports, July–August 1945

Air Group 6 Aircraft Action Reports, July–August 1945

Air Group 16 Aircraft Action Reports, July–August 1945

Air Group 27 Aircraft Action Reports, July–August 1945

Air Group 31 Aircraft Action Reports, July–August 1945

Air Group 34 Aircraft Action Reports, July–August 1945

Air Group 47 Aircraft Action Reports, July–August 1945

Air Group 49 Aircraft Action Reports, July–August 1945

Air Group 50 Aircraft Action Reports, July–August 1945

Air Group 83 Aircraft Action Reports, July–August 1945

Air Group 85 Aircraft Action Reports, July–August 1945

Air Group 86 Aircraft Action Reports, July–August 1945

Air Group 87 Aircraft Action Reports, July–August 1945

Air Group 88 Aircraft Action Reports, July–August 1945

Air Group (N) 91 Aircraft Action Reports, July–August 1945

Air Group 94 Aircraft Action Reports, July–August 1945

British Fleet Air Operations July–August 1945

History of *USS Anzio* (CVE-57) to September 1945

Report of Anti-Submarine Action, *USS Lawrence C. Taylor* (DE-415), 16 July 1945.

Second Carrier Task Force Report, 2 July–15 August 1945
Task Force 37 (British) Report, July–August 1945
Task Group 38.1 Action Report, 1 July–15 August 1945
Task Group 38.3 Action Report, 1 July–15 August 1945
Task Group 38.4 Action Report, 1 July–15 August 1945
Third Fleet War Diary, July–August 1945
Third Fleet Operational Summaries of Carrier Strikes, July–August 1945
USS Bataan War Diary, July–August 1945
USS Belleau Wood War Diary, July–August 1945
USS Bennington War Diary, July–August 1945
USS Bon Homme Richard War Diary, July–August 1945
USS Cowpens War Diary, July–August 1945
USS Essex War Diary, July–August 1945
USS Hancock War Diary, July–August 1945
USS Independence War Diary, July–August 1945
USS Monterey War Diary, July–August 1945
USS Lexington War Diary, July–August 1945
USS North Carolina War Diary, August 1945
USS San Jacinto War Diary, July–August 1945
USS Randolph War Diary, July–August 1945
USS Shangri-La War Diary, July–August 1945
USS Ticonderoga War Diary, July–August 1945
USS Yorktown War Diary, July–August 1945
USS Wasp War Diary, July–August 1945

INDEX

Italicized letters and page numbers indicate illustrations in insert sections A and B. Maps are indicated with *map* following the page numbers.

American celebrations of, 235,
243, *B16*
Japanese response to terms of,
5, 131, 155, 195, 212, 234,
236, 251
Japanese submarine escorted
after, *A13*
terms of, 7, 114, 131, 155, 195
Suruga Wan, 171
Susaki, 124, 127
Suttsu, 56
Swinden, Elbert, 221
Symonds, Alfred, 109

Tabbys (Nakajima L2D transports),
196, 271
Tabler, Rodney, 97
Tachibana, 34–35
Tachikawa Airfield, 70
Taira, 179
Takahagi Airfield, 5
Takasago, 100
Takasaki, 29, 158
Talbot, Robert, 29
Tamatsukuri, 65
Tambaichi Airfield, 158, 160, 161
Tanabe, 126
Tano, 126
Tarabusi, Arthur, 223
targets of opportunity, defined, 272
Task Force 37, 83, 212
Task Force 38 (Fast Carrier Task
Force of the American
Pacific Fleet). *See also specific
Task Groups, air groups, and
squadrons*

composition, 11–12
defenses, 13–14
definitions, 268, 272
geographic positioning, *ixmap,
viiimap*
missions, 11
pilot training and experience,
12–13
Task Group 34, 43–44
Task Group 35.3, 112
Task Group 35.4, 65
Task Group 38.1. *See also Air Groups
1, 6, 31, 49, 94*
composition of, 11–12, 13
sailing strategies, 13
strike leaders of, 70, 142
Task Group 38.3. See also Air
Groups 16, 34, 47, 83, 87
composition of, 11–12, 13
sailing strategies, 13
Task Group 38.4. See also Air
Groups 27, 50, 85, 86, 88, 91
carrier and destroyer maneuvers
of, *B11*
composition of, 11–12, 13
sailing strategies, 13
Tateyama Airfield, 65, 72, 218,
220, 222
TBMs. *See* Avengers
Teaff, Perry, 1, 2
Tenryu Airfield, 156
Thomas, Robert, 48
Thompson, George, 89
Thompson, James, 105
Thurston, William, 43

11/26/2019